15.99

Figure 1: Black Amun

35. When a message is sent in heaven it is heard in Anu, and is repeated in Hetkaptah to the Beautiful Face. It is done into writing in the letters of Djehuti, and dispatched to the city of Amun with their things. The matters are answered in Newt (Thebes).

From The Hymns of Amun

1

P. O .Box 570459
Miami, Florida, 33257
(305) 378-6253 Fax: (305) 378-6253

The author is available for group lectures and individual counseling. For further information contact the publisher.

Ashby, Muata
EGYPTIAN YOGA VOLUME II: The Supreme Wisdom of Enlightenment ISBN: 1-884564-39-9

Library of Congress Cataloging in Publication Data

1 Yoga Philosophy2 Ancient Egyptian Philosophy, 3 Eastern Philosophy 4 Esotericism 5 Meditation, 6 Self-Help.

For a complete listing of books, audio and video titles send for the free

Egyptian Yoga
Catalog

Sema
Institute of Yoga

Sema (‡) is an Ancient Egyptian word and symbol meaning *union*. The Sema Institute is dedicated to the propagation of the universal teachings of spiritual evolution, which relate to the union of humanity and the union of all things within the universe. It is a non-denominational organization, which recognizes the unifying principles in all spiritual and religious systems of evolution throughout the world. Our primary goals are to provide the wisdom of ancient spiritual teachings in books, courses and other forms of communication. Secondly, to provide expert instruction and training in the various yogic disciplines including Ancient Egyptian Philosophy, Christian Gnosticism, Indian Philosophy and modern science. Thirdly, to promote world peace and Universal Love.

A primary focus of our tradition is to identify and acknowledge the yogic principles within all religions and to relate them to each other in order to promote their deeper understanding. Also our goal is to show the essential unity of purpose and the unity of all-living beings and nature within the whole of existence.

The Institute is open to all who believe in the principles of peace, non-violence and spiritual emancipation regardless of sex, race, or creed.

EGYPTIAN YOGA VOLUME II:
The Supreme Wisdom of Enlightenment

Is the sequel to the

EGYPTIAN YOGA:
The Philosophy of Enlightenment

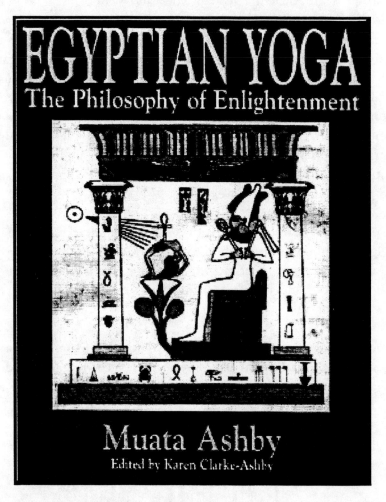

An original, fully illustrated work, including hieroglyphs, detailing the meaning of the Egyptian mysteries, tantric yoga, psycho-spiritual and physical exercises. Egyptian Yoga is a guide to the practice of the highest spiritual philosophy which leads to absolute freedom from human misery and to immortality. It is well known by scholars that Egyptian philosophy is the basis of Western and Middle Eastern religious philosophies such as *Christianity, Islam, Judaism,* the *Kabbalah,* and Greek philosophy, but what about Indian philosophy, Yoga and Taoism? What were the original teachings? How can they be practiced today? What is the source of pain and suffering in the world and what is the solution? Discover the deepest mysteries of the mind and universe within and outside of your self. **216 Pages 8.5" X 11" ISBN: 1-884564-01-1 Soft $18.95 U.S.**

DEDICATION

TO

Vijaya

Swamiji

And

AMUN, the Hidden Self in All

The Ram of Amun

Symbol of Amun incorporating the Sundisk (Ra), the hawk (Horus-Ptah) and the scarab (Kheper).

Foreword

It is my great pleasure to bring forth this new volume. It has been referred to, by those who have read it in its previous rendering as the "Hymns of Amun," as one of the most important books on the mystical philosophy of Ancient Egypt. I believe that it is so important that I have added two new sections to it, which expand on the mysticism of the parts of the spirit and how they relate to the Trinity of Creation. Further, the mystical understanding of the mind which was presented in the book *Egyptian Yoga: The Philosophy of Enlightenment* is herein expanded and brought to its height.

This book is written in the form of a journey of discovery. The section which deals with the Hymns of Amun, in particular, is a wonderful text which when understood in its deep mystical significance, can lead a person to spiritual enlightenment. In reality, the entire book is designed to explain these extraordinary teachings.

The success of *Egyptian Yoga: The Philosophy of Enlightenment* has brought a renewed vision of Ancient Egyptian Mystical Philosophy to the world. This volume acts as a consummation of fulfillment of the philosophy that was introduced in that volume.

I wish to thank all those who made the creation of this volume possible. In particular, I would like to thank my spiritual partner, Karen "Vijaya" Ashby for her support and love as well as her work as editor of this volume. Also I would like to thank my Spiritual Preceptor, Swami Jyotirmayananda, whose teachings on Yoga, which I have studied for many years, have allowed me to understand all that I had previously learned as a student of Egyptology.

Dr. Muata Abhaya Ashby January 26, 1998

Preface

Who Were the Ancient Egyptians and what is Yoga Philosophy?

The origins of Yoga.

The Ancient Egyptian religion (*Shetaut Neter*), language and symbols provide the first "historical" record of Yoga Philosophy and Religious literature. Egyptian Yoga-*Smai Taui or Smai Heru Set* is what has been commonly referred to by Egyptologists as Egyptian "Religion" or "Mythology," but to think of it as just another set of stories or allegories about a long lost civilization is to completely miss the greatest secret of human existence. Yoga, in all of its forms and disciplines of spiritual development, was practiced in Egypt earlier than anywhere else in history.

This unique perspective from the highest philosophical system which developed in Africa over seven thousand years ago provides a new way to look at life, religion, the discipline of psychology and the way to spiritual development leading to spiritual Enlightenment- *Nehast*. Egyptian mythology, when understood as a system of Yoga (union of the individual soul with the Universal Soul or Supreme Consciousness), gives every individual insight into their own divine nature and also a deeper insight into all religions and Yoga systems.

Diodorus Siculus (Greek Historian) writes in the time of Augustus (first century B.C.E.):

The Ethiopian origins of the early Egyptians.

"Now the Ethiopians, as historians relate, were the first of all men and the proofs of this statement, they say, are manifest. For that they did not come into their land as immigrants from abroad but were the natives of it and so justly bear the name of autochthones (sprung from the soil itself), is, they maintain, conceded by practically all men..."

"They also say that the Egyptians are colonists sent out by the Ethiopians, Osiris having been the leader of the colony. For, speaking generally, what is now Egypt, they maintain was not land, but sea when in the beginning the universe was being formed. Afterwards, however, as the Nile during the times of its inundation carried down the mud from Ethiopia, land was gradually built up from the deposit...And the larger parts of the customs of the Egyptians is, they hold, Ethiopian, the colonist's still preserving their ancient manners. For instance, the belief that their kings are Gods, the very special attention which they pay to their burials, and many other matters of a similar nature, are Ethiopian practices. The shapes of their statues and the

forms of their letters are Ethiopian. The two kinds of writing which the Egyptians have, that which is known as popular (demotic) is learned by everyone, while that which is called sacred (hieratic), is understood only by the priests of the Egyptians. They learnt it from their Fathers as one of the things, which are not divulged, but among the Ethiopians, everyone uses these forms of letters. Furthermore, the orders of the priests, they maintain, have much the same position among both peoples. All are clean who are engaged in the service of the gods, keeping themselves shaven, like the Ethiopian priests. They have the same dress and form of staff, which is shaped like a plough and is carried by their kings who wear high, felt hats which end in a knob in the top and are circled by the serpents which they call asps. This symbol appears to carry the thought that it will be the lot who shall dare to attack the king to encounter death-carrying stings. Many other things are told by them concerning their own antiquity and the colony, which they sent out that became the Egyptians, but about this there is no special need of our writing anything.

Two kinds of writing which the Egyptians have...

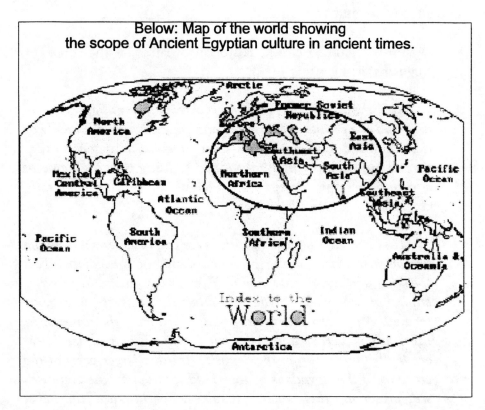

Below: Map of the world showing the scope of Ancient Egyptian culture in ancient times.

Figure 3: The World

The Ancient Egyptian texts state:

*"Our people originated at the base of the mountain of the Moon,
at the origin of the Nile river."*

"KMT"
"Egypt," "Burnt," "Land of Blackness, Land of the Burnt People."

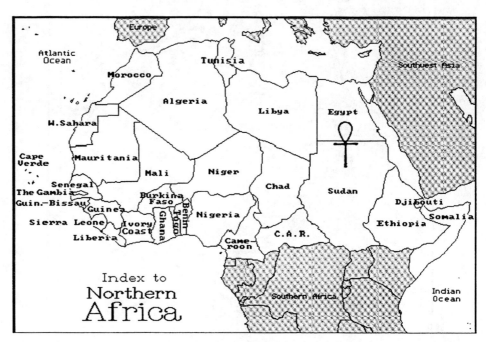

Figure 2: North Africa

KMT (Ancient Egypt) is situated close to Lake Victoria in present day Africa. This is the same location where the earliest human remains have been found, in the land currently known as Ethiopia-Tanzania.

Ancient Egypt and India as colonies of Ethiopia.

The Ancient Egyptian legend of Asar (Osiris) tells of the time when the earliest inhabitants of Egypt migrated from Ethiopia.

"Ancient Egypt was a colony of Nubia - Ethiopia. ...Asar having been the leader of the colony..."
"And upon his return to Greece, they gathered around and asked, "tell us about this great land of the Blacks called Ethiopia." And Herodotus said, "There are two great Ethiopian nations, one in Sind (India) and the other in Egypt."[1]

---

[1] **Recorded by Egyptian high priest *Manetho* (300 B.C.) also Recorded by *Diodorus* (Greek historian 100 B.C.)**

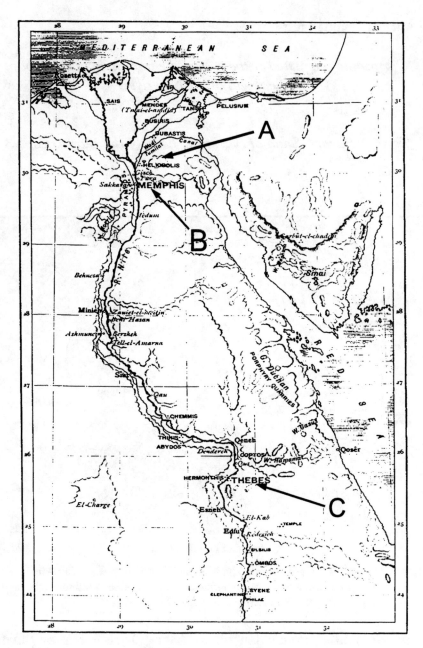

Figure 3: Ancient Egypt

The land of Ancient Egypt is located in the north-eastern corner of the African Continent. The cities wherein the theology of the Trinity was developed are outlined as follows. A- Anu (Heliopolis), B- Hetkaptah (Memphis), and C- Newt (Waset, Thebes).

What is Yoga?

In modern times the word "Yoga" has become popular in society. However, most people think of Yoga as an exercise or as meditations to calm the mind. This is a very limited understanding. Yoga is a vast philosophy of spiritual life which encompasses several spiritual disciplines to aid a person in succeeding in the struggle of life and discovering their Higher Self. Therefore, Sheti is nothing more than Yoga disciplines which the Ancient Egyptians practiced many thousands of years ago. In this volume we will see how their teachings were adopted by Christians and Yogis in India and then we will begin to study the teachings of Sheti so that we may begin to spiritualize our lives. Thus we will concentrate our study on Egyptian Yoga, Indian Yoga and Christian Yoga. The relationship between these three spiritual philosophies will become evident. One important similarity is that they all used the symbol, ♀ , known as the *Ankh* of ancient Egypt.

So what is Yoga? The word "Yoga" is a Sanskrit term meaning to unite the individual with the cosmic. In Ancient Egypt the term "Smai" meant the same thing. The English terms have been used in certain parts of this book for ease of communication since the word "Yoga have received wide popularity in recent years. The disciplines of Yoga fall under five major categories. These are: *Yoga of Wisdom, Yoga of Devotional Love, Yoga of Meditation, Tantric Yoga* and *Yoga of Selfless-Righteous Action.* Within these categories there are subsidiary forms which are part of the main disciplines.

So the practice of any discipline that leads to oneness with the Supreme Consciousness can be called Yoga. If you study, rationalize and reflect upon the teachings, you are practicing *Yoga of Wisdom.* If you meditate upon the teachings and your Higher Self, you are practicing *Yoga of Meditation.* If you practice rituals which identify you with your spiritual nature, you are practicing *Yoga of Ritual Identification* (which is part of the Yoga of Wisdom and the Yoga of Devotional Love of the Divine). If you develop your physical nature and psychic energy centers, you are practicing *Serpent Power* (*Kundalini or Uraeus*) *Yoga* (which is part of Tantric Yoga). If you practice living according to the teachings of ethical behavior and selflessness, you are practicing *Yoga of Action* (Maat) in daily life. If you practice turning your attention towards the Divine by developing love for the Divine, then it is called *Devotional Yoga* or *Yoga of Divine Love.* The practitioner of yoga is called a yogin (male practitioner) or yogini (female practitioner), and one who has attained the culmination of yoga (union with the Divine) is called a yogi. In this manner, yoga has been developed into many disciplines which may be used in an integral fashion to achieve the same goal: Enlightenment. Therefore, the aspirant should learn about all of the paths of yoga and choose those elements to concentrate on which best suit his/her personality and practice them all in an integral, balanced way.

All forms of spiritual practice are directed toward the goal of assisting every individual to discover the true essence of the universe both externally, in physical creation, and internally, within the human heart, as the very root of human consciousness. Thus, many terms are used to describe the attainment of the goal of spiritual knowledge and the eradication of spiritual ignorance. Some of these terms are: *Enlightenment, Resurrection, Salvation, The Kingdom of Heaven, Moksha or Liberation, Buddha Consciousness, One With The Tao, Self-realization, Know Thyself*, etc. Also, many names have been used to describe that transcendental essence: *God, Allah, Asar, Aset, Krishna, Buddha, The Higher Self, Supreme Being* and many others.

EGYPTIAN YOGA

The name **"Egyptian Yoga"** comes from the Ancient Egyptian terms:

Shetaut Neter meaning: "The way of the hidden Supreme Being" and

Smai Taui meaning: "The union of the two lands."

Smai means union and the following determinative terms give it a spiritual significance, at once equating it with the term "Yoga" as it is used in India..

The "two lands" refer to Upper and Lower Egypt as well as Horus and Set who represent the Higher Self and the Lower Self of every human being respectively.

Thus, we also have the Ancient Egyptian term: *Smai Heru-Set.*

Yoga means "Union." The philosophy of YOGA as espoused by the ancient Egyptians incorporated no less than four words whose exact meanings are equal to the Indian word *"YOGA"* which means *"spiritual union".* The four hieroglyphic symbols used on the front cover of this book represent the four words in Egyptian Philosophy which mean *"YOGA".* They are: *"Nefer", "Sema", "Ankh"* and *"Hetep²"* (See below). A more detailed examination of these symbols may be found in Chapter Seven: Symbols.

---

² Also pronounced "Hotep."

Integral Yoga

The personality of every human being is somewhat different from every other. However the Sages of Yoga have identified four basic factors which are common to all human personalities. These factors are: Emotion, Reason, Action and Will. This means that in order for a human being to evolve, all aspects of the personality must progress in an integral fashion. Therefore, four major forms of Yoga disciplines have evolved and each is specifically designed to promote a positive movement in one of the areas of personality. The Yoga of Devotional Love enhances and harnesses the emotional aspect in a human personality and directs it towards the Higher Self. The Yoga of Wisdom enhances and harnesses the reasoning aspect in a human personality and directs it towards the Higher Self. The Yoga of Action enhances and harnesses the movement and behavior aspect in a human personality and directs it towards the Higher Self. The Yoga of Meditation enhances and harnesses the willing aspect in a human personality and directs it towards the Higher Self.

Emotion	Reason	Action	Will.
↑	↑	↑	↑
Devotion	Wisdom	Service	Meditation

Yoga is a discipline of spiritual living

Thus, Yoga is a discipline of spiritual living which transforms every aspect of personality in an integral fashion, leaving no aspect of a human being behind. This is important because an unbalanced movement will lead to frustration, more ignorance, more distraction and more illusions leading away from the Higher Self. For example, if a person develops the reasoning aspect of personality he or she may come to believe that they have discovered the Higher Self, however when it comes to dealing with some problem of life, such as the death of a loved one, they cannot control their emotions, or if they are tempted to do something unrighteous, such as smoking, they cannot control their actions and have no will power to resist. The vision of Integral Yoga is a lofty goal which every human being can achieve with the proper guidance, self-effort and repeated practice. There is a very simple philosophy behind Integral Yoga. During the course of the day you may find yourself doing various activities. Sometimes you will be quiet, at other times you will be busy at work, at other times you might be interacting with people, etc. Integral Yoga gives you the opportunity to practice yoga at all times. When you have quiet time you can practice meditation, when at work you can practice righteous action and selfless service, when you have leisure time you can study and reflect on the teachings and when you feel the sentiment of love for a person or object you like you can practice remembering the Divine Self who made it possible for you to experience the company of those personalities or the opportunity to acquire those objects. From a higher perspective you can practice reflecting on how the people and objects in creation are expressions of the Divine and this movement will lead you to a spontaneous and perpetual state of ecstasy, peace and bliss which are the hallmarks of spiritual enlightenment. The purpose of Integral Yoga is therefore to promote integration of the whole personality of a human being which will lead to complete spiritual enlightenment. Thus Integral Yoga should be understood as the most effective method to practice mystical spirituality.

The important point to remember is that all aspects of yoga can and should be used in an integral fashion to generate an efficient and harmonized spiritual movement in the practitioner. Therefore, while there may be an area of special emphasis, other elements are bound to become part of the yoga program as needed. For example, while a yogin may place emphasis on the Yoga of Wisdom, they may also practice Devotional Yoga and Meditation Yoga along with the wisdom studies. Further, it must be understood that as you practice one path of yoga, others will also develop automatically. For example, as you practice the Yoga of Wisdom your faith will increase or as you practice the Yoga of Devotion your wisdom will increase. If this movement does not occur your wisdom alone will by dry intellectualism or your faith alone will be blind faith. So when we speak of wisdom here we are referring to wisdom gained through experience or intuitional wisdom and not intellectual wisdom which is speculative. If you do not practice the teachings through the Yoga of Action, your wisdom and faith will be shallow because you have not experienced the truth of the teachings and allowed yourself the opportunity to test your knowledge and faith. If you do not have introspection and faith, your wisdom and actions you will externalized, agitated and distracted. Your spiritual realization will be insubstantial, weak and lacking stability. You will not be able to meet the challenges of life nor will you be able to discover true spiritual realization in this lifetime or even after death. Therefore, the integral path of yoga, with proper guidance, is the most secure method to achieve genuine spiritual enlightenment.[3]

The balanced practice of all forms of Yoga.

---

[3] See the book Initiation Into Egyptian Yoga: The Secrets of Sheti by Muata Ashby.

"Smai taui"

("Egyptian Yoga.")

CHAPTER I

Who is AMUN?

Introduction

The wisdom of Ancient Egypt has long fascinated the world due to the massive structures and the plentiful inscriptions telling of a vast culture which was capable of unimaginable feats of engineering while at the same time being spiritually rooted.

The spiritual roots of Ancient Egypt were the backbone of the society in every aspect. The strength that came from spiritual awareness was the force that engendered the creation of the most spiritually advanced society in our history.

In Part 1 of this volume we will present an Introduction to the Hymns of Amun. This work will provide a basic understanding of what is referred to as *Theban Theology*. It will also provide an introduction to the mystical philosophy of Ancient Egypt through the philosophy as it was practiced in the Ancient Egyptian City of *Waset* or *Newt*, also known as *Thebes* by the Western countries. Before entering into the introduction to the Hymns of Amun, we must first understand some basic principles of Ancient Egyptian Religion and Mythology. Then we will need to have a basic understanding of the period of time in which the Ancient Egyptians lived and who they were as a people.

Waset is the city of Ancient Egypt that was named Thebes by the Greeks, who knew it also, as *Diospolis* ("heavenly city"). Thebes is the city identified in the Old Testament as *No* ("city"), *No-Amon* ("city of Amon"), *Anu* (city of Ra) and *Hetkaptah* (city of Ptah). In Ancient Egypt, Waset was synonymous with the *Beautiful West* or the mythical city where the Supreme Being in the form of Amun, Ra, Ptah or Asar abides. Thus the *West* was the highest goal of every human being because it was the place where unity with God is possible and where supreme peace and bliss can be experienced for all eternity. In much the same way as the sun is born in the east, rises and sets in the west, every human being is seen as a traveler. He or she comes into the world of human experience and one day dies with the hopes of reaching the west, where God, in the form of the sundisk (Ra), also ends up each day to complete the cycle of time. So where is this coveted western land? Is it simply a myth or is it actually possible to find this peace and bliss even in our own times? This question is the objective of our study.

The Ancient Egyptian city of Waset.

Religion and Yoga

The word *religion* comes from the Latin "Relegare" which means, "to link back." This implies, to link the individual human soul back to its original source, the Universal soul. The word *Yoga* is an Indian term meaning to "Yoke" or "Join," implying, to join individual consciousness to universal consciousness. Yoga is the practice of mental, physical and spiritual disciplines that lead to self-control and self-discovery by purifying the mind, body and spirit, so as to discover the deeper spiritual essence, which lies within every human being and object in the universe. In essence, the goal of yoga practice is to unite or *yoke* one's individual consciousness with universal or cosmic consciousness. Therefore, Ancient Egyptian religious practice, especially in terms of the rituals and other practices of the Ancient Egyptian temple system known as *Shetaut Neter* (the way of the hidden Supreme Being), may be termed as a yoga system: *Egyptian Yoga*. In this sense, religion, in its purest form, is a yoga system, as it seeks to reunite people with their true and original source.

Religion encompasses three levels, *myth, ritual* and *mystical philosophy*. Many students of Ancient Egyptian religion have focused on the religious stories of Ancient Egypt as mythical fables or superstitious rantings from a long lost civilization. In the *Egyptian Yoga Book Series* we successfully showed how the teachings of mystical spirituality were carefully woven throughout Ancient Egyptian Mythology.

Three levels of
Religion

> The body belongs to the earth; The soul belongs to heaven.
>
> Ancient Egyptian Proverb

Ancient Egyptian Religion centers on the understanding that every human being has an immortal soul and a mortal body. Further, it holds that creation and the human soul have the same origin. How can this momentous teaching be proven and its reality experienced? This is the task of Mystical Spirituality (religion in its three phase's and/ or the practice of Yoga disciplines).

The disciplines of Yoga come under five major categories. These are: *Yoga of Wisdom, Yoga of Devotional Love, Yoga of Meditation, Tantric Yoga* and *Yoga of Selfless-Righteous Action*. Within these categories there are subsidiary forms which are part of the main disciplines. The emphasis, in the Ausarian Myth, is on the Yoga of Wisdom, Yoga of Devotional Love and Yoga of Selfless-Righteous Action. The important point to remember is that all aspects of yoga can and should be used in an integral fashion to effect an efficient and harmonized spiritual movement in the practitioner. Therefore, while there may be an area of special emphasis, other elements are bound to become part of the yoga program as needed. For example, while a yogin may place emphasis on the Yoga of Wisdom, they may also practice Devotional Yoga and Meditation Yoga along with the wisdom studies.

So the practice of any discipline that leads to oneness with Supreme Consciousness can be called Yoga. If you study, rationalize and reflect upon the teachings, you are practicing *Yoga of Wisdom*. If you meditate upon the teachings and your Higher Self, you are practicing *Yoga of Meditation*. If you practice rituals which identify you with your spiritual nature, you are practicing *Yoga of Ritual Identification* (which is part of the Yoga of Wisdom and the Yoga of Devotional Love of the Divine). If you develop your physical nature and psychic energy centers, you are practicing *Serpent Power* (*Kundalini or Uraeus*) *Yoga* (which is part of Tantric Yoga). If you practice living according to the teachings of ethical behavior and selflessness, you are practicing *Yoga of Action* (Maat) in daily life. If you practice turning your attention towards the Divine by developing love for the Divine, then it is called *Devotional Yoga* or *Yoga of Divine Love*. The practitioner of yoga is called a yogin (male practitioner) or yogini (female practitioner), and one who has attained the culmination of yoga (union with the Divine) is called a yogi. In this manner, yoga has been developed into many disciplines which may be used in an integral fashion to achieve the same goal: Enlightenment. Therefore, the aspirant should learn about all of the paths of yoga and choose those elements to concentrate on which best suit his/her personality and practice them all in an integral, balanced way.

Yoga defined

Enlightenment is the term used to describe the highest level of spiritual awakening. It means attaining such a level of spiritual awareness that one discovers the underlying unity of the entire universe as well as the fact that the source of all creation is the same source from which the innermost Self within every human heart arises.

All forms of spiritual practice are directed toward the goal of assisting every individual to discover the true essence of the universe both externally, in physical creation, and internally, within the human heart, as the very root of human consciousness. Thus, many terms are used to describe the attainment of the goal of spiritual knowledge and the eradication of spiritual ignorance. Some of these terms are: *Enlightenment, Resurrection, Salvation, The Kingdom of Heaven, Moksha or Liberation, Buddha Consciousness, One With The Tao, Self-realization, to Know Thyself,* etc.

Nebertcher: The All-God

Figure 4: Neberdjer[4]

"The All-encompassing God."

The All-God unites the attributes of all Egyptian deities, Khepri, Amun, Amsu, Ra, two plumes symbolizing Aset and Nebethet (Aset and Nephthys) and a male phallus, etc., with male emphasis.

"Neberdjer: Everything is Amun-Ra-Ptah, three in one."

Ancient Egyptian Proverb

The idea of a Supreme Being

Ancient Egyptian Mythology centered around the Creation of the universe out of a Primeval Ocean.[5] This ocean was formless and homogenous. From this original essence, the Supreme Being arose in the form of an all-encompassing Supreme Being known as *Neberdjer* (All-encompassing existence) or *Pa Neter* (The Supreme Being). Neberdjer is an androgynous, formless being. However, Neberdjer received many symbolic names and forms throughout the vast Ancient Egyptian history. Neberdjer, also known as *Pa Neter* or "The God," distinguishing the Supreme Divinity from the neteru, the Gods and Goddesses , which symbolizes cosmic powers through which the Supreme Being manifests. Many forms were associated with the Supreme Divinity. These included both male and female

God as male and female

forms. Thus, the Ancient Egyptian gods, Asar and Amun, who were male, were also known as Neberdjer. The Ancient Egyptian cow goddess, Mehurt, was also known as Neberdjer, the source of creation. In order to engender Creation, Neberdjer transformed into a Trinity, Amun-Ra-Ptah. This signifies that from a self-existent, singular and formless mass (Nu, the

---

[4] Also pronounced as *Nebertcher.*

[5] Also referred to as the Primeval Waters.

Primeval Ocean) the phenomenal universe consisting of objects with forms that have been given names, arises. For our study, we will use the words Supreme Divinity, Supreme Being, Pa Neter, Neberdjer, God, Divine Self, and The Self, interchangeably, to refer to the same Supreme Spirit.

Above: The All-God- Neberdjer encompassing all the aspects of other divinities and in control of nature as symbolized by the seven animals encircled by the serpent and the ones being held with the left hand.

The teaching of Neberdjer: Amun-Ra-Ptah is a profound study of mystical philosophy which encompasses the nature of Creation, Divinity and the origins and destiny of human life. It involves a study of the very makeup of the human heart (consciousness) and the way towards realizing the greatest goal of human existence. Thus, to believe that Ancient Egyptian Mythology and Mystical Religion is merely a fictitious yarn about some mythical characters is to entirely miss a most important teaching about the purpose of human life and the supreme goal of human existence, Spiritual Enlightenment, the discovery of the nature of God.

Ancient Egyptian Religion developed over a period of tens of thousands of years.[6] Each segment of the four-fold system of mystical philosophy (Neberdjer, Amun, Ra, Ptah) in Ancient Egyptian Theban Religion as it is known today, originates in the Ancient Egyptian city of *Anu*, known to the Ancient Greeks as Heliopolis or the city of the sun. The presiding symbol of the Supreme Divinity was known there as *Ra*.

Four-fold system of mystical philosophy

------

[6] See the book *The Cycles of Time*, by Dr. Muata Ashby.

In the creation story involving the Ausarian Mysteries[7], Asar assumes the role of Khepera and Tem:

"Neb-er-tcher saith, I am the creator of what hath come into being, and I myself came into being under the form of the god Khepera, and I came into being in primeval time. I had union with my hand, and I embraced my shadow in a love embrace; I poured seed into my own mouth, and I sent forth from myself issue in the form of the gods Shu and Tefnut." "I came into being in the form of Khepera, and I was the creator of what came into being, I formed myself out of the primeval matter, and I formed myself in the primeval matter. My name is Ausares (Asar).

I was alone, for the Gods and Goddesses were not yet born, and I had emitted from myself neither Shu nor Tefnut. I brought into my own mouth, *hekau,* and I forthwith came into being under the form of things which were created under the form of Khepera."

Neberdjer

(All-encompassing divinity-eternity-the absolute)

Amun

(Hidden essence of creation-witnessing consciousness)

Ra

(Mind and senses-Life force of creation)

Ptah

(Heaven and earth-the physical universe)

---

[7] See the books *The Ausarian Resurrection: The Ancient Egyptian Bible* and *The Mystical Teachings of The Ausarian Resurrection: Initiation Into The Third Level of Shetaut Asar.*

These passages all point to the fact that while the name of the Supreme Being has changed under the different priesthoods, these are merely different expressions of the same principles and teachings which even use the same wording, therefore, there is no discontinuity or confusion within the theology. More importantly, the last passage reminds us that all of the names and forms are merely outward expressions of the Supreme Being, *Neb-er-tcher*, in its physical manifestation. Neberdjer who signifies the all-encompassing being is the source of the Trinity. Neberdjer includes all male and female aspects of the Trinity and is therefore to be understood as the androgynous and primordial being from which arose all names and forms, all Gods and Goddesses , all creation.

The Trinity as manifestation of Neberdjer.

The other important point in this passage is that Asar states that he brought himself, and thereby creation, into being by the just uttering his own name. The idea of the primeval utterance which emerges out of the hidden regions of existence and into the realm of time and space is taken up here by the priests of Asar.

Sekhmet-Bast-Ra
The All - Goddess

She is the union of the vulture (Mut), lioness (Sekhmet), human female with wings, two plumes (Aset and Nebthet) and a male phallus.

An important, but less known form of the Ancient Egyptian Goddess is known as *Sekhmet-Bast-Ra*. Sekhmet-Bast-Ra is a composite depiction of the Goddess encompassing all of the attributes of the goddesses as well as the attributes of the gods. This is a recognition that all things in Creation are not absolutely female or male. All of Creation is a combination of male and female elements. Therefore, since Creation is androgynous, so too Divinity and the human soul are also androgynous. This understanding is reflected in the following instruction from Aset to Horus from the Ausarian Resurrection.

"Sex is a thing of bodies, not of souls"

The Mystical Creation Myth

Ra-Tem
⇩
Hathor
Djehuti
Maat
⇩
Shu ⇔ Tefnut
⇩
Geb⇔Nut
⇗   ⇩   ⇘

Set — Nebthet   Asar ⇔ Aset   Asar⇔ Nebthet
⇩   ⇩
Horus   Anubis

The emergence of the Gods and Goddesses on the boat of Ra.

The diagram above shows that the *Psedjet* (Ennead), the creative principles that are embodied in the primordial neteru (Gods and Goddesses) of creation, emanated from the Supreme Being. Ra or Ra-Tem arose out of the *Nu*, the Primeval Ocean, the hidden essence, and began sailing the *"Boat of Millions of Years"* which included the Company of Gods and Goddesses . On his boat emerged the neteru, the Gods and Goddesses who symbolize the cosmic principles of Creation. The neteru of the Ennead are Ra-Atum, Shu, Tefnut, Geb, Nut, Asar, Aset, Set, and Nebthet. Hathor, Djehuti (Ṭehuti) and Maat represent attributes of the Supreme Being as the very *stuff* or *substratum* which makes up creation. Shu, Tefnut, Geb, Nut, Asar, Aset, Set, and Nebthet represent the principles upon which creation manifests. Anubis is not part of the Ennead. He represents the feature of intellectual discrimination in the Ausarian myth. "Sailing" signifies the beginning of motion in creation. Motion implies that events occur in the realm of time and space, thus, the phenomenal universe comes into existence as a mass of moving essence we call the elements. Prior to this motion, there was the primeval state of being without any form and without existence in time or space.

Above: The Creation: Ra emerges from the Nu (primeval waters) along with the Company of Gods and Goddesses .

God rises out of the primeval waters and His continuous motion through the cosmos sustains the universe. This same barque is constantly attacked by the evil forces headed by the serpent Apep. Apep represents the fetters of the soul. It is the task of the initiate to eradicate the obstructions (Apep) from the path of spiritual progress. Sublimating the Setian forces, the lower self, represented by Set, can do this.

Above: The Great Trinity of Ancient Egypt including both male and female principles. A-Amun and Amenit or Amunet (Mut), B- Ra and Rai, C- Ptah and Sekhmet.

The Mysteries of Anu are considered to be the oldest exposition of the teachings of Creation and they formed a foundation for the unfoldment of the teachings of mystical spirituality which followed in the mysteries of the city of *Hetkaptah* through the Divinity in the name Ptah, and the Mysteries of *Newt (Waset or Thebes)*, through the Divinity in the name Amun. With each succeeding exposition, the teaching becomes more and more refined until it reaches its quintessence in the *Hymns of Amun*. Thus, while each of the divinities in the Ancient Egyptian Trinity (Amun-Ra-Ptah) are related,

The oldest known mystery teachings.

in their own tutelary way they assume the form of the *High Divinity* or *Supreme Being* with name and form. However, as we have seen, they are only representations or symbols (representation with name and form) of the transcendental androgynous Divinity which is without name or form who is referred to as Neberdjer. This understanding holds vast implications for the comprehension of Ancient Egyptian Religion and its message in reference to the human soul because the human soul is related to Neberdjer just as the Trinity is related to Neberdjer. How is this possible? This is the teaching of the Hymns of Amun.

This work represents an introduction to the sacred scriptures from one segment of the Ancient Egyptian Trinity. It is provided for those who would like to begin their studies of Theban Theology and to practice the teachings contained therein. These sacred scriptures encompassed in the Hymns-*Hessu* are to be used for praying, chanting, memorizing and repeating, and should be studied ardently. When they are propitiated-*Amma,* in this manner, they bestow spiritual wisdom-*Sâa*, mental calm and spiritual upliftment.

The Deeper Aspect of Amun

The concept behind the teaching of Amun is the central theme of not only Ancient Egyptian Religion and mystical philosophy, but also of every world religion and of modern physics as well. The idea of Amun has been mythologized by Sages in such a fashion that the continuous study of the teachings and myths reveal increasingly more profound layers of the mystery of life. The outer layers are shed through understanding of the philosophical ideas and teachings. When understanding reaches an intuitive level through the study and practice of the teachings, the core wherein lies the discovery of the true essence of mystical religious philosophies is revealed.

The name *Amun* appears in the remotest times of Egyptian history and came to prominence in the ancient city of Waset (Thebes), Egypt. The mysteries of Amun represent a quintessence of Egyptian philosophy concerning the nature of the un-manifest aspect of all existence and the understanding of human consciousness. This teaching speaks of God as an un-manifest, nameless, formless *Being of Light* which is the source of all that is manifest. The formless *Being of Light* also became known as the *Nu, the Watery Abyss* and as Amun, the Witnessing Self. In the Ancient Egyptian Shabaka Inscription, this teaching was espoused with *Ptah* assuming the role of the manifestation of the un-manifest Self.

In Egypt, the concept of God, the ultimate and absolute reality-*Un maat* behind all physical manifestations, was called *Amn* or *Amun*[8] or *Neberdjer* or *Pa Neter*. In Hindu mythology, it is *Brahman*, to the Taoists, it is *The Tao*, in Judaism it is referred to as *Yahweh*, in Islam it is *Allah*, in Christianity it is *God the Father* and *The Kingdom of Heaven*, and to modern physics it is *Energy*. In Indian mystical philosophy the inner Self is referred to as *Antar Amin*. The similarity in the terms used to denote *The Self* in Ancient Egypt and India is evident.

Since the most ancient times of Egyptian civilization, a nameless, formless, gender-less "Supreme God," was also referred to as "*Neter Neteru*" (*God of gods*), and as "*The Hidden One*," until later times when myths were constructed for the understanding of the common people which made use of symbols or forms. Thus, representations of God began to appear, first in zoomorphic forms (using animals to convey a symbolic image), and then in anthropomorphic (human) forms. "*Pa Neter*" or "The God" was thought of as a Father-Mother Creator God and must not be confused with the "*neteru*" or "gods and goddesses," which represented the cosmic forces of the Universe which emanate from Pa Neter.

Pa Neter and the neteru.

Prior to creating, the Creator is viewed as both female and male until creation is created, at which time creation becomes the female principle (Creation) and the mover-vivifier (God), becomes the male principle (Spirit) . This is the beginning of duality coming out of non-duality. From an advanced point of view however, God is neither male nor female, but God is the source from which the Gods and Goddesses (neteru), men and women and all creation comes. Therefore, the concept of "*Pa Neter*" encompasses a concept that goes beyond ordinary human - mental understanding of God. For the "common folk," "*Pa Neter*" was referred to as Amon - Ra - Ptah, the Holy Trinity, or as Asar, Aset, Horus, Hathor, etc., and was represented by various symbols such as the Sundisk or a single flag, as well as other symbols. These symbols contain deep mystical significance and hold formulas which convey mystical teachings about ourselves and the nature of existence.

Each divine aspect and symbol for the Divine carries with it certain specific pieces of information which, when put together through intuitive understanding, reveal the wholeness of creation and of human consciousness. Thus, through each major High God and his Consort, different levels of mystical wisdom are revealed. In three of the major cosmological systems of Ancient Egypt, mystical wisdom is revealed through the symbolic representation of the deities and through their relationships.

---

[8] Other spellings include *Amun, Amen, Amon, Amonu, Amunu.*

The relationships of the deities constitute the different "Companies" (*Paut Neteru*) of gods who are in the following of the High (Supreme) God (*Neter Neteru*). Further, the Companies reveal that the Supreme Being exists in the un-manifest form and manifests as a Trinity (*Amun-Ra-Ptah*), and also as the different principles which are represented by the various Gods and Goddesses (*Neteru*). In this manner, the ancient texts themselves proclaim that *Amun* is One and Alone, *Ptah* is One and Alone, and *Ra* is One and Alone. All deities are *One* because they represent the One Supreme Being, so there is no conflict because there are no differences between them; they are only symbols of certain characteristic principles of the same Divine Self, so their differences are of appearance only. Thus, the concept of the High God must be interpreted in a much broader sense than in the stricter dogmatic religious philosophies. The High God is androgynous, therefore, male or female deities may serve the role of High God as is needed for the particular doctrine and wisdom teaching. Thus, Amun, Ra, Ptah, Asar, Horus, Khepera, Aset, Hathor, Mut, Nut, etc., are all representatives or representations of the Supreme Deity which is beyond name and form, though manifesting with name and form.

The gender of the Supreme Being in Ancient Egyptian Philosophy.

By looking at the various deities with an insight into the principles they represent and their relationships to the absolute Supreme Being (*Pa Neter*), the correct understanding emerges with respect to the androgynous nature and origin of the soul. In ancient texts, Aset informs Horus that *sex is a thing of bodies and not of souls* and elsewhere, we are instructed that *the body belongs to the earth and the soul to heaven*. Therefore, you are to understand that the task of the mysteries of Yoga involve a shifting of your conscious identification from the body to the soul essence. With this understanding, the concept of *Pa Neter* includes the female element. So when Aset says she is *All that is and All that shall ever be* and Hathor is described as *One and Alone*, you can understand these statements as all being true.

Furthermore, all deities of other religions (Jesus, Krishna, Buddha, etc.) are *One* as well, in that they are symbols and representations of the One ultimate reality behind all names and forms. So whatever deity is chosen for worship, there is no conflict because the true object of worship is the transcendental reality behind the form of the deity. In this manner, religion progresses from the ritualistic level where the external form of the Divine is worshipped to the mythical level, wherein the particular deity is worshipped as a representation of the Divine. Finally, religious movement progresses to the metaphysical or mystical level where the deities are intentionally understood to be representations of the divine essence underlying all things, which is the innermost reality of yourself. With this understanding, the essence of God within the innermost recesses of your heart is revealed.

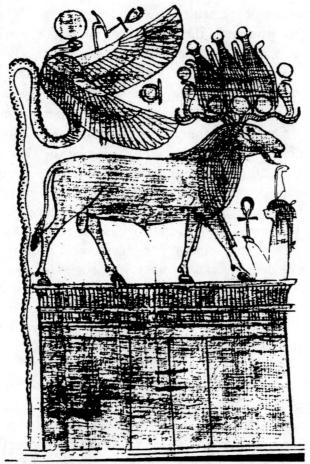

Above: **The ram of Amun and the Uraeus Goddess.**

In the same manner that Hindu deities such as Shiva and Krishna are pictures with their consorts Parvati and Radha, respectively, who represent their *shakti* (manifesting energy or power), Amun is pictured with his female *Sekhem* or power in her name as Arat (the Uraeus).

So any deity may be chosen according to the level of understanding and *meskhenet* (karmic) inclination of the individual. There are varied forms of religions and yoga disciplines in existence because there are varied human personalities. Further, since all things in creation are in reality manifestations of God, everything in creation is divine and is therefore worthy of deification and reverence. The goal of each and every discipline of yoga is the attainment of the beatific state of Enlightenment wherein all Creation is understood as being Divine.

The Symbols of Amun

Making images of God and the Gods and Goddesses in human likeness can be either helpful or dangerous for the follower. The mind is a wonderful tool for accomplishing seemingly impossible tasks. When it is captivated by something it holds onto it tenaciously and every effort is made to achieve the desired goal. However, it easily indulges in emotion and imagination-*Iab*, developing attachment to that which it understands, and fear and hatred towards that which it does not.

The danger in religious symbolism.

The danger in religious symbolism arises when the mind becomes fixed on the image or symbol rather than the essence of the symbolic meaning of the symbol or deity being worshipped. Instead of worshipping those qualities and developing them in one's self, the worshipper might believe that those qualities belong to the statue, spiritual entity, painting or "some special person who lived long ago.' They do not realize that symbols such as Horus, Christ, and Buddha represent qualities which lie deep within every individual human being and not somewhere "out there" but "right in here," inside the heart. In ancient times, the wise sages chose images which were so far from the norm that the attachment-oriented human mind would not get "hung up" on the "picture," and thereby concentrate on the meaning. For example: The hawk, the symbol of Horus, the God of light, signifies the qualities of heaven, accurate vision and speed. When looking at the hawk, ⤤, you should be immediately drawn to those qualities of accurate vision or discrimination between what is real and what is not real, tenacity, speed and freedom, expansion, righteousness, justice, truth, etc.

How the mind understands things.

Symbols have a great psychological significance because, without them, there would be no possibility for the mind to exist, function and interact with creation. A deeper examination of symbols reveals that they are more than just representations of images or ideas. The human mind understands things by first making a mental picture of it and then associating that mental concept with other ideas and thoughts. When you think of a chair, a three dimensional mental image appears in the mind as to what a chair looks like. You do not think of the letters that make up the word C-H-A-I-R. Therefore, symbols are far superior to literary and verbal forms of communication, to efficiently and quickly convey an idea or thought. In literary or verbal forms of communication ideas are expressed through lengthy discussions and explanations. With the hieroglyphic system or other forms of visual-symbolic communication, extremely complex ideas and concepts are conveyed at the speed of the mind's perception through the senses. After reading this book, you will find that having learned about the symbols, just a glance at them will convey the ideas, thoughts and feelings associated with them.

Above Left: The Supreme Divinity, Amun, depicted with a zoomorphic form using the head of a ram and the body of a human being.

Above Right: Amun-Ra: The combination aspect of Amun and Ra in the form of a hawk-headed human.

What is absolute reality?

When you understand that you are not the body, but spirit, it becomes obvious that all your mental notions are only elaborate symbols. In fact, all the objects in creation are really symbols or ideas, not absolute realities, just as the objects in a dream-*Resu* are only representations based on your unconscious mind and not absolute realities. Therefore, symbols are a vital key to understanding the workings of the mind and the nature of existence. Thoughts themselves are symbols. In Egyptian mythology and philosophy, as well as in other mythological and philosophical systems, it is often necessary to learn about a symbol's meaning(s) by its relation to other symbols.

Amun as the Creator of human beings.

One of the sacred symbols of Amun is the *Khnem* ram. Amun is associated with the ram because of its virility and pugnacity or power and will to fight. In reference to virility, this metaphorical reference is more of a tantric symbolism than a sexual one. One of God's most important attributes is the ability to engender or cause the existence of an infinite universe. This infinitude is symbolized by the sexual power of the ram. Khnemu is the aspect of Amun as the *Creator Of Men*. He sits at the potter's wheel, fashioning the form of all things in creation. *Khnemu* also means *to join, to build* or *to unite*. Amun is the breath of life and also the breath that is breathed.

Above: Amsu-Min

Another symbol of Amun is a pregnant woman, representing the essence or generating Life Force that causes life to exist and be engendered. In much the same way, Amun is associated with *Amsu–Min* or *Menu*, the ithyphallic (erect penis) form of Horus symbolizing the source of the sexual energy which causes arousal and the generation of life in the realm of time and space (phenomenal universe), and the sublimation of that energy.[9] This same sexual energy, when sublimated, is the power that Horus uses in the form represented by *Amsu-Min* to overthrow the fetters of Set (see the book *The Ausarian Resurrection*). In the same manner, *Amunet*, as the consort of Amun, is an androgynous fertility goddess associated with *Min* and the goddesses *Neith-Amunet, Ahat-Amunet* and *Aset-Amunet*. In association with the vulture as *Mut*, she represents nature, the feminine power which assimilates, recycles and regenerates dead matter and brings it back to life again. Therefore, Mut is the *Great Mother*, nature itself, which is the field in

[9] see *Egyptian Tantra Yoga: The Art of Sex Sublimation and Universal Consciousness.*

which material things come to life and to which they return at the time of death, She is the consort of the Spirit (The Self).

Above: Khnemu or Khnum, a form of Amun as the "fashioner of men," is seen here creating a human being. Knum in the act of creating a child and it's Ka. He fashions the body in accordance with the fortune and destiny that has been allotted to it by Djehuti. This outlines the span of life of each human being according to his or her karmic past and the persons evolutionary needs.[10]

Above left and right: *The anthropomorphic form of Amun with double plumes, moon-bulls tail, "ankh amulet" and "Was scepter."*

---

[10] See verses 15, 16, 40 and 43 of the Hymns of Amun.

Above: *The forms of Khonsu, The Traveler, offspring of Amun and Mut (Amunet).*

In short, Amun is the origin and essence of all things and is the innermost reality of all human beings. Amun is the same Life Force essence which manifests through the sun (Ra), therefore, Amun is known as *Amun-Ra.* Since *Amun* and his consort *Amunet (Mut)* are in reality one being who manifests as a duality, encompassing all the pairs of opposites, Amun is also known as *Ka-Mut-F* or the *Bull Of His Mother*, signifying that the hidden soul within all things has the power to exist and generate life from within itself. Therefore, all life is an expression of the self-existent being, beyond time and space though manifesting as time and space, and all objects in creation. Amun is shown in the *Books of the Duat*[11] holding a serpent-shaped scepter. This serpent was called *Kam-at-f*, "He who hath finished His moment." This serpent, representing creative power, enshrines the soul of Amun. As Amun is neither alive or dead, the serpent surrounding his soul represents creation and the soul is the source and power which sustains creation.

Amun

Mut

Ka-Mut-F

[11] *Duat* is the Ancient Egyptian name for the Astral Plane or Netherworld. It also is written as Duat or Duat.

Ancient Egyptian writing did not record the vowels in words. This accounts for the wide variety of word spellings and different uses for the same symbols. Further, the symbols may carry a phonetic value, a symbolic value and or a determinative value.

Ancient Egyptian scripture sometimes holds a phonetic value which relates to its spoken characteristics such as pronunciation. The symbolic value relates to its mystical meaning which transcends the ordinary idea of the picture. For example, the eye has the ordinary symbolic value as an organ of vision, however, when used in conjunction with Asar (Asar), it means the "all-seeing," "witnessing" power of God. The determinative value serves to direct us towards the specific object or idea being spoken about. Determinatives may relate to a single group, an entire class or to gender. Also, symbols may convey a secret value when used in certain unusual ways.

Above: The ram of Amun in the four-headed aspect symbolizing the all-encompassing nature of the Divine. The Supreme Being encompasses all directions, everything within the directions of East, West, North and South. Also, this motif recalls to mind the four-fold nature of existence, Neberdjer: Amun-Ra-Ptah (Absolute: Causal-Astral-Physical Planes). It must be clearly understood that the Absolute (God) has no planes of existence or aspects. These terms are used as concepts to assist the mind in grasping the necessary teachings which will allow the mind to transcend its ignorance and thereby expand in understanding and inner discovery. The Self is the ever pure, non-dual essence. The many names and descriptions are used only for instruction.

On the whole, Egyptian hieroglyphic writing was produced for those who had an idea about the philosophy and the context of the teachings. In other words, they were meant for those who had previously been initiated into the mystery teachings. Therefore, the elementary levels of instruction and the esoteric meanings of those symbols were not recorded, but were transmitted orally from generation to generation and meant for those who could decipher the meanings by deductive and intuitional reasoning. Once the principles of mythology are known, the inner meanings of a particular mystical philosophy can be reconstructed by piecing together the references of different symbols in relation to each other and then placing them within a context of a whole teaching. This way of "reading" a mythological system is a key to understanding all mythology. It is a universal principle which reveals the hidden teachings of the mystical meanings of world mythologies.

The symbols of the name of Amun are derived from ⟨symbols⟩ = *hidden god, hidden wisdom*. In Ancient Egyptian language, the phonetic value of the word ***Amun*** is ⟨symbol⟩=ä with the "a" being as the "o" in *bottle* or "*i*" as in *bite*, ⟨symbol⟩= *me* or *mu*, ⟨symbol⟩= *n* as in *Nu*, the primeval waters of creation. Symbolic meanings include ⟨symbol⟩= flowering reed, ⟨symbol⟩= water ⟨symbol⟩= established. The determinative value is: ⟨symbol⟩= God, ⟨symbol⟩= hidden or un-manifest. Therefore, we have: Å-M-U-N (*a-mun*), *the God who is the flowering Life Force which is hidden and established in the waters of consciousness.* The similarity to the Hindu name of God, *A-U-M (Om),* should be noted. In the *Leyden Papyrus,* a late Ancient Egyptian Magical Papyrus, the word *Om* appears as one of the names of Amun-Ra. In Column IX entitled *Divination by Chons (Khonsu),* lines 5 and 6 read as follows:

> (5) "Great" is thy name, "Heir" is thy name, "Excellent" is thy name, "Hidden" is thy name. "Mighty one of the gods" is thy name," "He whose name is hidden from all the gods" is thy name, "Om," (6) "*Mighty Am*" is thy name, "*All the gods*" is thy name, "*Lotus-lion-ram*" is thy name, ...

Left: Mut as the vulture goddess and consort of Amun.

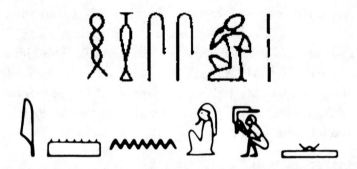

Hessu Amun

(The Hymns of Amun)

CHAPTER II

"THE HYMNS OF AMUN"

The following utterances are translations from Ancient Egyptian Hymns of Amun. A hymn is usually defined as: "A song of praise or thanksgiving, especially to God." The hymns were written upon papyruses, steles, reliefs and other inscriptions. Each verse is to be considered as Hekau or Words of Power, a mantram which when correctly understood and recited or chanted-*Hesi*, imparts wisdom which has a transformative effect on the human mind. This process of transformation leads the reciter towards divine awareness and communion with the Higher Self.

The Hymns of Amun

(i) *O Åmen, O Åmen, who art in heaven, turn thy face upon the dead body of the child, and make your child sound and strong in the Underworld.*

(ii) *O Åmen, O Åmen, O God, O God, O Åmen, I adore thy name, grant thou to me that I may understand Thee; Grant thou that I may have peace in the Duat, and that I may possess all my members therein...*

(iii) *Hail, Åmen, let me make supplication unto Thee, for I know thy name, and thy transformations are in my mouth, and thy skin is before my eyes.*

(iiii) *Come, I pray Thee, and place Thou heir and Thine image, myself, in the everlasting underworld... let my whole body become like that of a neter, let me escape from the evil chamber and let me not be imprisoned therein; for I worship thy name..*

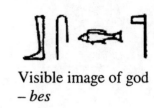

Visible image of god – bes

(see glossary)

1. *He is self-created and as He fashioned Himself none knows His forms.*

2. *He became in primeval time, no other being existed, there was no other god before Him, there was no other god with Him to declare His form, all the gods came into being after Him.*

3. *He had no mother by whom His name was made; He had no father who begat Him, saying, "It is even myself." He shaped His own egg. He mingled His seed with His body to make His egg to come into being within Himself.*

4. *His unity is Absolute. Amun is One One.*

5. *He is the creating wind which was over the waters of NUNU.*

6. *He is the Breath of Life, the spirit which permeates and vivifies all things.*

7. *He took the form of TANEN in order to give birth to the PAUTTI gods.*

8. *He hides His name from His children in this His name of Amun.*

9. *He makes Himself to be hidden.*

10. *The One, Amun, who hides Himself from men, who shrouds Himself from the gods; His color and appearance is not known.*

11. *The gods cannot pray to Him because His name is unknown to them.*

12. *His name is victory.*

13. *He, the One Watcher, who neither slumbers nor sleeps.*

14. *Amun drives away evils and scatters diseases.*

15. *He is the physician who heals the eye without medicaments; He opens the eyes; He drives away inflammation.*

16. *He delivers whom He pleases, even from the Duat (underworld).*

17. *He saves a man or woman from what is His lot at the dictates of their heart.*

18. *To Him belong both eyes and ears, on every path of them whom He loves.*

19. *He hears the petitions of they that appeal to Him.*

20. *To them that call Amun, He comes instantly.*

21. *He lengthens life; He cuts it short.*

22. *To them whom He loves. He gives more than hath been decreed for them.*

23. *When Amun casts a spell on the water, and His name is on the waters, if this name of His be uttered, the crocodile loses power, the winds are driven back, the hurricane is repulsed.*

24. *At the remembrance of Amun the wrath of the angry man dies down; He speaks the gentle word at the moment of strife.*

25. *He is a pleasant breeze to Him that appeal to Him.*

26. *He delivers the helpless one.*

27. *He is the wise God whose plans are beneficent.*

28. *He is more helpful than millions to the man who hath set Him in His heart.*

29. *One warrior (who fights) under His name is better than hundreds of thousands.*

30. *Indeed He is the beneficent strong one.*

31. *He is perfect and seizes His moment; He is irresistible.*

32. *All the gods are three, Amun, Ra and Ptah, and there are none other like unto them.*

33. *He whose name is hidden is Amun, Ra belongeth to Him as His face, and the body is Ptah.*

34. *Their cities are established on earth forever, Thebes, Anu, Hetkaptah.*

35. *When a message is sent in heaven it is heard in Anu, and is repeated in Hetkaptah to the Beautiful Face. It is done into writing in the letters of Djehuti, and dispatched to the city of Amun with their things. The matters are answered in Thebes.*

36. *His heart is understanding, His lips are Taste, His Kau are all the things that are in His mouth.*

37. *He enters, the two caverns are beneath His feet. The Nile appears from the hollow beneath His sandals. His soul is Shu, His heart is Tefnut. He is Horus of the two horizons in the upper heaven.*

38. *His right eye is day. His left eye is night. He is the leader of faces on every path. His body is Nu. The dweller in it is the Nile, producing everything that is, nourishing all that is.*

39. *He breaths breath into all nostrils.*

40. *The luck and destiny of every man and woman are with Him.*

41. *His wife is the Earth; He united with her.*

42. *His seed is the wheat plant, His effluxes are the grain.*

43. *Thou art Temu, who did create beings endowed with reason; Thou make the color of the skin of one race to be different from that of another, but, however many may be the varieties of mankind, it is Thou that make them all to live.*

44. *Thou art the lord of intelligence, and knowledge is that which proceed from Thy mouth.*

45. *Thou make every work to proceed; Thou work in the sky and Thou make to come into being the beauties of the daylight; the gods rejoice in Thy beauties, and their hearts live when they see Thee.*

46. *Thy beauties take possession of and carry away all hearts, and love for Thee make all arms to relax, Thy beautiful form make the hands to tremble, and all hearts melt at the sight of Thee.*

47. *Amen...Thou Being above who make the earth according to Thine own designs.*

48. *...at whose utterance the gods come into being, and food is created, ... and all things are come into being; the traverser of eternity, the old man who make himself young (again) through myriad's of pairs of eyes and numberless pairs of ears...*

Above: Amun as the Zoomorphic[12] Ram.

---

[12] Symbolism which uses animal images to depict spiritual or mystical principles.

CHAPTER III

Sheti Hessu Amun

**"The Mystical Teachings and Implications
of
The Hymns of Amun"**

The following is a commentary highlighting the most important mystical teachings presented in the Hymns. The individual hekau utterances will be discussed in detail. Each commentary is preceded by the symbol of Amun: ⚕ .

A Commentary On The Hymns of Amun

(i)- O Åmen, O Åmen, who art in heaven, turn Thy face
upon the dead body of the child, and make your child sound
and strong in the Underworld.

The opening line of any spiritual scripture is important because it gives a sense or tone of what is to follow. Those who are familiar with the Christian Bible will recognize that this line is similar to the *Lords Prayer*: "Our Father who art in Heaven, Hallowed be thy name...." Immediately the first hekau of the Hymns of Amun indicates the divine name of God, Amen, and invokes the Supreme Divinity to turn his attention toward the supplicant. There also is an immediate kinship established here between the one being prayed to and the one praying. There can be no closer human relationship than a relationship between a parent and a child, since along with the emotional attachment there is a biological bond. Thus the parent-child relationship is used as a metaphor to signify that you, as the one praying, are in reality closely related to God. But how can this be? How can it be possible for you to be related to God? Aren't you made of flesh, blood and other elements? Isn't God a spirit? Why should you seek help from a spirit to give you strength in the Underworld and what is the nature of this Underworld?

> Our relationship with the Divine Self.

The relationship between you and the Supreme Divinity is at the heart of all spiritual texts from Ancient Egypt, but it is perhaps most expressly outlined in the Hymns of Amun. Your body is essentially dead. It is in reality not any more alive than a stone or a piece of metal. It is the Spirit, the innermost reality of your soul, which enlivens it. Once the soul departs from the body, the body becomes "lifeless" and dissolves into the earth. The elements which comprise the body disintegrate and once again assume the form which they had before they became part of your body. From a higher perspective, you are dead in consciousness if you believe that you are the body and that when the body dies you will die. Therefore, it is said that those who have not realized their divine nature are spiritually dead. So where is life? What is it within you that can be said to be alive?

> Innermost Heart, Horus - *Abtelab Heru.* (see glossary)

The answers to these questions lie in the last word of the last line in the opening verse: Underworld. The Ancient Egyptian concept of creation includes three realms. These are the Earth ⟶ TA, Heaven Pet, and Duat, the Underworld. Duat (Ṭuat) is pronounced with the "Ṭ" sounding as a "D" in much the same way as the "*Tao*" of Taoism is pronounced "*Dao.*" The Duat is the abode of the gods, goddesses, spirits and souls. It is the realm where those who are evil or unrighteous-*N maat,*

> The pronunciation of the Ancient Egyptian Word for Netherworld.

are punished, but it is also where the righteous live in happiness. It is the "other world," the spirit realm. The Duat is also known as Amenta since it is the realm of Amen (Amun). The Duat is where Ra, as symbolized by the sun, traverses after reaching the western horizon, in other words, the movement of Ra between sunset and sunrise, i.e. at night. Some people thought that the Duat was under the earth since they saw Ra traverse downward and around the earth and emerged on the east, however, this interpretation is the understanding of the uninitiated masses. The esoteric wisdom about the Duat is that it is the realm of the unconscious human mind and at the same time, the realm of cosmic consciousness or the mind of God. Both the physical universe and the Astral Plane, the Duat, are parts of that cosmic consciousness.

The "Duat" is conceived of as a circular region which mirrors the physical world. It is a plane known as the "Astral World" which is devoid of physicality. It is the realm of the mind and senses. It is the place where the soul goes after the death of the physical body. If the person led a righteous life while alive, the experiences there will be heavenly. However, if the person led an unrighteous life then there will be hellish experiences. The Duat is the body of Asar. In the center of it is the Pillar of Asar, the Djed. A righteous person has the choice to go to the Djed and abide in Asar, to merge with him, or they can await the time when Ra traverses through the Duat illuminating it as He passes in his Barque. If they choose Ra, they will be picked up and be loaded unto the barque where they will merge with Ra and experience peace, bliss and happiness for all time. If they choose to stay in the Duat they will lead a life similar to that on earth but with very important differences. These differences are outlined in Chapter 175 of the Ancient Egyptian Book of Coming Forth By Day:

The Asar, the scribe Ani, whose word is truth, saith:- Hail, Temu! What manner of land is this unto which I have come? It hath not water, it hath not air; it is depth unfathomable, it is black as the blackest night, and men wander helplessly therein. In it a man cannot live in quietness of heart; nor may the desire for love-making be satisfied therein.

Temu: The state of the Spirit-souls has been given unto instead of water and air, and the satisfying of the longings of love, and quietness of heart has been given instead of cakes and ale.

It is important to understand that when the word "chooses" is used here it does not imply a conscious choice. Peoples preferences and desires, even in ordinary human life, are based on deeply rooted impressions in the unconscious which are stimulated when the person comes into contact with

The Pillar of Osiris.

objects in Creation. At the time of contact the innermost desires express themselves as an attachment or rejection of the objects based on the past karmic association with that objects. This is why some people like certain things and others hate those same things. In the same way that people make choices in life without understanding the reason, a soul in the astral world will choose based on the unconscious desires. This is why it is important to set up positive impressions so that they will manifest at the right time in life and the life hereafter. This is done through the various disciplines of yoga and mystical spirituality.

Sexuality and the physical pleasures which human beings seek are activities which can only be performed in the physical realm when there is a physical body and the mind and senses with which to experience. The Sahu or Spirit-Soul (living-soul, enlightened) state is beyond physicality and beyond time and space. Thus, in order to achieve this level of consciousness it is necessary to renounce and leave behind the ignorant and egoistic notions of the lower desires and the needs of the body. This process is outlined in the *Ausarian Resurrection Myth* as well as in the *Book of Coming Forth By Day*.

All human experiences occur in the mind.

All human experiences occur in the mind. Think about it. When you experience a dream, everything occurs in the mind. When you experience the sense of touch, it is not your body which is experiencing it, but your mind. Your mind registers sensation via messages which are sent to it through the nerves which have their connection to the brain. The brain registers the sensations and the mind interprets them in a particular way according to its conditioning. For example, the sensation of touching something soft is understood as softness because the mind has learned to interpret it as such. However, what are you experiencing when you are asleep having a dream? You are not using the senses or other parts of the body and yet there are sensations and feelings. In the Dream State, when you are sleeping or also when you are lost in a day dream, you are experiencing the Duat or the astral world. When you die you go to this world and have various experiences based on the life you led while on earth. If you were righteous, you will be led to heavenly experiences; if you were unrighteous, you will be led to hellish conditions.

In reality, you are the Spirit who is using a body to have physical experiences. Having forgotten about your true nature, you experience the pleasure and pain of the body, thinking that pleasure or pain is experienced because of something that the body does. In reality, it is your spirit which enlivens the brain and nervous system and allows them to bring sensations which you call experiences. The body acts as a safety valve in reference to pleasure and pain. If there is too much pain, the body automatically swoons and there is a cessation of the experience. If there is too much pleasure or elation, then again the body swoons. However, when the body dies, the mind survives and has perception of the astral (mental) world in much the same way as you have various experiences tumbling from one dream to another during a night's sleep. In this condition, the soul is led to experience various situations of pleasure or pain according to its past history of good or bad deeds (karma), and also according to its level of spiritual realization. This means that if you believe that you are the body, an individual personality, then you will continue to experience existence in that way. You will see yourself as an individual lost in a maze of situations which the mind can create endlessly. These situations are based on your deep-rooted unconscious desires and your level of ignorance about yourself.

The consequences of indulging in the pleasures of the senses.

There is a big difference in the level of intensity with which the experiences of the Astral Plane are perceived. In the bodiless state there is no safety valve to control the levels of pain or pleasure, and therefore, it is possible to experience unimaginable levels of pain as well as pleasure. These are known as hell or heaven, respectively. In the bodiless state the unconscious mind and the subtle senses remain with the soul when a person has not reached the heights of spiritual enlightenment (complete detachment from mind and senses). The unresolved desires in the unconscious emerge to impel the soul to move on in the search for fulfillment of those desires even though they are unreal and unnecessary. Imagine if you could do whatever you wanted to do but without restriction. If you wanted to eat pizza you can eat continuously without getting overweight or sick. If you want to do violence against certain people you will be able to do so in an unrestricted manner. If you want to indulge in any pleasures of the senses such as sex, music, beautiful sights, etc. you can do so. In so doing the intellect becomes overwhelmed and therefore unused. Thus the intellect becomes weak and atrophied. The senses take control and direct the path of the soul. At some point the astral experience is exhausted and then the soul, with its remaining unconscious impressions, returns to the physical realm in order to once again gain experiences as a living human being. If enlightenment is not attained, this cycle of birth, death and astral experiences is repeated over and over again, indefinitely.

What is "Purity of Heart."

This is why the process of yoga and mystical spirituality has as its primary goal to cleanse the unconscious impressions of the mind. In Ancient Egyptian terms this process, known as *Maak-heru* or "Purity of Heart," was the central mission presented in the *Ancient Egyptian Book of Coming Forth By Day*.

There is a special realm within the Duat. This is the abode of Asar as well as the ultimate destination of those who become enlightened. It is the realm of Supreme Peace. It is known as *Sekhet-Aaru* or in other times

Amentet. Amentet is a reference which unites the symbolism of Asar with that of Amun (Amen) because *Djed*, 𓊽, refers to the Djed or Djed Pillar of Asar. The Djed symbolizes the awakening human soul who is well "established" in the knowledge of the Self. *Djedu*, 𓊽𓊽𓏤𓇋𓏤𓊖, refers to the abode of Asar. This is what the following line from the *Egyptian Book of Coming Forth By Day*, Chapter I: 13-15, is referring to:

"I am steadfast, son of steadfast, conceived and born in the region of steadfastness."

The special realm within the Duat.

This special realm is shrouded in the deepest darkness and it is untouched by the myriad of cries, dismemberments and sufferings of unrighteous souls (the enemies of Ra) as well as the cries of happiness of the righteous souls who are experiencing heavenly or pleasurable conditions according to their good deeds of the past. This part of the Duat is composed of seven *Arits* or Halls. It transcends time and space as well as the mind and thoughts. It is absolute existence. The rest of the Duat as well as the physical world is relative reality. In this special realm, there is no growth of any kind. There is no birth and no death, no passage of time, just eternity. This is the meaning of the following hekau-utterance from The Egyptian *Book of Coming Forth By Day*, Chapter 125:1-17:

> The Asar, the scribe Ani (initiate), whose word is truth, saith: "I have come unto thee. I have drawn close to you in order to experience thy beauties. My hands are extended in adoration of thy name of "Maat" (Truth). I have come. I have drawn myself to the place where the cedar tree existeth not, where the acacia tree does not put forth shoots, and where the ground neither produces grass nor herbs. Now I have entered into the place of hidden things, and I hold converse with the god Set.... Asar the scribe Ani, hath entered into the house of Asar, and he hath seen the hidden and secret things which are therein....

The special hidden place.

That which is in the place where nothing grows-**Nrutef,** is the place of absolute stillness *Urti-hat*. It is a region that is devoid of forms or mental concepts of any kind. It is the primeval or celestial waters from which creation arises. It is the place which is "hidden" from that which is in motion, the relative reality. Therefore, it is hidden to those whose minds are in constant motion due to desires, cravings, emotional attachments, greed, etc. That which is relative or temporal emanates out of that which is absolute and eternal. The relative reality emanates from this hidden place of stillness. It is to this place of stillness where one must go and have "communion" with God. When this occurs, that which is hidden is revealed.

The mystical symbolism of darkness.

This deepest and most dark realm of the Duat is Asar, himself, and this is why Asar is referred to as the "Lord of the Perfect Black" and is often depicted as being black or green of hue. It is also why Nut, Aset, and Hathor are also described as "dark-skinned."[13] They are emanations from this realm of blackness which is described as a void or "*nothingness*" in the hieroglyphic papyrus entitled *The Laments of Aset (Aset) and Nebethet (Nebthet)*. This notion of nothingness is akin to the Buddhist notion of *Shunya* or the "void," which refers to the area of consciousness which is devoid of mental concepts and thoughts. When there are no thoughts or forms in the mind, it is calm, expansive and peaceful. When there are thoughts in the mind, the mental awareness is narrowed and defined in terms of concepts. If the mind is confined to these concepts and narrow forms of thought, then it is confined to that which is limited and temporal. If it eradicates its desires, cravings and illusions, then it becomes aware of the innermost reality and it realizes its connection to the entire cosmos. Thus, the teaching of the Duat (Amentet, Re-Stau, etc.) gives insight into the nature of the human mind. It is a description of the mental landscape, its demons, gods and goddesses (everything that leads to ignorance and mental agitation) as well as the way to discover the abode of the innermost Self (everything that leads to peace, harmony and wisdom). Therefore, the task of a spiritual aspirant is to eradicate the concepts, agitation, desires and cravings in the mind and to discover the "hidden" innermost reality which is Hetep (Supreme Peace), eternal and pure.

From a higher level of understanding, the Duat is the unconscious mind and Asar is that level which transcends the thinking processes... its deepest region. It is the level of consciousness that is experienced during deep dreamless sleep. Therefore, it is the "hidden" aspect of the human heart, and thus, it is also known as Amun.

---

[13] From an inscription in the temple of Denderah, Egypt.

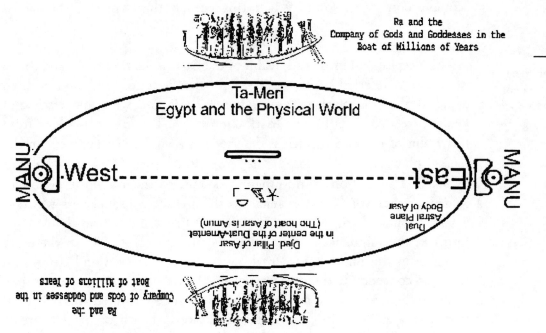

Left: Two dimensional rendering of the Physical plane and the Astral plane based on the Ancient Egyptian Mystical Teachings.

The experience of the Divine.

Having explored this most hidden region of the Duat (unconscious mind) through the practices of yoga and meditation, the initiate can now affirm that he or she has had experience of the Divine. Those who attain this experience are called Sages and/or Saints. Those who are established in this state of awareness, meaning that they have a continuous divine awareness based on this experience, are called enlightened Sages. Due to their mystical experience, anything that an enlightened Sage says is considered to be directly inspired by the Divine. Thus, they are considered to be "enlightened human Beings." This is the meaning of the following hekau-utterance from The *Egyptian Book of Coming Forth By Day*, Chapter 125:13-17:

> "I have entered into the House of Asar and I have removed the head coverings of Him that is therein. I have entered into Rasta, (1) and I have seen the Hidden One (2) who is therein. I was hidden but I found the boundary. (3) I journeyed to Nerutef (4) and He who was therein covered me with a garment....Verily He (Asar) (5) told me the things which concerned Himself."

The mystical meaning behind the hekau just presented is very important to the understanding of what is meant by the terms "enlightenment" and "mystical experience." (1) Rasta or Restau refers to the site of the grave of Asar; (2) "Hidden One" of course refers to the Shetai or Hidden Supreme Being who is known as Asar-Amun, (3) Here, the Initiate discovered that he/she was able to find the boundary and to discover the abode of the "Hidden One." The initiate was able to discover the difference between what is real and what is illusion, and was therefore able to traverse the illusory Duat and discover the special location wherein there is Supreme peace and immortality. (4) Nerutef refers to the mythological site of the grave of Asar or the innermost shrine. (5) This line imparts the wisdom that God him/herself is the one who ultimately gives the highest wisdom about God. All of the teachings of the scriptures are only incomplete and indirect descriptions of God because God transcends any and all mental concepts. Even though the spiritual scriptures are given by Sages and Saints who are in communion with God, the medium of communication, words and concepts, remain in the realm of the mind (relative reality). Therefore, the study of the scriptures and various rituals cannot in and of themselves confer enlightenment or the mystical experience of union with the Divine. For this to occur, it is necessary to actually experience the Divine and in order for this to occur, it is necessary to discover one's true essence as one with God, for only by becoming one with something can that thing be known. In this form of knowing, there is experience, unlike intellectual knowledge which does not confer experience. If a teacher tells you about China, you have "intellectual knowledge." If you visited China, you have "experience."

There is no way to describe the kind of knowledge that is gained through actual experience. Therefore, in order to truly have knowledge of the Divine, it is necessary to commune with the Divine. All other forms of knowledge are incomplete and will not lead to abiding peace-*Menu hetep* either while living on earth or in the Duat. This does not mean that acquiring intellectual knowledge is not important. Before you can harvest fruits, you must first plant the seeds. Before you plant the seeds, you must clear the land and prepare the soil. Intellectual knowledge tills the soil, removing the weeds and shrubs of mental agitation, egoism, selfishness and negativity. A seed planted in this fertile soil will grow into the tree of the subtle, purified intellect. Then it is possible to harvest the fruits of intuitional realization of the Self or Enlightenment. Shai and Rennenet are found in the judgment scene in the Hall of Maat wherein Djehuti records the result of a person's deeds and level of spiritual understanding. The hands of Djehuti (god of wisdom) are the goddess "Shai" which means "fate" or "destiny" and the goddess "Rennenet" which means "fortune and harvest." The implication is that you reap (harvest) the result of your actions (destiny) according to your level of wisdom. Thus, you yourself are the determiner of your own actions, the judge of your own actions and the determiner of your own fate and fortune or the fruits you will reap for those actions.

The metaphor of agriculture, sowing and reaping.

Those who are enlightened and have come to understand their oneness with Asar go to rejoin Asar in the *Beautiful West* (the Land of the Setting Sun- Ra) also known as Amenta, and become one with him. When you succeed in cultivating an intuitive intellect (*Saa*) which understands the nature of creation and the oneness of all things in the one "Hidden God," then you will achieve *Saa-Amenti-Ra*, the intelligence or knowledge of the Amenti of Ra, the hidden world. Those who do not achieve this level of spiritual realization are subjected to the various experiences which can occur in the Duat. Notice that the teaching of the Duat incorporates the main characters of the Ancient Egyptian religion, Amun, Ra and Asar, thus showing the uniformity of its understanding and the synchronicity of its teaching throughout Ancient Egypt.

The destiny of those who become enlightened.

It is of interest here to note the synchronicity between the Duat of Ancient Egypt and the Heaven in Christian symbolism. In the Bible, the book of Genesis speaks of how Adam and Eve, the primordial human beings, lived in a land of harmony and oneness, where all desires were fulfilled and there was an experience of unity with the Divine as well as immortality, and there was no desire because there was fulfillment. In this respect, the Garden of Eden may be likened to the special realm of Asar, Amentet.

Above: Osiris' body bent in a circle surrounded by the Primeval Ocean of Creation.

The body of Osiris (God) is the eternal Life Force which sustains Creation. The body of Osiris itself is the heart of the Ṭuat or Astral Plane and the supreme abode of Osiris as well as the goal of all spiritual practice.

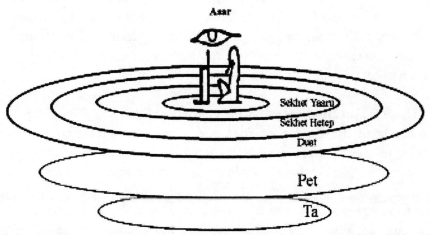

Above: A three dimensional diagram of existence based on the teachings of the Prt M Hru (Book of the Dead) and the Book of Am Duat (Book of What is in the Duat). It contains the Ancient Egyptian concept of Creation includes three realms. These are the TA, ═══ⅠⅠ (Earth), Pet, ═══□◠ (Heaven), and the Duat ★🐦◠▭ (the Netherworld). Notice that the earth plane is the smallest and the more subtle planes are larger and the abode (Aset) of Asar is in the center of Creation.

Adam and Eve were tempted by a serpent to eat from a fruit which had been forbidden to them. Prior to the eating from the *Tree of Knowledge of Good and Evil*, Adam and Eve did not have any special feeling of differentiation between themselves or with nature. Everything was the same, equal. However, desire in their hearts led them to eat from the tree of knowledge of good and evil, and this knowledge immediately caused them to see differences between themselves, within nature and between themselves and God.

The serpent is the symbol of Life Force energy which courses through every human being. It engenders desires and impels a human being to action. The *Tree of Knowledge of Good and Evil* is therefore, a symbol of the pairs of opposites. Instead of there being just oneness, pure awareness of one consciousness, singularity, now there is awareness of multiplicity and duality, the pairs of opposites, good-evil, you-me, here-there, up-down, male and female. Consciousness is now aware of individual parts of itself, as it were. Instead of being aware that the tree, the squirrel and themselves have the same origin and the same essence (God), there is forgetfulness and a feeling of separateness. Having eaten from the tree, everything became as if transformed by magic. The Garden of Eden seemed to be transformed from a place of joy and bliss into the world of multiplicity, separateness, duality and conflicting egos and desires which is perceived by ordinary human beings. The eating from the Tree of Knowledge of Good and Evil represents their leaving of the Garden of Eden. In effect, Adam and Eve have caused their own exile from the garden due to their desire filled minds. Thus, having been cast out of the garden they now experience mortality instead of immortality, and the pains and sorrows of human experience.

There is also another tree in the Garden of Eden, the *Tree of Life*. It is in the center of the Garden of Eden and it represents regeneration and the return to the primordial state of being. This is the tree of knowledge (wisdom) upon whose realization, humankind achieves whole consciousness. This wisdom includes consciousness of that which is mortal and changeable and also of that which is immortal and changeless. This is the state of Enlightenment which Jesus expresses in the words: *"I am Alpha and Omega, the beginning and the ending..."* from Revelations 1:8. In the same way that Horus of Egypt and Krishna of India are masters of *"Above and Below"* (mortal consciousness and divine consciousness), Jesus is also. Both trees are in the same place, human consciousness. Therefore, the Tree of Knowledge of Good and Evil has caused us to forget about the Tree of Life. In the psycho-mythology of Ancient Egypt there is also a Tree of Life which is propitiated for its sustaining food and drink which is given by the goddess of creation. In Egyptian mythology there is also a serpent. He is called *Apophis* and he represents the distracting, mischievous nature of the mind

The symbolism of the serpent.

The tree of knowledge of good and evil.

The Tree of Life.

which diverts the soul from its consciousness of oneness into the world of time and space, duality. This is the same serpent which distracted Adam and Eve and which afflicts humankind today, every time you are distracted by emotions, anger, hate, greed, passion, desire, etc. Through these feelings and emotions, your mind is driven away from the peace of pure, undifferentiated consciousness, however, if you learn the art of mystical living (practice of yoga) it is possible to eradicate stress and mental unrest in order to uncover the peace of the Self which is always there patiently awaiting rediscovery.

The Modern Christmas Tree

In the development of early Christianity, there was a tradition which held that Jesus was crucified on the Tree of Knowledge of Good and Evil. Jesus, like Asar, represents the soul who is leaving the Garden of Eden in order to come into the field of human experience (duality, multiplicity, happiness and sorrow, etc.). Therefore, the soul is being crucified by duality and multiplicity. This is the same idea of Asar being dismembered by his evil brother Set. Asar' dismemberment represents the scattering of the consciousness of the soul due to desires, egoism and ignorance. It was not until later that the tree symbol gave way to the cross symbol due to the numbers of Christian martyrs who were crucified by the Roman Empire. However, the mystical symbolism of the Christian Cross is that it represents time and space (duality and multiplicity) consciousness. In a subtle way, this mystical symbolism may be seen in modern day Christmas Trees since they are cut in such a way that they taper towards the top, ending in a point surmounted by the single star. This is the same symbolism represented in the great pyramids wherein each side represents duality and opposing forces which unify at the top and are transcended in the *Capstone* or uppermost point.

The Ancient Egyptian Pyramid

Therefore, the way to rediscover the original essence is to find the Tree of Life. In the New Testament, John 11:25, Jesus says that "I am the resurrection, and the life: he that believes in me, though he were dead, yet shall he live.." Like Jesus, Horus was the symbol of: "The resurrection and the life" and he, as the son of God (Asar), was also known to walk on water. Thus, by following the examples and teachings of Horus and Jesus, spiritual enlightenment is achieved.

The project of Enlightenment from a Christian point of view is to regain the knowledge of your divine nature (Tree of Life) and thus achieve complete consciousness within yourself. In this sense the Christian Tree of Life is equal to the *Caduceus* of Djehuti-Hermes or the Djed Pillar of Asar of Egypt, the *Chakras of Kundalini* Indian Yoga and the *Sefirotic Tree of Life* in the Cabalah.

The Pillar of Asar

Thus, The Tree of Life in Christian symbolism may be likened to the Pillar of Asar. In the myth of Asar and Aset, after Asar was killed by Set, his body grew into a tree. The pillar of Asar was made from this tree. The tree had developed such beauty and fragrance that a king discovered it and cut it into the shape of a pillar for his palace. Aset discovered the whereabouts of her dead husband and then revived him. This is the source of the Ancient Egyptian ritual of "Raising the Djed." The Pillar of Asar is a mystical symbol representing the four highest stages of spiritual experience. It also refers to the four higher psycho-spiritual energy centers of the subtle human (astral) anatomy which are developed through the various practices of mystical spirituality (yoga) outlined here. Aset represents wisdom, therefore, it is through the practice and discovery of the ultimate wisdom, your true Self, that you can return to, rediscover or resurrect your essential reality as an immortal, eternal being who is united with the source of all creation, the Divine Self.

The mind which is weakened by ignorance and lacks will and self-control will fall sway to the myriad visions and experiences of the Duat just as you fall prey to the experiences of a dream during sleep. These experiences can range from peaceful to violent and it is the reason why utterance (i) of the Hymns of Amun requests strength in the Duat and the next utterance (ii) makes supplication for peace in the Duat.

Through the practices of yoga (control of senses, dispassion and detachment toward sense objects, meditation, etc.), a yogi is able to gain control of the mind so not as to be caught up in the illusions of the Duat and thereby, he/she is able to discover Asar within him/herself and becomes *sound and strong in the Underworld*, i.e., he or she attains Enlightenment.

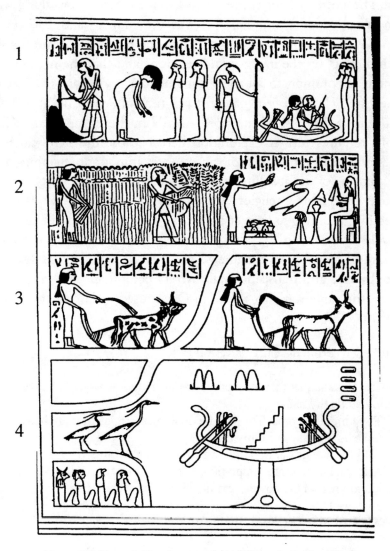

Above: The Tuat - Sekhet-hetepet of Anhai from the *Book of Coming Forth by Day of Initiate Anhai.*

1- Lady Anhai pays homage to her parents.
2- Anhai binds wheat into bundles.
3- Anhai is seen ploughing.
4- The Celestial Boat.

> (ii)- *O Åmen, O Åmen, O God, O God, O Åmen, I adore*
> *Thy name, grant Thou to me that I may understand Thee;*
> *Grant Thou that I may have peace in the Duat, and that I*
> *may possess all my members therein...*

As stated earlier, the Hymn of Amun is similar to the Christian Lord's Prayer. The Lord's Prayer is presented in its entirety below along with two Indian Yoga-Vedanta prayers, *The Gayatri Mantra* and *The Prayer for Universal Welfare*, to reinforce the fact that the Hymns of Amun have had a profound effect on the major world religions and that the highest spiritual sentiment is common to all the great religions. Compare the last part of Matthew 6:9, *Hallowed be thy name*, to Hymns of Amun hekau (ii) above, *I adore thy name*. The use of the word AMEN in the Egyptian and Christian religions requires further exploration here because the significance of the word Amen in Egyptian mythology connotes important teachings as to the understanding of the absolute reality, the Transcendental Deity or Supreme Being. In the Hebrew religion, the word Amen is usually explained as an interjection, meaning *so be it*. It is used at the end of a prayer or to express approval. However, in Egyptian mythology and symbolism, the source of *Amen*, Amen signifies an extremely sophisticated and elaborate explanation of the absolute and transcendental mystery behind all physical phenomena in much the same way that the term *Om* is used in Hindu mythology and religion.

Matthew 6 (From the Christian Bible)

9. After this manner therefore pray ye: Our Father who art in heaven, Hallowed be thy name.
10 Thy kingdom come. Thy will be done on earth, as [it is] in heaven.
11 Give us this day our daily bread.
12 And forgive us our debts, as we forgive our debtors.
13 And lead us not into temptation, but deliver us from evil: For thine is the kingdom, and the power, and the glory, for ever. Amen.

The Gayatri Mantra (From Hinduism)

We pray to that Divine Self,
who illumines the three planes of existence:
physical, astral and causal.
Who is effulgent as the sun.
May the Divine Self illumine our intellect.

The Prayer for Universal Welfare continues[14]:

Lead me from untruth to truth.
Lead me from darkness to light.
Lead me from death to immortality.

The mystical symbol "AUM."

In Indian-Vedantic mysticism, Om is known as the root of all mantras or words of power. Thus, almost all Indian mantras begin with Om. The mystical meaning behind Om is to be found in the formula of its construction. Om is made up of four letters. These are A, U, M and ( ). "A" represents the physical reality, the Waking State of consciousness where you are aware of the physical body and day to day activities. "U" represents the Dream State of consciousness where you are conscious of the astral body and the Dream State. "M" represents the deep Sleep State of consciousness where you go beyond the waking and Dream States. This is the realm of the causal body. Here one is in contact with the real Self, although not at the conscious level. "( )" represents the silence after the "M" sound is finished. It symbolizes the transcending of the three previous states of consciousness into the realm of experiencing the Absolute Truth of reality which is not possible through the intellectual (thought) process. Our true consciousness, the constant spectator of the previous three states of consciousness may be realized by waking up from these three states through meditation. If you pronounce the letters A, U and M, you will notice that all of the possible sounds that can be created with the mouth are contained between the sounds "A" and "M." Therefore, AUM encompasses all sounds in creation. Sound is the medium of creation. This concept was translated into Christianity as the "WORD" or "LOGOS" contained in the son of God the Father, Jesus. In this sense, Jesus became the *Word made flesh*. However, thousands of years before the creation of Christianity, Horus, the son of Asar, was known as the *Word made flesh*.

The Ancient Egyptian teaching of Heka and the Indian

Heka is equivalent to the Hindu concept of *Maya* or cosmic magical illusion, wherein the world, which is Pure Consciousness (*Brahman*), appears as other than what it really is. In Hindu mythology, *AUM (Om)* was the first sound uttered by God, and with its utterance creation came into being. Likewise, much earlier in Ancient Egypt, the word "Heka" was used for the same purpose and in the same way. According to the ancient hieroglyphic texts, the first sound uttered by God was "*HEKA.*" This utterance constituted the first act which brought creation into being. In the creation story of *Neb-Er-Djer* (Neb-er-tcher), the creator says: *I was One by myself for they* (the gods-nature-creation) *were not born and I had not produced Shu and I had not produced Tefnut. I brought my own mouth, my name as HEKA.* Thus, *Heka* was the first utterance of creation which turned the primeval

---

[14] (From Hinduism)

waters into the visible universe. Heka is also an act of mind and not a physical act, as the Creator explains: *I found no place on which to stand* (solid objects), *I used a spell* (Hekau) *in my heart* (mind - pure consciousness - primeval waters), *and so formed the designs* (forms) *of the material objects which subsequently came into being.*

Om is a universal word of power which was used in Ancient Egypt and is used extensively in India by yogis. Om or AUM[15] is related to the word Amun from Ancient Egypt and Amun is related to the Amen of Christianity. Therefore, Om is generally useful for spiritual practice. Om* is also not related to a particular deity but is common to all. It is also the hekau - mantra of the 6th energy center at the point between the eyebrows known as the Ancient Egyptian *Arat* or Uraeus serpent and the *Third eye of Shiva* in India.

> The mystic word of power: Om.

While *Om* is most commonly known as a *Sanskrit* mantra (word of power from India), it also appears in the Ancient Egyptian texts and is closely related to the Kemetic *Amun* in sound and Amen of Christianity. More importantly, it has the same meaning as Amun and is therefore completely compatible with the energy pattern of the entire group. According to the Egyptian Leyden papyrus, the name of the "Hidden God," referring to Amun, may be pronounced as *Om,* or *Am.*

Om is a powerful sound; it represents the primordial sound of creation. Thus it appears in Ancient Egypt as Om, in modern day India as Om, and in Christianity as Amen, being derived from Amun. Om may also be used for engendering mental calm prior to beginning recitation of a longer set of words of power or it may be used alone as described above. One Indian Tantric scripture (*Tattva Prakash*) states that Om or AUM can be used to achieve the mental state free of physical identification and can bring union with *Brahman* (the Absolute transcendental Supreme Being - God) if it is repeated 300,000 times. In this sense, mantras such as Om, Soham, Sivoham, Aham Brahmasmi are called *Moksha Mantras* or mantras which lead to union with the Absolute Self. Their shortness promotes greater concentration and force toward the primordial level of consciousness.

Knowing the name of something is knowing the essence of that thing. Knowing the name of God means having the key which opens the entire universe for discovery. Chanting (repetition of hekau-mantras) and understanding the mystical implications of the names are the way to unlock the door to self-discovery.

---

[15] For more detailed information on hekau-mantras see *Initiation Into Egyptian Yoga* by Dr. Muata Ashby.

In present day Egypt, the followers of mystical Islam, known as Sufism, can be heard chanting the Divine name *Allah* continuously for hours in hopes of being swept away into the ecstasy of divine awareness. Sufis go to the Ancient Egyptian temples and perform rituals which are a mixture of esoteric Islam and the Shetaut Neter (Mysteries of Ancient Egypt) and incorporate the African drum beats and dancing forms. The purpose of the chanting, dancing and drumming practices is to engender an ecstasy which shifts the state of consciousness. The rituals, hymn chanting and other rituals in Ancient Egypt directed to the various Ancient Egyptian Gods and Goddesses had the same purpose, namely, to transport the practitioner to a different level of consciousness wherein the Divine may be experienced. This state may be likened to a trance or meditative state of mind. In the same way, Jesus exhorted his followers to exalt the name of God. This practice is also very important part of Hindu worship.

Saa, the Intellectual capacity of a human being.

Another important feature of Hymns of Amun hekau (ii) is the appeal for understanding (*Saa*). As stated earlier, understanding the mystical implications of the teaching is a most important facet of mystical spiritual practice. Therefore, the supplication for understanding is of paramount importance both in the Ancient Egyptian and Indian prayers. The Ancient Egyptian god of intellect, *Saa*, is being invoked here. The mind is capable of taking any direction it is given, provided the mind is disciplined and controlled. The practices of studying the wisdom teachings, chanting the divine name, meditation, control of the senses, etc., lead the mind in the direction of greater and greater understanding of the Divine. Understanding is possible only when the mind is not distracted by the ignorance, delusions and restlessness of desires which are always besieging the heart (unconscious mind). The hymn proceeds to unfold the greatest mystical teachings, knowing which, a spiritual aspirant may attain the highest level of self-knowledge.

The solar barque of Amun-Ra and the Company of gods and goddesses of Amun

(iii)- *Hail, Åmen, let me make supplication unto Thee, for I know thy name, and Thy transformations are in my mouth, and Thy skin is before my eyes.*

Along with having knowledge of the Divine Name, the next most important point is to have at least intellectual or indirect knowledge about the nature of the Divine. The mouth is a symbol of creation. In the same manner as a human being creates ideas and manifests those by means of speech, God creates the entire universe by means of the utterance of sounds which transforms that which is unformed into the phenomenal universe. This point, already discussed above, will be further elaborated on in the commentary to hekau #5.

The mouth is also the symbol of memory-consciousness. It is the symbol of reawakening or remembrance of one's true nature. In the "*Opening of the Mouth*" ceremony, the mouth of the initiate is opened up through the force of the hekau, the ritual itself and the force of the spiritual practices which have been leading up to the initiation ritual. Knowing the process of creation, you as the spiritual aspirant must realize that you are also endowed with creative powers since you are essentially the "child" of God. Therefore, realizing that everything is a manifestation of the Divine, there is an acknowledgment that the various transformations and multiplicity which are found in nature is nothing more than expressions of the Divine. All is God. Thus knowing and understanding this wisdom brings about the realization that God is before your eyes, at every moment, expressing Himself/Herself as everything that you see or perceive with any of the senses.

> (iiii)- *Come, I pray Thee, and place Thou heir and Thine image, myself, in the everlasting Duat... let my whole body become like that of a neter, let me escape from the evil chamber and let me not be imprisoned therein; for I worship Thy name..*

Identity with the Divine.

There is an important realization in the hekau (iiii). It relates to the understanding that you are not only the heir of God, but that you are yourself, the image of God. God expresses as the phenomenal universe which includes you and all people and living things. With this understanding, the next line requests that God should open up that special portion of the Duat or Underworld which is everlasting.

As you begin to realize your innate divinity, the desire to cease your identification of yourself with your mortal body and personality arises. You begin to understand that your mortal personality is not abiding. Your spiritual awareness is opening you up to the fact that you can transform yourself into a neter, meaning that you can become one with the cosmic forces or expressions of God (Neter) who manifests in the form of neteru or cosmic forces of creation. The various Gods and Goddesses who comprise the company of Amun, Asar, Ra or Ptah are neteru.

The deeper implication of the relationship between Neter and neteru is that the neteru are expressions of Neter in much the same way as light is an expression of the sun. Therefore, when you begin to consciously realize your Divine nature and to move towards it as opposed to allowing yourself to become more and more deeply involved in worldly entanglements and concerns which carry your thoughts and aspirations, you are truly waking up to the ever-present reality which was always there, though forgotten.

As your intuitional realization of the teachings grows, you are becoming aware of the fact that you are indeed a spirit who has identified and associated with the mortal body, and that this association has deluded you into believing that you are mortal and limited. In reality, you are a free spirit and not bound to the confines of the physical body or any physical location. The Spirit pervades the entire universe, therefore you, as one with the Divine, encompass the entire universe. From this aspect, the body may be seen as the "evil chamber" which holds the soul in an "imprisoned" state. This state of imprisonment is due to the fact that the mind is beset with ignorance and is unaware of its true nature.

From an advanced perspective, when you begin to realize your innate Divinity, you will discover that the physical body is nothing more than an expression of your mind in much the same way that this universe is an expression of the mind of God. Knowing this, there will no longer be a contradiction between what is divine and what is not divine. This entire universe, from beginning to end, from the smallest particle to the largest celestial bodies of planets and stars, is an expression of the Divine. The human soul, as a special expression or reflection of Divine Consciousness, has been endowed with the power to create thoughts, a physical body, and the experiences which the body encounters in the course of ordinary human life. Thus, YOU are the creator of your body as well as the situations you experience in life, be they positive or negative. Through spiritual studies and practice, you can consciously come into harmony with creation (becoming like a neter), and thereby improve your human conditions while leading yourself to the highest levels of self-discovery wherein there is transcendence of all which is mortal, finite and affected by ignorance.

1. He is self-created and as He fashioned Himself, none knows His forms.

2. He became in primeval time; no other being existed; there was no other god before Him; there was no other god with Him to declare His form, all the gods came into being after Him.

3. He had no mother by whom His name was made. He had no father who begat Him, saying, "It is even myself." He shaped His own egg. He mingled His seed with His body to make His egg to come into being within Himself.

4. His unity is Absolute. Amun is One - One.

God is the Self. The Self is a self-existent being which transcends concepts of creation and created. The Self emerged out of the Self and what emerged is none other than the Self. Creation and the Self are one and the same. God assumes the names and forms which human beings call objects and the varied life forms which are in existence. Although the Self is the sustaining force behind all phenomena and all life, human beings are ignorant of the existence of this force and thus see themselves as the source of their own existence. They are ignorant to the fact that their very existence is sustained by the Self. Through this process of ignorance, human consciousness is fooled into believing that its thoughts and ideas are its own and that its memories and experiences constitute its unique existence. This concept of a unique and separate existence is what constitutes egoism in human existence and the separation from Divine Consciousness. (See also the explanation of hekau-utterance 44)

5. He is the creating wind which was over the waters of NUNU.

Nu: the Primeval Ocean

The teaching of the Primeval Ocean occurs in Jewish and Hindu mysticism.

Egyptian Mythology is filled with stories of Gods and Goddesses, but all of them are related in a harmonious manner which, when understood correctly, helps to unlock the mysteries of the human heart. Egyptian mythology begins with the existence of the Nu, the Primeval Ocean. The creation stories of the Bible, the Cabalah (Jewish Mysticism) and the Upanishads (Indian Mysticism) are remarkably similar in the notion of the original primeval formlessness and in the subsequent names and forms (differentiation and objectification of matter) which arose later.

Ancient Egyptian Shabaka Inscription:

"Ptah conceived in His heart (reasoning consciousness) all that would exist and at His utterance (the word - will, power to make manifest), created Nun, the primeval waters (unformed matter-energy).

Then, not having a place to sit Ptah causes Nun to emerge from the primeval waters as the Primeval Hill so that he may have a place to sit. Atom (Atum) then emerges and sits upon Ptah. Then came out of the waters four pairs of gods, the Ogdoad (eight gods):

From Genesis 1 (Bible):

1. In the beginning God created the heaven and the earth.
2. And the earth was without form, and void; and darkness [was] upon the face of the deep. And the Spirit of God moved upon the face of the waters.

From the Sepher (Sefir) Yezirah:[16]

These are the ten spheres of existence, which came out of nothing. From the spirit of the Living God emanated air, from the air, water, from the water, fire or ether, from the ether, the height and the depth, the East and the West, the North and the South.

---

[16] Cabalism

From the Zohar:

Before God manifested Himself, when all things were still hidden in him... He began by forming an imperceptible point; this was His own thought. With this thought, He then began to construct a mysterious and holy form...the Universe.

From the Laws of Manu (Indian):

Manu is a Sage-Creator, God of Indian Hindu-Vedic tradition who recounts the process of Creation wherein the *Self-Existent Spirit* (God) felt desire. Wishing to create all things from His own body, God created the primeval waters (Nara) and threw a seed into it. From the seed came the golden cosmic egg. The Self-Existent Spirit (Narayana) developed into Brahma (Purusha) and after a year of meditation, divided into two parts (Male and Female).

When you think of your body you don't differentiate between the left leg and the right, the lips and the face, or the fingers and the arm. In a mysterious way, you consider all the parts as a whole and call this "me." In the same way, in the state of Enlightenment, the entire universe is understood as "me." Consciousness is essentially pure until the association with the ego develops. Then multiplicity and duality appear to exist, but as the following passages explain, the multiplicity of creation is merely the forms which energy takes on as it moves and interacts in different polarities or the pairs of opposites. This concept of vibrations being the underlying cause of the phenomenal world existed within the Egyptian mystical text called *The Kybalion*. The teachings of the Kybalion will be discussed in the commentary to verse 45 of the Hymns of Amun.

From the Cabalah:

Polarity is the principle that runs through the whole of creation, and is in fact, the basis of manifestation. Polarity really means the flowing of force from a sphere of high pressure to a sphere of low pressure, high and low being always relative terms. Every sphere of energy needs to receive the stimulus of an influx of energy at higher pressure, and to have an output into a sphere of lower pressure. The source of all energy is the Great Un-manifest (God), and it makes its own way down the levels, changing its form from one to the other, till it is finally "earthed" in matter.

The pure impulse of dynamic creation is formless; and being formless, the creation it gives rise to can assume any and every form.

The following passage comes from *Lao-Tzu*, the classical Taoist writer who popularized Taoism in China at the same time that *Buddha* and *Mahavira* developed Buddhism and Jainism in India. He further illustrates the idea of undifferentiated versus differentiated consciousness.

There was something undifferentiated and yet complete, which existed before heaven and earth. Soundless and formless, it depends on nothing and does not change.
It operates everywhere and is free from danger.
It may be considered the mother of the universe.

The same idea of *"formlessness"* or *"undifferentiated"* matter occurs in the *Rig* (Rik) *Veda*, the Upanishads and the Bhagavad Gita from India as well. The only difference between the following texts is that the Gita takes all of the attributes of the manifest and un-manifest nature of divinity and incorporates them in the anthropomorphic personality of Krishna.

From the Rig Veda:

There was neither non-existence nor existence then; there was neither the realm of space nor the sky beyond. There was no distinguishing sign of night nor of day... Desire came upon that one in the beginning; that was the first seed of mind.

From the Upanishads:

There are, assuredly, two forms of the Eternal: the formed and the formless, the mortal and the immortal, the stationary and the moving, the actual and the illusory.

Gita: Chapter 9:17

I am the Father of the universe; I am the Mother, the sustainer, as well as the Grandfather. I am the goal of Vedic knowledge, I am the sacred Om, I am verily the Vedas in the form of Rik, Yaju and Sama.

The Ancient Egyptian Primordial Ocean

Before there was any god or goddess, even Ra or Asar and Aset, and before there was any physical matter, the planets, the sun, animals, human beings, etc., there was the Primeval Ocean and from it emanated all that exists. There are stories of a Primeval Ocean in other cultures. Hinduism also includes teachings in reference to the Primeval Ocean and the Christian Bible begins with creation emanating out of primeval waters, in the book of Genesis. The oldest notion and greatest emphasis on the concept of the Primeval Ocean comes from Ancient Egypt.

In the same manner that waves arise out of the ocean, and appear to be of different shapes, sizes and textures, the objects of the phenomenal universe, the sun, stars, planets trees, animals and all living beings, arise out of this Primeval Ocean. But this rising did not only occur once in the "beginning of time;" it is continually occurring. All objects in nature are continuously sustained by an "unseen" force which modern science cannot fully explain. However, science does explain some characteristics of the phenomenal universe and these reveal an ocean of energy wherein all things are interrelated and bound together, as opposed to the ordinary thinking of a universe full of separate objects which are composed of different elements. In fact, modern science reveals that all objects in the universe are composed of the same "stuff." All of the "elements" have the same basis, energy. Further, all matter is merely a manifestation of that same essence, but in different modes of manifestation. This facet of matter was explained thousands of years ago by the Sages of mystical wisdom.

The Sages have shown that consciousness or pure awareness is the basis of all matter, just as when you are not thinking, there are no thoughts or vibrations in the consciousness of your mind. In the same way, this universe is a manifestation of the thought process of the Supreme Being. Therefore, it is possible to have an infinite number of elements and combinations of those elements just as it is possible for you to create anything in your mind out of your consciousness when applied towards the imaginative and dream processes.

When the body dies, it returns to the earth from whence it arose. Where does the soul go? It returns to the ocean of consciousness, as represented by the Duat, and if it is not enlightened, returns to this Physical Plane of existence to have more human experiences. When enlightenment is attained through the practice of yoga, one communes with the ocean of pure and infinite consciousness which is an ever existing reality beyond the grasp of those who are devoid of spiritual sensitivity. Your limited mind is like a wave in the ocean of the Supreme Being. However, though the waves seem to be separate and you seem to be alone, in reality God is always there and is the very fabric of all physical objects as well as the very source and sustenance of human consciousness. It is due to the distractions of the mind caused by desires, illusions, cravings, longings and ignorance that the innermost recesses of your unconscious mind is veiled from conscious awareness. Nevertheless, the exterior world and the internal world are nothing but manifestations of the primeval waters, God, the Higher Self within all beings.

Sheti defined.

When you delve deeply into the mysteries of the ocean of consciousness within your mind, you are able to discover the deeper truths about your real essence, origin and purpose. This is the process called *Sheti*. Sheti is the intense study of the teachings through good association-*Smait,* with Sages and others who are spiritually elevated personalities. When the wisdom teachings are studied deeply and the mystical implications are understood, a special form of transformation occurs which leads to the discovery of the highest spiritual truths within one's heart. Discovering this glorious truth of your true nature. This is the goal of yoga and all mystical philosophies.

Thus, in the same way as a form is within a stone and can be carved into a sculpture, all objects in creation exist, arise and dissolve into the Primeval Ocean. In other words, from the singular, preexistent ocean of consciousness arises all that exists as a thought in the mind of God, in the form of a Trinity or Triad of consciousness. Therefore, from the one arises the three.

The Self, God, is a sea of pure consciousness (NUNU or NUN), and out of that same sea came creation. Creation, then, is the sea which has been rippled with waves by the wind of thought vibrations. These thought vibrations are the result of desires of the mind. In the same way a placid lake reflects the unbroken image of the moon and when disturbed by a rock develops ripples, the pure consciousness of the mind is fragmented, rippled as it were, by the thought waves caused by desire for worldly experiences. Because of this rippling of consciousness, there appears to be many moons when there is in reality only one. If the lake of the mind were to be calmed, if there were no desires, then the mind would reflect its essential unity and non-duality. The primeval waters never changed into creation. Creation is the primeval waters itself and is continuously changing according to the winds of Cosmic vibration as prescribed by the Cosmic Mind (God). Therefore, creation is a continuous process which occurs at every moment by God's consciousness, i.e. God's very presence.

The relentless decay of matter.

All matter is in reality cosmic mental thought substance in varying degrees of vibration and varying degrees of subtlety. The subtlest material is the Self, God, and the Self permeates all other things from the less subtle material which composes the astral world (Duat) to the grosser material which composes the physical world. Nevertheless, all matter is in a state of vibration and its existence is continually being sustained by the Self. This process of sustaining creation occurs every instant of every day just as the form and structure of the human body is sustained by a continuous process of new cells being created to substitute for those which are dying off. Every cell in the body is changed every year. Therefore, you do not have the same body you had a year ago. In the same way, the atoms of the house you live in are not the same as they were yesterday even though the house "looks" to be the same as before. Thus, what is considered to be "solid" matter is not solid at all. This is also the reason why things break down. If you were to allow a longer time to pass, say fifty years, this process would be more obvious. No object escapes the power of time which withers everything away. Sooner or later, everything breaks down and dissolves back into its original state. Even the most spectacular monuments and architectural creations will someday deteriorate to the point of no longer being usable or recognizable. Look at the Pyramids and the Sphinx. Having withstood the ravages of time for over 12,000 years, they are showing signs of deterioration. Even the most perfectly constructed machines or objects cannot escape the movement of time and eventually breaks down.

Think of a building. What is its life span? Say that it will last one hundred years and then will have to be torn down to build a new one. Every year there is a certain amount of destruction or dissolution which occurs in the atoms of the building. It could be said that it breaks down one hundredth of its life span every year. The movement of dissolution is slow, and those who do not reflect on it, those who do not acknowledge the hidden mystical teaching are missing the opportunity to discover the hidden essence which underlies the phenomenal world of time and space. You must study and understand the teachings of mystical spirituality now while there is "time," prior to the time of your death.

Another important teaching to understand about "matter" is that the substratum of all objects is the same and therefore, all objects can be transmuted or transformed into others. Even the most foul smelling rotten matter can be rearranged at the molecular or subatomic level and changed into the most fragrant substance. Solid matter can be converted into energy and then back into solid material form once again. These findings have been confirmed by modern physics experiments.

The underlying power of time comes from the continuous process of movement in creation. In the same manner that the human mind does not "stand still," the universe is continuous motion. Even at subatomic levels, matter, regardless of how solid it may appear to be, changes. The physical universe is in constant dissolution and creation. This is the reason why the solar and lunar barque of Amun-Ra (⛵) traverses the heavens perpetually, and must constantly battle the forces of chaos and disorder

The continuous process of movement in nature.

(Set). Amun-Ra constantly establishes Maat (cosmic order) and thereby maintains the phenomenal universe in existence. The barque traverses through the heavens, and every evening is consumed by the cow-goddess, Nut. Every morning she gives birth to it, renewing its life.

This utterance is the progenitor of the Christian and Hebrew idea of creation described in the book of Genesis where God or the Spirit hovers over and stirs the primeval waters. The original Biblical texts express the creation more in terms of an act of sexual union: *Elohim* (Ancient Hebrew for gods/goddesses) impregnates the primeval waters with *ruach*, a Hebrew word which means *spirit*, *wind* or the verb *to hover*. The same word means *to brood* in Syriac. Thus, as the book of Genesis explains, creation began as the spirit of God moved over the waters and agitated those waters into a state of movement. In Western traditions, the active role of Divinity has been assigned to the male gender while the passive (receiving) role has been assigned to the female gender. This movement constitutes the dynamic *female* aspect of the Divine in Tantric (Eastern and African) terms while the potential-passive aspect is male. Creation is therefore understood to be a product of the interaction between these two aspects of the same reality: spirit (male) and primeval waters (female).

Since God is all that exists, then God is also the spirit and the primeval waters at the same time. Therefore, God interacts with himself/herself and emanates creation out of himself/herself. So within this teaching of the Bible lies the idea that creation and God are one and the same in a mysterious unexplained way. Some important questions arise here. If the Spirit is God and the primeval waters of creation are also God, then what is creation and where is the *Kingdom of Heaven?* Is creation separate from God or is creation held in the palm of God's hand? Where is God? Where did God come from? What is our relationship to God?, and so forth. What does this all mean? The study of Ancient Egyptian and Indian creation stories provides answers to these questions.

The Ancient Egyptian and Indian creation myths.

The Ancient Egyptian and Indian creation myths originate in the far reaches of antiquity, 5500 BCE and 3000 BCE respectively. The primeval Egyptian creation myth is similar in many respects to the creation story from the Indian mythology associated with the *Laws of Manu*. God felt desire. Wishing to create all things from his own body, God created the primeval waters from which all creation emerges. In the Bhagavad Gita, Lord Krishna reiterates the wisdom of the primeval waters as he proclaims that he is the same Supreme Being who arose and formed creation. As in the Ancient Egyptian pantheon of gods, all gods represent the Supreme Divinity, therefore Krishna and Narayana are manifestations of the same Self. In the Vibhuti Chapter of the Gita text Lord Krishna explains that among all Created things He is the foremost essence in all. The following verse is of keen interest in our study.

> 27. Among the horses know Me to be Uchhaihshrava that arose during the churning of the ocean; I am Airavata among the elephants, and the King among human beings.
>
> Bhagavad Gita: Chapter 10
> Vibhuti Yogah--The Yoga of Divine Glories

The teaching of the Primeval Ocean points to another mystical implication. The mind is like a lake of consciousness which is being buffeted by the winds of thoughts which have their origins in the feelings of desire, greed, hatred, anger, fear, attachment, elation, sorrow and impatience which are constantly blowing across its surface, creating waves of agitation and distractions in the mind. If these waves were to be calmed, if it were possible to make the mind free of the waves of desires, it would be possible to have clear insight into the depths of one's consciousness, just as it would be possible to see the bottom of a lake if it is free of waves. A most important task of every spiritual aspirant is to train the mind so that it not affected by the winds of emotion, desire and thoughts based on ignorance. When this practice is perfected, equanimity arises in the mind. This equanimity allows you to discover the depths of the lake of the mind and the Self within. In order to practice this teaching, it is necessary to have a keen understanding of the mystical nature of the universe and of one's own being. Then it is necessary that you live your life according to these teachings and remain mindful of every thought and emotion that enters your mind, rejecting those which are contrary to Maat (order, righteousness, truth) and accepting those that are in line with Maat.

From a yogic perspective, when you act with reason and uphold justice, correctness and virtue in your life, you are living in accord with Maat, and when you live in harmony with Maat, you are moving into harmony with the entire universe, God. When you live according to the whims, desires and feelings of the mind which are based on ignorance, anger, greed, fear, hatred and so on, you are living according to chaos and mental agitation. This is known as a hellish existence. Therefore, you must strive to cultivate peace, harmony and love toward humanity and the universe within your heart. These qualities will lead you to discover and experience the deeper essence of your being just as a swimmer dives below the waves and discovers the depths of the ocean. In the same way, you can dive below the waves of mental agitation (ignorance, anger, greed, fear, hatred, etc.) and discover the ocean-like Divine Self within you.

How to move in harmony with the universe.

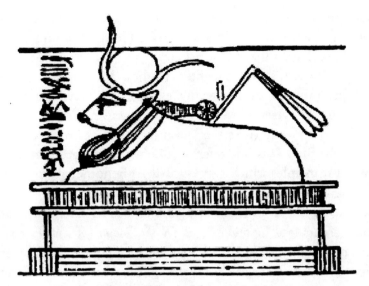

Above: The goddess *Mehurt.*

Perhaps the most important teaching to be derived from the Primeval Ocean is in reference to its fullness. As a metaphor for consciousness, which holds within itself infinite possibilities for expression as the universe, the Primeval Ocean is said to be "full." This "fullness" implies that it is complete, in much the same way as you are complete, even as entire dream worlds arise from your mind during sleep. The dream world is apparently "full" also. It seems to contain all of the necessary elements of a "real" world wherein there are people, objects, situations and you, as a subject who assumes various identities. Nevertheless, you are the real support of your dream. Its basis lies within your consciousness. In the same way, this entire universe lies within the consciousness of God who is the substratum of this entire creation, just as you are the substratum of your dreams. This teaching of the fullness of the Primeval Ocean is to be found in the *Book of Coming Forth By Day* (xvii. 76,79; lxxi. 13; cxxiv. 17). The hekau-utterance in Chapter xvii gives an exact description of this concept. The initiate says:

> "Behold Ra who was born yesterday from the buttocks of the Goddess Mehurt." In the answer to the question: "What then is this?," it is explained: "It is the watery abyss of heaven, or as others say, It is the image of the Eye of Ra in the morning at His daily birth. Mehurt is the Eye (Utchat) of Ra."

Mehurt was originally the female embodiment of the watery matter, the Primeval Ocean from which the substance of the world was formed. Her name ⳡⳆⳆ, means **"mighty fullness."** She was the infinite source of matter which was impregnated by the male spirit. This is one of the reasons why one of the symbols of Amun is a pregnant woman

𓃒 . Of course, the female primeval matter and the male spirit are both aspects of the same energy. This is expressed in the last line of the utterance where it is explained that Mehurt herself is the "image" of the "Eye of Ra." The Eye of Ra is his own daughter, Hathor. Mehurt is depicted as a cow goddess brimming with life giving essence. This symbol is common to Hathor, Nut and Aset as well. The cow goddess is often referred to as a "seven fold deity" known as the "seven Hathors" who preside over the life of each individual. This title refers to the further differentiation of the three primordial principles which express as the phenomenal universe through a series of sevens. This number, *seven*, is expressed in all levels of creation. It is expressed in the seven levels of the human subtle anatomy with the seven spiritual centers (see *Egyptian Yoga: The Philosophy of Enlightenment* and *The Serpent Power*), and also as the seven primary colors of the rainbow. This principle of sevens translated into the Gnostic idea of the "seven planetary spirits" and Archangels, known as the *Heads of the Celestial Host,* and were titled the "Seven Archangels of the Presence." Aset-Hathor in Ancient Egypt symbolized the source of creation. The *Milky Way* was produced by her udder and she was "the Great Cow which gave birth to Ra, the Great Goddess, the mother of all the Gods and Goddesses ...the lady who existed when nothing else had being as yet and who created that which came into being."

> The "Seven Hathors."

In Indian Mythology, the cow holds the same symbolism as that of Ancient Egypt. The cow is known as the "fountain of milk and curds." In a mystical sense the world is also a curd of the milk which emanated from the Celestial Cow (God). To this day, the cow is held to be sacred in India. It is associated with Purusha or the Supreme Self in the Avatara personality of Krishna, who is know as the "milker of the cow." Krishna is an incarnation of Vishnu (God) in the same way that Horus (Heru) of Ancient Egypt is an incarnation of Asar (God). One of Krishna's titles is "Govinda." Govinda means "cow finder, milker, herder." In a symbolic sense, Krishna is the milker of the Upanishads. He extracts the essence of their wisdom teachings and this essence is presented in the *Bhagavad Gita* text. The Sanskrit word *"go"* (cow) also means "sacred treasure," and is variously known as the philosopher's stone." The Upanishads are the sacred mystical wisdom texts which expound the teachings of mystical philosophy in much the same way as the "Metu Neter" (Words of The God or Neter Metu - Divine Speech) known as the hieroglyphic texts of Ancient Egypt. The Upanishads are known as "divine speech" or the "words of God," which not surprisingly, is also the definition of *Metu Neter.* These similarities point to the essential synchronicity of Ancient Egyptian and modern Indian mystical philosophy.

> The mythology of the cow

The Company of the gods and goddesses of Amun.

1-Amen-Ra
2-Mut
3- Khonsu
4- Min
5- Isis
6- Djehuti
7- Maat
8- Lady of Amenti (aspect of Hathor)
9- Osiris
10- Un-Nefer-Khenti-Amenti
11- Horus of the two Horizons
12- He of the embalming chamber
13- Het-Her (aspect of Hathor)
14- Governor of the house of the physician
15- Nephthys

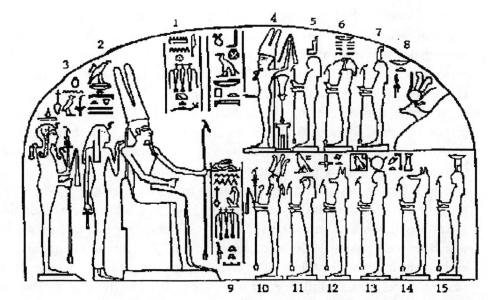

The Eye of Ra (𓂀) is Ra's creative principle in this aspect. Thus, creation itself is an image of God. The primordial essence from which creation arises and that which arises as creation are images of God in much the same way as your thoughts and dreams are images of your consciousness.

The interplay of duality which leads to multiplicity.

Through the interplay of the male and female principles, an infinite variety of forms can arise. This is the cause of the multiplicity that is seen in creation. The multiplicity of chemical elements and the infinite varieties, shapes and forms which are possible through their combinations are in reality expressions of the two principles, the opposites, duality, which are an expressions of the one, singular and non-dual essence. All of the multiplicity is in reality an expression of the two principles (duality) which, when examined closely with keen philosophical reason and an intuitive mind, are found to be in reality a singular or non-dual principle. This is the deeper meaning of the Ancient Egyptian teaching: *I became from God one, gods three,* which was presented earlier, where God tells us he was one essence and then transformed himself into three. These three constitute the basis of the multiplicity of creation; the duality, along with the interaction between the two, make three principles. However, the substratum of all creation (the trinity and duality) is oneness and this oneness has been translated into religion as the concept of monotheism and the Trinity. However, monotheism as it is understood in Western religions such as Orthodox Christianity, Orthodox Islam, Orthodox Judaism and others, is not the same monotheism implied in the teachings of Yoga and mystical religions such as the Egyptian Mysteries, Vedanta, Sufism, Buddhism, the Tao, etc.

In Western religion, monotheism implies that there is one God who exists in fact and is watching over his creation. God is conceptualized as a male figure who is separate from creation and manages it from afar. In the mystical sciences, monotheism implies that God is the only being that truly exists and therefore all that exists is an expression of the Divine. God expresses as nature, the stars, your body, your thoughts, your senses, all physical objects, all good and evil people, etc. God is everything, just as everything in your dreams is in reality an expression of your own consciousness. God is not separate from creation, but is immanent in creation. God is never far from you, but is as close as your every thought, every breath, every sensation, every feeling. Thus, that which transcends the phenomenal world of time and space is "full" and the phenomenal world which is an expression of the eternal is also "full." At every moment you are embracing the glory of God. At every moment , regardless of your life's circumstances, you are full. Even if you were to become blind or to lose an arm or leg, you would remain full. Just as the injuries of your dream personalities do not affect you as you lay on your bed, so too your transcendental Self is unaffected by any condition that is experienced by your body or mind (ego-personality).

The Western idea of monotheism.

This exact teaching of the "fullness" of God and the "fullness" of creation may be found in the Indian Upanishads in the following prayer:

Purnamadah Purnamidam Purnat
Purnamudachyate Purnasya
Purnamadaya Purnamevavahisyate.
Om Shantih, Shantih, Shantih.[17]

That (Absolute) is full, this (world, being a manifestation of the Absolute) is full. When this (world-process) is taken away (by transcending it through Self-realization), what remains is full (the Absolute). May there be Peace, Peace, Peace.

A striking example of the integration of the female principle into Ancient Egyptian mythology is to be found in Chapter 78, Line 47, of the Egyptian *Book of Coming Forth By Day*, where it is stated to the initiate:

"To the son (initiate), the gods have given the crown of millions of years, and for millions of years it allows him to live in the Eye

---

[17] From Mantra, Kirtana [Kirtan], Yantra and Tantra by Sri Swami Jyotirmayananda.

(Eye of Horus), which is the single eye of God who is called Neberdjer, the queen of the gods."

The previous passage is of paramount significance since it states that the primary Trinity, *Neberdjer,* the High God of Egypt, which is elsewhere primarily associated with male names, *Amun-Ra-Ptah,* is also *"the queen of the gods."* Therefore, the primary *"Godhead* or *Supreme Being* is both **male and female.** Even in dynastic times, the goddess was attributed equal status and importance for the salvation of humanity. All high deities were considered to be bisexual or androgynous, possessing a male and female aspect.

In the Hymns of Amun by *Her* and *Suti,* Amun is called *"Glorious Mother of gods and men."* Thus, either the male, female or androgynous aspect of the Divine is emphasized according to the particular idea being expressed. Since the Divine encompasses all genders and that which transcends genders, there is no conflict in any of these interpretations. The conflict in theological study arises when the mental concept of God is concretized and held onto steadfastly as an absolute reality, or when it is held to be a historical fact, rather than a psychological symbol of a deeper reality which is within the human heart and which is also the essence of the universe. This has the effect of stunting spiritual development because eventually, on the way to enlightenment, all concepts must be left behind. Concepts are necessary for the formulation of theories and for understanding ideas, however, concepts must always be understood as signs, signals or symbols leading toward the Divine, rather than as definitive, absolute truths. This is the idea behind the statements of various Ancient Egyptian hymns:

> "No man has been able to seek out God's likeness. Though God can be seen in form and observation of God can be made at God's appearance, God cannot be understood... God cannot be seen with mortal eyes..."

These statements signify that no one who looks for God with the understanding of the ego-concept will be able to see God. What they will see is the world of time and space, and deities created out of the imagination, because they are looking through the impure intellect, mind and senses. In order to understand God, one must transcend the human ego and thus become like God. It is only then that the correct understanding will dawn. The same idea is more explicitly stated in the Hindu *Upanishads* and the Taoist *Tao Te Ching*:

> "He truly knows Brahman who knows him as beyond knowledge; he who thinks that he knows, knows not. The

ignorant think that Brahman is known, but the wise know him to be beyond knowledge."

Kena Upanishad

"The Tao that can be told is not the eternal Tao.
The name that can be named is not the eternal name.
The nameless is the beginning of heaven and earth."

Tao Te Ching

When God is personified and given a specific name, it is like trying to circumscribe the unconscious mind. Is there a limit in the unconscious mind? Is there a clear identity to the farthest reaches of your unconscious? No, therefore it cannot be circumscribed with any term or description. The concepts should only serve as temporary crutches for the mind to assist it in understanding the transcendental nature of the Divine until it is ready to grasp infinity and non-duality. Concepts should never be held onto because any and all concepts are faulty since the human mind is limited. Therefore, any attempt to classify God or circumscribe God with any description, location, name or form will be erroneous and idolatrous. God cannot be defined in terms of time and space because God transcends these. In reality, the word "God" is a metaphor for that which transcends all human categories of thought and all mental concepts. The word "God" and the disciplines of religion and yoga philosophy are supposed to be a vehicle to get you in touch with the depths of your own being, but if you hold onto them as absolute realities, you will miss the point which is being conveyed through the metaphors.

> The personification of God.

This way of holding onto the idea of God as a male personality or as a Savior figure represents an erroneous understanding of religious symbolism, and is a source of strife among religions, social groups and in the relations between men and women. However, when you are able to transcend your own mind through the practices of yoga, then you are able to commune with that which is real, non-dual, perfect and supremely "FULL."

6. He is the Breath of Life, the spirit which permeates and vivifies all things.

The Self is the source of all existence. All manifestations emanate and are supported by the Self because they are essentially the Self's body. The idea that there is the Self and then there is creation is wrong. The rays of the sun and the sun are one and the same. In the same way, creation and the Self are one. Just as you sustain your body by breathing, drawing Life

Force energy from the atmosphere, so too it is God's breath (Life Force) which sustains this universe (God's body so to speak).

7. He took the form of TANEN in order to give birth to the PAUTTI gods.

Tanen refers to the earth god. The Self is nameless, formless, unborn, transcendental and undying. Assuming a name and form as the earth, the Self has projected creation within itself along with the properties and principles represented by the *Pautti* (Company of gods cosmic laws of nature) under which it exists. These are the laws by which the ripples in the primeval waters reflect the light of consciousness. In the Papyrus of *Nesi-Khensu*, a similar scripture reads: *Amen...the first divine matter* (primeval *paut*) *which gave birth unto subsequent divine matter* (other *pautti*)*!* This second rendering is important because it establishes the divine source of existence (*paut*) as being the Divine Self (Amen, Amun) and in concordance with Memphite Theology, it establishes that that which is created (*pautti*) is also divine matter which has assumed different forms according to the will of the Divine. This idea is in accordance with the tenets of modern day Quantum Physics theory which hold that matter is in reality energy which has assumed various forms according to laws which they still cannot fully understand.

The insubstantial nature of matter.

According to Memphite Theology and to this Hymn of Amun, which constitutes Theban Theology, what is considered as solid matter is in reality nothing more than the same form of matter which is experienced in the Dream State of consciousness. Thus, the "physical" world is composed of the same material as the dream world and is therefore subject to vanish as surely as a dream. However, the phenomenal world, being part of God's dream, or projection, as opposed to that of a human being, is longer lived. It may last billions of years from the standpoint of a human lifetime, however, it is only a flash in the realm of eternity. Thus, the human concept of "time" is only a minute segment within the stream of eternity. The concept of relativity of time is expressed in a hieroglyphic text entitled: *The Songs of The Harper.* In one verse, the relativity of the passage of time is explained as follows:

> **"The whole period of things done on the earth is but a period of a dream."**

Consider your dreams. They may seem to occur over a period of hours, days, months or years. Yet upon waking up, you realize that the entire time you were in bed asleep for a short time. In the same way, the entire period of the existence of the universe is nothing but the span of a short dream in the mind of God.

From an advanced perspective, neither time nor space can be said to exist as something which is real, just as time, matter, and physical objects within a dream cannot be called "real." The entire dream world exists in the mind and does not require real time or space. The phenomenal, world which is experienced in the Waking State of consciousness, is also not real and does not exist except in the mind of God. This teaching is not only confirmed by the Hymns of Amun, but it is also a primary teaching of Memphite Theology presented in the *Shabaka Inscription*. In reality, only eternity is real, and God is eternity. Since all matter is in reality constituted of the thought energy of God, and changes in the matter are called time, it must be clearly understood that God is the only reality which exists.

God is eternity, and the limited perceptions of the mind and senses are what human beings refer to as "time" and "space" awareness. However, the perception of time and space is due to the limitations and conditioning of the human mind and body. If you had the ability to perceive the entire universe at once, an eternal view which is not restricted to time and space, then you would discover that there is only oneness. This is the view that the cosmic mind (God) has towards creation. Recall the teachings of Memphite Theology on the creation of the universe by Ptah through thought alone. Thus, the task of the spiritual aspirant is to grow out of the limitations of the mind and body and discover the cosmic vision which lies within. When this is accomplished, there is a new perception of the universe. This represents the death of the ego in a human being and the birth of the spiritual life in the human being.

God has assumed the form of the neteru or Pautti (Company of Gods and Goddesses). These "neteru" are cosmic forces and energies that sustain the universe and which constitute "physical matter." Therefore, this "physical" universe is in reality the body of God and everything in it is Divine, from the smallest atom to the largest celestial bodies in the heavens.

8. He hides His name from His children in this His name of Amun.
9. He makes Himself to be hidden.
10. The One, Amun, who hides Himself from men, who shrouds Himself from the gods; His color and appearance is not known.
11. The gods cannot pray to him because His name is unknown to them.

The Self appears to be hidden from the world to those who do not look beyond the physical reality they have in front of them. Accepting the visible alone as the only reality, they are as if mesmerized by creation. Further, due to the ignorance of egoism, people see themselves as separate individuals and are thus unable to behold their deeper nature, the Self. As long as the constant pressure of egoistic thoughts and pursuit of fulfillment through the world continues, so long the illusory separation between the soul and the Self will continue. The soul will continue to travel through time and space and the astral and physical realms through many dimensions until it realizes its error. The Gods and Goddesses, like human beings, exist in time and space. They also, are aware only of events which occur in the subtle plane or the physical. The subtle plane is more fluid than the physical world of human beings, but it is nevertheless still located in time and space. Therefore, even the Gods and Goddesses must transcend this Astral Plane in order to achieve the Cosmic Vision of the transcendental Self.

The finite nature of the gods and goddesses.

When a human being dies, the consciousness shifts from the physical body to the astral body. It is this body and its senses which allows the soul to have experiences on the Astral Plane. However, this plane exists in a different time frame and therefore, hundreds of years may pass there while thousands may pass in the physical earth plane of human beings. The Astral Plane is more fluid, meaning that events can occur and entire circumstances can change instantly according to the desires and thoughts of the mind. Thus, the Astral Plane is related to the mind and senses more than to the gross physical body of earthbound existence. It is also experienced in part during the Dream State when sleeping. When sleeping, you are carried away with the thoughts and events of the dream world. You believe it is real and you believe it has always been real. However, when you awaken, you come to believe it was not real and call it imagination, and forget about the dream. However, when falling into the Sleep State, the physical reality is lost to you; it becomes "unreal."

Likewise, when you "die," you will undergo an experience of swooning and your past personality is lost. However, you will take with you the psychic impressions in the unconscious mind. These deep rooted desires and prejudices remain and impel you to move on in the Astral Plane searching for fulfillment and happiness. This Astral Plane, though more subtle than the Physical Plane of existence, cannot provide true happiness and supreme peace because it is as illusory and "unreal" as a dream world is discovered to be unreal upon waking up. Further, both the Astral Plane (Duat or Underworld) and the Physical Plane are emanations from the Self, so both are relative planes of existence which emanate from the Absolute (God). Since they are relative and transitory, it is not possible to find abiding satisfaction or fulfillment in them. Only when the Absolute and transcendental Self is discovered can there be true peace and happiness.

It is in this plane where the soul experiences either hellish or heavenly conditions according to its actions, feelings and thoughts while on the earth plane. It is these actions, thoughts and feelings that constitute the karmic history and destiny of the soul. If you have lived un-righteously while on earth, you will experience hellish conditions after death which are of your own making. Since the Astral Plane is more "fluid" than the physical, it is recommended that the spiritual aspirant diligently practice the teachings of mystical spirituality so as to gain control over the mind and senses and not to be susceptible to the whims, desires and negative thoughts of the mind.

Hell and heaven.

12. His name is victory.

The victory being described here is not like a victory that is experienced as a result of winning a war or a competitive sport. The victory which is being referred to here is the victory of attaining enlightenment, the discovery of your true Self. Having discovered the hidden, absolute essence within, one has discovered the name of God. This discovery bestows victory over all maladies and adversities. It is the definition and abode of that which is auspicious and triumphant. It is the goal and aim of all teachings and the supreme prize before which all worldly luxuries pale in comparison. The Self, when turned to with devotion-*Uah abr Neter*, is the source that bestows the victory of enlightenment (salvation) from the bondage of time and space.

13. He the One Watcher who neither slumbers nor sleeps.

Many thousands of years prior to the development of the *Sakshin Buddhi* concept in Vedanta philosophy and the *Mindfulness* concept of Buddhism, the concept of the *witnessing consciousness* was understood in Ancient Egypt. This watcher or witnessing consciousness is related to three other important utterances (33-35) which explain the relationship between the witnessing consciousness of the mind, the perceptions through the senses and the physical world. Here we will focus on understanding the watcher or witnessing consciousness which is the innermost essence of the human mind.

The witnessing nature of the Self.

The Self is the eternal and silent witness to all that goes on in the mind of every human being. It is the mind, composed of memories and desires stored in the subconscious and unconscious, which believes itself to be real and independent. But when you begin to ask "Who is this that I call me?," you begin to discover that you cannot find any "me." Is "me" the person I was at five years of age? at twenty? or am I the person I see in the mirror today? Am I the person I will be in ten years from now or am I the person I was 500 or 1000 years ago in a different incarnation? Where is "me"? Is "me" the body? Am "I" the legs, or am "I" the heart? Am "I" the brain? People have lost half their brain and continue to live, not in a vegetable state but as human beings, with consciousness. Since body parts can be lost or transplanted, these cannot be "me." What does this all mean?

As a child you acted a certain way. As an adolescent you acted in another way. As an adult you act yet another way. All the while, your body is growing, changing, and gradually moving towards death. You have experienced all of these changes and through mental conditioning, you have come to believe that all of these characters are you. Initiatic teaching proves through philosophical argument and through intuitional enlightenment that these are only transitory characters with no real substance. So what is real? Your witnessing Self is real. It was the witnessing consciousness, identified with the ego-self-consciousness, who experienced the pains and pleasures, disappointments and successes. That witnessing consciousness which withdraws at the time of sleep and experiences dreams, that witnessing consciousness that observed all of the changes like a silent onlooker waiting to be noticed, is your innermost Self.

The real "me" is that which causes the existence of the body and uses it to have worldly experiences. The body-mind complex, its problems and concerns, failures and successes, pleasures and pains, life and death, cannot affect the real "me." The project of yoga is to discover the illusoriness of the ego-personality (mind and body) and to discover the real "me," the *Watcher who never slumbers*. From the point of view of the ocean, the problems, failures, successes, pleasures, pains, life and death of the waves is of no concern since none of these occurrences affect its essential nature. The conditions of the waves do not add or detract from the fullness of the ocean. The ocean encompasses all of the waves. Regardless of whether the waves are rising or falling, the ocean remains full. Likewise, you, the real you, is always embracing the fullness of the Divine Self at every moment. Just as the sun shines and sustains all the activities of the world, the consciousness of God is as a light which shines on all things and allows them to exist. In the same way that you are the sole witness and support of the entire world which arises out of your mind during a dream and you are not affected by any situations which occur in your dreams as you lay peacefully in your bed, the Self is the unaffected witness and support of this entire world process. This silent witnessing is the kind of vision you must engender in your mind as opposed to the one which is constantly agitated and upset by the things you like-*Mer* and therefore seek to acquire, the things you have come to see as hateful-*Fat* and therefore seek to move away from, and the passing problems of human existence. This is the Divine vision that leads an aspirant to spiritual enlightenment.

God is always aware of the fact that the entire creation, the universe and all of the various planes of existence within it are nothing more than a thought. Ordinary human beings who have not practiced yoga or sought to attain spiritual enlightenment are not aware of the fact that this creation is a dream, so they believe it is a reality and become caught in the dream of the world process as it were. They are caught in the desires and illusions of their own as well as the dreams, desires and illusions of others. This leads to myriad of human complications and entanglements which all lead to disappointment and sorrow in the end. Along with this needless pain and suffering, it is ironic that in the end all human activities, no matter how grand or glorious they may appear to be, are in reality perishable and fleeting much like a dream, albeit a longer lasting dream. Therefore, unenlightened human life is an ignorant state of consciousness in all states (waking, dream, dreamless-deep-sleep).

As stated earlier, ordinary human experience is as a dream. The ignorance that besets the mind causes a kind of ignorant movement from one state of mind to another. The mind moves from the waking to the Sleep State, from sleep to dream, and from dream once again back to waking. The soul is caught up in the illusory trap of its own ignorance.

The innermost realm of the unconscious is beyond the mind and senses. Therefore, if life is lived in the realm of the mind and senses alone, you are only aware of that which is temporal and unreal. Consider how life would be if you went to sleep and fell into a dream out of which you could wake up. Having forgotten about the Waking State of consciousness, you would be tumbling from one experience to another because you are "ignorant" as to your "true" Self who is sleeping. Your only salvation would be if someone were to come along within your dream and remind you that this dream character is not the real you and that the real you is comfortably sleeping, and all you need to do to escape the pain and suffering you are experiencing in the dream is to wake up.

"The wise wake up early to their lasting gain while the fool is hard pressed."

"Salvation is the freeing of the soul from its bodily fetters, becoming a God through knowledge and wisdom, controlling the forces of the cosmos instead of being a slave to them, subduing the lower nature and through awakening the Higher Self, ending the cycle of rebirth and dwelling with the neteru who direct and control the Great Plan."

Ancient Egyptian Proverbs

In the same way, the dreams you have when sleeping as well as your experiences in the Waking State are all in the realm of the mind and senses, therefore, all of them are illusory, like a dream. Your mortal existence and all of your incarnations throughout time and space are in reality the experience of a dream from the point of view of your innermost Self. While your mind changes, your dreams change, you are born, grow old and die only to be reborn again in a new family, country, etc., these events are all in the realm of time and space. However, when you discover your innermost reality, then you discover that which is timeless, changeless, immortal and eternal. Therefore, you must "drawn close" to the innermost essence within you in order to discover your true identity beyond the mind and senses.

Just as if you were trying to escape a terrible danger in your dream, the best solution would be to wake up, the only way out of the illusion of the world process is to wake up from the triads of Seer-Seen-Sight and the waking-sleep-Dream States entirely. These three states are part of the relative realm of time and space. The task is to transcend them all and to reach attunement with the level of the ever-present *Watcher*, the witness behind all things, the real "me."

What is Consciousness?

Consciousness is the primordial state of existence. As referred to in Egyptian and Indian mythology, pure consciousness or the *Primeval Waters* are considered to be *Unformed Matter, The Self, God*. Pure consciousness is the stuff of which everything will be composed and it is the matter of which thoughts are composed. It may be referred to as awareness without specificity or the mind without thoughts. In the same way that modern physics has discovered the same underlying basis behind all matter (energy), the ancient Sages discovered that there is one underlying substance, *Pure Consciousness*, behind all things, matter, thoughts, energy, etc. The "Primeval Waters" is a metaphor referring to pure consciousness, unmodified or unconditioned into any particular form in time and space. Through the process of thought, consciousness is able to become whatever it desires, that is, to take on any form by the power of vibration. Vibration causes ripples in consciousness and these ripples are what constitute movement, shape, color, dimension, sound, light, etc.

The metaphor of the Primeval Ocean as a teaching relating to Consciousness.

In human life consciousness refers to the awareness of being alive and of having an identity. The consciousness or awareness of being an individual, living, thinking being is the characteristic which separates humanity from the animals and one individual human being from another. Animals cannot become aware of their own existence and ponder the questions such as: Who am I? Where am I going in life? Where do I come from? They cannot write books on history and create elaborate systems of social history based on ancestry, etc. Ironically, this tendency to name things, to categorize and intellectualize is what causes the awareness of differences and separations.

Thus, consciousness is characterized by the quality of existence. It exists, as opposed to non-existence. However, all that exists then can be said to be conscious, the earth, the trees, the sun, etc. What makes human existence special is the awareness of existence and individual identity. This quality of existence, coupled with the quality of awareness, is what constitutes the higher level of consciousness in human beings. In human beings consciousness expresses itself in three modes. These are: Waking, Dream-Sleep and Dreamless-Sleep.

In the primordial state there is only The Self, Pure Consciousness. There is not even a thought about anything other than itself. Upon the emergence of the first thought immediately there is something besides the Self, an objectified form. Now there is the experience of duality and of the triad because the Self can now perceive something alongside itself. It is only through illusion that the self is able to see anything as if it is other than itself. In order for this to be possible there must be a triad of seer-seen-sight or subject-object-interacting media. This is the function of the mind. It allows the illusion of the triad to exist. However, this objectified form is composed of the same Self. The material out of which dreams and waking consciousness arise is the same. Sages have discovered that Pure Consciousness (God) is the underlying basis of the human mind but when thoughts arise, consciousness takes and identifies with the various forms.

God creates him/her self

At this time God is said to have created him/herself in the form of that which is created in the same way as a person dreaming takes on the forms of the dream. When consciousness becomes something, anything, from the grossest form to the subtlest, a tree, a rock, a planet, a human body, air, radiation, etc., then it is said to have created a physical object; creation is created. The Self no longer simply just exists in complete peace and stillness. When The Self enlivens a physical object such as an animal, a plant, a human body, with the soul (higher consciousness), then it is said to be living. When the Self becomes involved with the thoughts and forgets itself, thinking that it is the subject, then this process is called *Identification*. The Self which was pure consciousness has become involved in the thoughts through a process of becoming ignorant of its real nature.

The important factor to understand here is that each element of the Trinity represents a factor of absolute consciousness in the following order:

Soul ➔ Ego-Mind ➔ Body and Senses

Amun - Ra - Ptah

Through the understanding of this relationship the body and sense organs (physical nature) are related to the Cosmic Physical Self (Ptah). The mind and senses are related to the Cosmic Astral Self (Ra). The awareness or consciousness which is beyond the astral and physical planes (Watcher who never slumbers) is related to the Cosmic Causal Self (Amun). All of these arise out of Neberdjer, the Absolute Self.

14. Amun drives away evils and scatters diseases.

The Cause of Disease

The spiritual Self is the source of all life including the life of each individual human personality. It is also the spiritual Self which sustains the mental and physical selves. At this level you should understand that the spiritual Self exists in the realm of nature (time and space) and also in a another dimension, the spiritual realm, which is beyond time and space (movement and change), whereas, the mental and physical selves exist entirely in the realm of time and space. The body and mind, being instruments of the Soul, operate according to the laws of nature.

Contrary to the belief system which pervades modern day society that disease originates from factors outside of the body, it is the contention of yoga philosophy that the root cause of disease is ignorance of one's true nature as the Self. In the unenlightened state, you identify yourself with the mind, and through the mind and senses (which are merely an extension of the mind), with the body. When this occurs, the universal Self becomes deluded by the state of ignorance into believing in the concepts of death, disease, limitation, and individuality. Because death, disease and limitation are not characteristics of the true Self, conflict and contradiction develops deep within the unconscious mind which results in a disturbance of the mental function. This distorted or inharmonious state of mind translates into a disturbance within the Life Force Energy of the body and results in disease, because the flow of Life Force Energy (Sekhem, Prana, Chi) is blocked or otherwise disrupted throughout portions of the body. The Life Force Energy flows from the Soul to the Causal Body (unconscious mind), then to the Astral Body, which is composed of the mind and senses. Through subtle channels within the Astral body, the energy flows into the physical body and vivifies the organs. The presence of this energy is what constitutes "life." The absence of it is called "death."

The word disease itself gives a clue to this process by implying that disease results from a lack of (dis-) ease in the body. What is this ease? It is the ease of the true Self which is universal, free, all encompassing, immortal, and absolute bliss and peace (Hetep). Imagine how much dis-ease would be created if you tried to confine the ocean or the sky in a jar? How much dis-ease does a wild animal, which is used to roaming in the vast forest, experience when it is captured and placed in confinement? So when body identification occurs and the soul now identifies with concepts of individuality as opposed to universality, death as opposed to immortality, dis-ease or tension arises from within the soul level of the individual which becomes manifested in the mind as desire, fear, anger, hatred, greed, jealousy, envy and attachment. These in turn become manifested in the body as what we term illnesses and diseases, such as cancer, colds, fatigue, AIDS, and all other disease syndromes.

The word
"disease."

Thus, it is not surprising that modern medicine is finding that the most healthy activity a person can engage in is to sit quietly once or twice a day in a state of deep relaxation or meditation. Why is this? When the mind is filled with thoughts of a worldly nature, it creates ripples in the lake of consciousness, and just as the wind blows across a lake and creates ripples, the reflection of the sky is obstructed, so too the ripples created in the lake of consciousness by tension laden thoughts obstruct the reflection of the Self. When these thoughts are quieted through the relaxation or meditation process, then the Self reflects in the lake of consciousness, providing one with a feeling of expansion, a sense of peace, bliss and immortality. In this state of consciousness there is a free flow of healing Life Force Energy that maintains the body and mind healthy. This is what happens when you enter into deep dreamless sleep every night, however, because your consciousness is withdrawn during this process, you are ignorant of the experience. You only know that you feel rested and relaxed when you wake up. This is why you are told to get lots of rest when you are ill or you may feel that you are becoming ill and instinctively know that if you to go to bed early, the chances are that you will not become ill. The healing comes from embracing your true nature and letting go of your body identification (ego) by relaxing the desires of the mind and temporarily giving up worldly activities. Sleep is nature's way of providing you with this experience, however, it is not the only way to have this experience. This is where the practice of yoga comes in.

The goal of intuitional realization.

Through the process and disciplines of yoga, you are able to achieve the state where you can have this experience at all times, the state of enlightenment. The formal practice of meditation provides you with this experience initially, however, when the teachings become integrated into your consciousness, your wisdom and intuitional realization of the teachings will allow you to maintain this experience, even amidst the most chaotic circumstances. So, integral and foremost to the process of maintaining or regaining optimal physical or mental health is the practice of meditation and the other disciplines of yoga, because the ultimate state of total health-*Senbi,* is in the state of enlightenment. In Indian yoga philosophy "true health" is termed *"Swastat"* or being established in the Self (the state of Enlightenment). Although you need to have a healthy diet, proper exercise and rest to maintain health, these factors alone can never confer total health. You must engage in spiritual practices to discover your true nature to be truly healthy. The ancient medical traditions such as the Ayurvedic system of India and The Therapeutic system of Egypt recognized this and therefore, in addition to recommending and prescribing various diets and herbs for specific illnesses, also recommended mantras and hekau repetition to calm the mind as well as the practice of meditation to promote healing.

The goal of yoga is to promote integration of the mind-body-spirit complex in order to produce optimal health of the human being. This is accomplished through mental and physical exercises which promote the free flow of spiritual energy by reducing mental complexes caused by ignorance. There are two roads which human beings can follow, one of wisdom and the other of ignorance. The path of the masses is generally the path of ignorance which leads them to negative situations, thoughts and deeds. These in turn lead to ill health and sorrow in life. The other road is based on wisdom and it leads to health, true happiness and enlightenment.

It must be understood that being enlightened does not automatically confer a state of physical health. One's state of health is also subject to the law of karma, so even someone who is enlightened may undergo serious illnesses. There have been many enlightened Sages who have developed cancer, diabetes and other illnesses. However, this does not mean that you should not endeavor to live a healthy lifestyle. Suppose, based on karma from your previous embodiments as well as this embodiment, you develop some illness. You have the choice to promote a healthy diet and lifestyle (good karma) or an unhealthy diet and lifestyle in this lifetime. Promoting a healthy lifestyle may add years to your life, whereas ignoring proper nutrition and exercise may result in your dying at an earlier age, not to mention the karmic repercussions you will still have to deal with in future lifetimes.

The effect of previous karma on your health.

Promoting a healthy lifestyle is key to the practice of yoga because once you realize that your body and mind are tools to take you to the destination of absolute peace and bliss, you will want to take care of them as you would a car or some other important possession you have. In addition, unless one is very spiritually advanced, beyond identifying with the body and mind, illnesses can detract from spiritual progress because they keep the thoughts bound to the physical body. To understand this, just reflect on when you have a headache or stomachache. Where are your thoughts drawn? Usually they are more focused on the part of the body which ails you. Therefore, promoting a healthy lifestyle through proper nutrition and exercise are also very important disciplines in the quest to attain Yoga, union with your Higher Self.

Following the path which leads to the wisdom of the Self eradicates mental and physical afflictions and the miseries of life. All of the maladies of human life arise due to one's ignorance of one's true nature. When you discover that your deepest Self is one with Amun, who is the Self of all things, then there is no need or desire for any of the things which motivate ordinary human life. There is no need or desire for wealth, fame, name, power, etc., neither is there a need, desire or fear of the lack of any of these.

Note: For more on physical health and purification see the books *Initiation Into Egyptian Yoga: The Secrets of Sheti* and *Meditation: The Ancient Egyptian Path to Enlightenment.*

Ignorant human beings see life as a struggle in which they must strive to compete in a race to achieve certain goals or to acquire certain objects to secure happiness. When you discover that in reality, God is the underlying essence of all objects, and that God is indeed the true mover, the true watcher, the true director and the true and only support of your life, you can relax your endless desires and move into harmony with the Divine Will. Human struggle is a deviation from Divine Will, from Maat. However, when you begin to place trust in your true, divine Self, all evils are as if rendered null and void. How can there be evil within God if ALL is God? How can there be good either? All things move according to their own ideal. The wind blows, the waters of the ocean flow with the tides, the planets and stars move according to their own plan as prescribed by the mysterious divine source. The same occurs in human life. The circumstances you come across, the personalities you meet, the thoughts and desires in your mind and so on, are all provided for your spiritual movement. It is you who assign certain value to a certain situation over another and call one evil and another good. It is you who decide if a personality you meet is agreeable or not. It is you who decide if a plot of land is beautiful or not. These objects exist only by divine grace. They have no consciousness of their appeal to you, or their rejection by you, and they do not care. You say "I own this land," or "this is my house" and so on, but the land or house have no knowledge of this! If you were to inquire as to who "owned" the land a hundred years ago or who will "own" it a hundred years from now, how will this knowledge enhance your life at this very moment? If something is not true in the beginning, middle and end, then it is not true at all. Therefore, since you did not own land in the beginning and will not own it when you die, the entire situation is un-true, much like a dream. The answer is that ownership is an illusory concept which deludes people into a false sense of pride, vanity, greed and egoism. These negative human qualities are the chains of the soul which keep it tied to human suffering and cloud the intellect from discovering the truth, that there is a greater existence beyond the day to day world of ordinary human experience.

The idea being imparted here is that you must give up your egoistic ideas of your little individual self and thereby wake up to your true Self. You must give up the little things you are holding onto in order to gain the entire universe. Giving up should not be understood as a relinquishing of possessions necessarily. Many possessions only serve to complicate our lives but, certain objects and possessions are needed in life. However, it should be understood as giving up or relinquishing the attachment and worry over possessions. Therefore, it is more of a psychological attitude than a physical act. In order to do this, you must understand deeply within your heart that your true identity is not John, Robert, Cathy, Mary or whatever your name

How nature repudiates the selfish and greedy people.

may be. Your true identity is the transcendental, eternal, universal Self who is the sole watcher and witness to all things. It is this witnessing consciousness which is there awaiting your discovery if you stop the ignorant thoughts, beliefs, desires and illusions of the mind which agitate your consciousness and distract your awareness of your true identity. If you can accomplish this, you will become a "Knower of the Self," an enlightened human being. In fact, this is the true definition of a human being. Any other state of existence is in reality worse than an animal existence because while animals do not have awareness of their Divinity, they also do not have the capacity to experience the intense forms of human pain and suffering caused by worries and anxieties of the past, desires for the future and regrets of what might have been, but was not.

Through philosophical insight from the wisdom teachings you must rise above this pitiful condition to the status of Divinity by giving up the petty human desires and ignorant notions which compel you to seek happiness in the world of time and space which is never abiding and always perishable.

Note: For more on the Ancient Egyptian teachings in reference to diet, health, exercise and nutrition see the books *Meditation: The Ancient Egyptian Path to Enlightenment* and *The Egyptian Yoga Exercise Workout Book.*

15. He is the physician who heals the eye without medicaments; He opens the eyes; He drives away inflammation.

The Eye of Horus refers to the eye of spiritual intuition or inner spiritual realization of the truth of one's true nature within one's heart. In much the same way that inflammation around a physical eye obstructs vision, the fattening of the ego obstructs the vision of the intuitional eye. In this context, "fattening" of the ego may be defined as follows:

> By thinking of the objects of the world and by entertaining desires for the pleasures of the senses, the mind becomes increasingly involved in the world process. This is called fattening of the mind. By considering the body as the Self, and by developing attachment towards one's spouse and children, and towards the objects of the world, the mind becomes fattened.
>
> Yoga Vasistha 6:50

When you aquifer true insight into the nature of the Self, Amun, it means that you have glimpsed into eternity, your own eternity, your own divinity. This is true knowledge, born of your own experience of the Divine. When this occurs, it is like the moment you understand something which had baffled you for a long time. Imagine that you are given a box and asked to determine what is inside, but it is closed and you don't know how to open it. Its contents are described to you but still you cannot guess at what it is because you do not know enough about it. You are told that you will be given a great reward if you discover its contents, so you try very hard. Despite all of your efforts, you fail because you have not exercised the proper movement which will give you the knowledge which you need. However, if you are told that you need to move towards it, hold it in a certain way in order to open it, you are then in a position to discover what you need. Having done this and having opened the box and discovered its contents, there is irreversible knowledge which you have acquired. Now you "know" its contents by your own experience. Your life from now on incorporates this knowledge. There is no going back to the time when you did not know. This movement from ignorance to knowledge is what happens when true intuitional knowledge dawns in the human heart. It cures the mind of the complexes as if by magic, just as looking into the box and discovering its contents cured the malady of ignorance about the contents. Discovering the Self within your heart will dispel the malady of your ignorance about the contents of the universe. Having discovered the Self within your heart there will be nothing left to discover. All that is to be known will be known.

The
movement
from
ignorance
to
knowledge.

16. *He delivers whom he pleases, even from the Duat (Astral world).*
17. *He saves a man or woman from what is His lot at the dictates of their heart.*

The utterances above are directly referring to Meskhenet or karma. They also relate to hekau #40. The teachings of karma are mostly associated with Eastern religions. However, the study of African religions and the Ancient Egyptian religious system reveals that the teachings of karma were understood and practiced in Ancient Africa much earlier than anywhere else in history. Meskhenet is an Ancient Egyptian goddess aspect of Maat. Maat is a goddess aspect of Aset (Aset). Also, Meskhenet is associated with two other goddesses, Shai and Rennenet who represent fortune and destiny as well as Djehuti, who represents reason and rationality, the intuitive intellect. Along with her associates, the goddesses Shai, Rennenet and Meskhenet, Maat encompass the teachings of Karma and Reincarnation or the destiny of every individual based on past actions, thoughts and feelings.

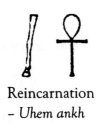

Reincarnation
– *Uhem ankh*

Meskhenet
(Karmic direction of an individual)
⬆
Shai and Rennenet
(Fortune and Destiny)

Djehuti
(Reason - Rationality - Understanding)
⬆
Maat
(Ethical standards of an individual)
⬆
Aset
(The support of Creation)

The diagram above illustrates the process of meskhenet. Creation itself is the field in which an individual is able to exist, carry out various activities and to learn, through various experiences, how to live either in prosperity or adversity. The results of one's actions are the teachers. A negative result should teach that a particular ac is not correct and henceforth a person can correct future actions and so on.

Maat is the principle of order, righteousness and truth. She is the standard by which all should be measured. Djehuti is a counterpart of Maat. He represents the wisdom which comes from correct reasoning, rationality based on truth, the knowledge of the inner self. Shai and

Rennenet are the hands of Djehuti. In the *Ancient Egyptian Book of Coming Forth By Day* Djehuti is the neter who records the results of the balance scales where the heart of the individual (the individual's acts, thoughts, speech and deeds while alive) are judged. With his hands (Shai and Rennenet) he records the results of the balance and then Meskhenet carries out the task of sending the soul of that individual into their new .

Thus, karma should be thought of as the total effect of a person's actions and conduct during the successive phases of his/her existence. But how does this effect operate? How do the past actions affect the present and the future? Your experiences from the present life or from previous lifetimes cause unconscious impressions which stay with the soul even after death. These unconscious impressions are what constitute the emerging thoughts, desires, and aspirations of every individual. These impressions are not exactly like memories, however, they work like memories. For example, if you had a fear in a previous lifetime or the childhood of your present lifetime you may not remember the event that caused the fear, but you will remember the "strange feeling" you have when you come into contact with certain objects or certain people. These feelings are caused by the unconscious impressions which are coming up to the surface of the conscious mind. It is this conglomerate of unconscious impressions which are "judged" in the Hall of Maat and determine where the soul will go to next in its spiritual journey towards evolution or devolution, also known as the cycle of birth and death or reincarnation as well as the experiences of heaven or hell. The following segment from the Ancient Egyptian "Instruction to Mer-ka-Ré" explains this point.

> *"You know that they are not merciful the day when they judge the miserable one..... Do not count on the passage of the years; they consider a lifetime as but an hour. After death man remains in existence and his acts accumulate beside him. Life in the other world is eternal, but he who arrives without sin before the Judge of the Dead, he will be there as a neter and he will walk freely as do the masters of eternity."*

The reference above to "his acts accumulate beside him" alludes to the unconscious impressions which are formed as a result of one's actions while still alive. These impressions can be either positive or negative. Positive impressions are developed through positive actions by living a life of righteousness and virtue (Maat). This implies living according to the precepts of mystical wisdom or being a follower of Horus (*Shemsu Hor*) and Aset. These actions draw one closer to harmony and peace, thus paving the way to discover the Self within. The negative impressions are developed through sinful (egoistic) actions. They are related to mental agitation,

---

What is judged in the Hall of Maati.

99

disharmony and restlessness. This implies acts based on anger, fear, desire, greed, depression, gloom, etc. These actions draw one into the outer world of human desires. They distract the mind and do not allow the intellect (Saa) to function. Thus, existence at this level is closer to an animal, being based on animal instincts and desires of the body, rather than to a spiritually mature human being, being based on reason, selflessness, compassion, etc.

(Purification of the heart)

How then is it possible to eradicate negative karmic impressions and to develop positive ones? The answer lies in your understanding of the wisdom teachings and your practice of them. When you study the teachings and live according to them, your mind undergoes a transformation at all levels. This transformation is the "purification of heart" so often spoken about throughout the *Egyptian Book of Coming Forth By Day*. It signifies an eradication of negative impressions, which renders the mind pure and subtle. When the mind is rendered subtle, then spiritual realization is possible. This discipline of purifying the heart by living according to the teachings is known as the Yoga of Action or Maat, Karma Yoga in the Indian Yoga system.

Eradicating negative karma.

The philosophy of Maat is a profound teaching which encompasses the fabric of creation as well as a highly effective system of spiritual discipline. In creation stories, Neberdjer (God) is said to have established creation upon Maat. Consequently it follows that Maat is the orderly flow of energy which maintains the universe. Further, Maat is the regularity which governs the massive planetary and solar systems as well as the growth of a blade of grass and a human cell. This natural process represents the flow of creation wherein there is constant movement and a balancing of opposites (up-down, hot-cold, here-there, you-me, etc.).

Most people act out of the different forces which are coursing through them at the time. These may be hunger, lust, fear, hatred, anger, elation, etc. They have no control over these because they have not understood that their true essence is in reality separate from their thoughts and emotions. They have *identified* with their thoughts and therefore are led to the consequences of those thoughts and the deeds they engender. You, as an aspirant, having developed a higher level of spiritual sensitivity, are now aware that you have a choice in the thoughts you think and the actions you perform. You can choose whether to act in ways that are in harmony with Maat or those that are disharmonious. You have now studied the words of wisdom and must now look beyond the level of ritual worship of the Divine to the realm of practice and experience of the Divine.

In ordinary human life, those who have not achieved the state of Enlightenment (the masses in society at large) perceive nature as a conglomeration of forces which are unpredictable and in need of control. However, as spiritual sensitivity matures, the aspirant realizes that what once appeared to be chaotic is in reality the Divine Plan of the Supreme Being in the process of unfoldment. When this state of consciousness is attained, the aspirant realizes that there is an underlying order in nature which can only be perceived with spiritual eyes.

The purpose of the injunctions of Maat.

The various injunctions of Maat are for the purpose of keeping order in society among ordinary people, people without psychological maturity and or spiritual sensitivity, meaning that they lack an awareness of spiritual principles and moral - ethical development. Also, they provide insight into the order of creation and a pathway or spiritual discipline, which when followed, will lead the aspirant to come into harmony with the cosmic order. When the individual attunes his or her own sense of order and balance with the cosmic order, a spontaneous unity occurs between the individual and the cosmos, and the principles of Maat, rather than a blind set of rules which we must strive to follow, becomes a part of one's inner character and proceeds from one in a spontaneous manner.

This means that through the deeper understanding of cosmic order and by the practice of living in harmony with that order, the individual will lead him or herself to mental and spiritual peace and harmony. It is this peace and harmony which allows the lake of the mind to become a clear mirror in which the individual soul is able to realize its oneness with the Universal Soul.

Maat signifies *that which is straight*. Two of the symbols of Maat are the ostrich feather (𝄐) and the pedestal (___) upon which God stands. The Supreme Being, in the form of the God *Ptah*, is often depicted standing on the pedestal.

Maat is the daughter of Ra, the High God, thus in a hymn to Ra we find:

The land of Manu (the West) receives thee with satisfaction, and the goddess Maat embraces thee both at morn and at eve... the god

*Djehuti and the goddess Maat have written down thy daily course
for thee every day...*

Another Hymn in the Papyrus of Qenna provides deeper insight into
Maat. Qenna says:

*I have come to thee, O Lord of the gods, Temu-Heru-khuti, whom
Maat directeth... Amen-Ra rests upon Maat... Ra lives by Maat...
Asar carries along the earth in His train by Maat...*

Maat is the *daughter of Ra*, and she was with him on his celestial barque
when he first emerged from the primeval waters along with his company of
Gods and Goddesses . She is also known as the *eye of Ra, lady of heaven,
queen of the earth, mistress of the Underworld and the lady of the Gods and
Goddesses* . Maat also has a dual form or MAATI. In her *capacity* of God,
Maat is *Shes Maat* which means *ceaseless-ness* and *regularity* of the course of
the sun (i.e. the universe). In the form of Maati, she represents the South
and the North which symbolize Upper and Lower Egypt as well as the
Higher and lower self. Maat is the personification of justice and
righteousness upon which God has created the universe and Maat is also
the essence of God and creation. Therefore, it is Maat who judges the soul
when it arrives in the judgment hall of Maat. Sometimes Maat herself
becomes the scales upon which the heart of the initiate is judged. Maat
judges the heart (unconscious mind) of the initiate in an attempt to
determine to what extent the heart has lived in accordance with Maat or
truth, correctness, reality, genuineness, uprightness, righteousness, justice,
steadfastness and the unalterable nature of creation.

In this sense, Maat is at once equivalent to the Chinese concept of the
Tao or "*The Way*" of nature. This "*Way*" of nature, from the *Tao-te-Ching*,
the main text of Taoism, represents the harmony of human and divine
(universal) consciousness. Also, Maat may be likened with the Indian idea
of *Dharma* or the ethical values of life and the teachings related to *Karma
Yoga*, the yogic spiritual discipline which emphasizes selfless service and the
attitude that actions are being performed by God who is working through
you instead of your personal ego-self. God is working through you to serve
humanity, which is also essentially God.

> Maat
> compared to
> the Tao, and
> Dharma.

"There are two roads traveled by humankind, those who
seek to live Maat, and those who seek to satisfy their animal
passions."

Ancient Egyptian Proverb

It is important here to gain a deeper understanding of what is meant by *action*. In primeval times, before creation, the primordial ocean existed in complete peace and rest. When that ocean was agitated with the first thought of God, the first *act* was performed. Through the subsequent *acts of mind* or *efforts of divine thought*, creation unfolded in the form of the various Gods and Goddesses who form the "Companies." They represent the qualities of nature (hot-cold, wet-dry, etc.) in the form of pairs of opposites.

When the first primeval thought emerged from the Primeval Ocean of pure potentiality, immediately there was something other than the single primordial essence. Now there is a being who is looking and perceiving the rest of the primordial essence. This is the origin of duality in the world of time and space and the triad of human consciousness. Instead of there being one entity, there appears to be two. The perception instrument, the mind and senses, is the third factor which comprises the triad. Therefore, while you consider yourself to be an individual you are in reality one element in a triad which all together comprise the content of your human experiences. There is a perceiver (the real you), that which is being perceived (the object) and the act of perception itself (through the mind and senses).

With this first primordial act, God set into motion events which operate according to regular and ceaseless motion or action. This is the foundation upon which the universe is created and it emerges from the mind of God. Therefore, if one is able to think and act according to the way in which God thinks and acts, then there will be oneness with God. Human beings are like sparks of divine consciousness, and as such, are endowed with free will to act in any given way. This free will, when dictated by the egoism of the individual mind, causes individual human beings to feel separate from God. This delusion-***Riba*** of the mind leads it to develop ideas related to its own feelings and desires. These egoistic feelings and desires lead to the performance of egoistic acts in an effort to satisfy those perceived needs and desires. This pursuit of fulfillment of desires in the relative world of the mind and senses leads the soul to experience pain, sorrow and frustration because these can never be 100% satisfied. Frustration leads to more actions in search of fulfillment.

The fleeting feelings which most people have associated with happiness and passion are only ephemeral glimpses of the true happiness and peace which can be experienced if the source of true fulfillment within you was to be discovered. Maat shows a way out of the pain and sorrow of human existence and leads you to discover Asar within you, the source of eternal bliss and supreme peace. If you choose to act according to your own will (ego), then you will be in contradiction with Maat. This means that you are contradicting your own conscience, creating negative impressions which will become lodged in the heart (unconscious mind) and will cause continuous mental agitation while you are alive and hellish experiences for yourself after death. The negative impressions rise up at given times in the form of uncontrolled desires, cravings, unrest, and the other forms of self-torment with which human life abounds.

It is important to understand that when the soul is attuned to a physical body, mind and senses, the experiences occur through these. Thus the experiences of pleasure and pain are regulated by how much the body, mind and senses can take. If there is too much pain the body faints. When there is too much pleasure the mind and senses become weakened and swoons into unconsciousness or sleep. If there is too much pleasure, there develops elation and the soul is carried off with the illusion of pleasure which creates a longing and craving for more and more in an endless search for fulfillment.

The body and senses as the regulators of experiences.

However, after death there is no safety valve as was explained earlier. Under these conditions the soul will have the possibility of experiencing boundless amounts of pleasure or pain according to its karmic basis. This is what is called heaven and hell, respectively. Therefore, if you have lived a balanced life (Maat), then you will not have the possibility of experiencing heaven or hell. Rather, you will retain presence of mind and will not fall into the delusion of ignorance. Therefore, the rewards of developing a balanced mind during life continues after death. This mental equanimity allows you to see the difference between the truth and the illusions of the mind and senses, in life as well as in death.

Thus, if you choose to act in accordance with Maat, you will be in a position to transcend the egoistic illusions of the mind and thereby become free from the vicious cycle of actions which keep the mind tied to its illusory feelings and desires and thereby, the soul in bondage to the world of time and space due to its *identification* with the mind. When the practice of Maat is perfected, the mind becomes calm. When this occurs, the ocean of consciousness which was buffeted by the stormy winds becomes calm. This calmness allows the soul to cease its identification with the thoughts of the mind and to behold its true nature as a separate entity from the mind, senses, feelings and thoughts of the ego-self.

Actions are the basis upon which the Cosmic Plan of creation unfolds. In human life, it is the present action which leads to the results that follow at some point in the future, in this life or in another lifetime. Therefore, if you are in a prosperous situation today or an adverse one, it is the actions you performed in the past which have led you to your current situation. Thus, both situations, good or bad, should be endured with a sense of personal responsibility and equanimity of mind (Maat). From a transcendental point of view, the Soul looks at all situations equally. This is because the Soul knows itself to be immortal, eternal and untouched by the events of human existence which it has witnessed for countless lifetimes. It is the ego, which is transient, that looks on life's situations as pressing and real, and therefore either tries to hold onto situations which it considers to be "good" or to get away from or eradicate situations which it considers to be "bad." All situations, whether they are considered to be good or bad by the ego, will eventually pass on, so you should try to view them as clouds which inevitably pass on, no matter how terrible or how wonderful they may seem to be. When life is lived in this manner, the mind develops a stream of peace which rises above elation and depression, prosperity and adversity. By looking at situations with equal vision and doing your best regardless of the circumstances, you are able to discover an unalterable balance within yourself. This is Maat, the underlying order and truth behind the apparent chaos and disorder in the phenomenal world. In doing this, you are able to attune your mind to the cosmic mind of the innermost Self which exists at that transcendental level of peace all the time.

This means that if you are, deep down, indeed the Universal Self, one with God, and if you have come to your current situation in life of bondage to the world of time and space due to your own state of mental ignorance, then it follows that if you undertake the practice of certain disciplines of knowledge (studying the teachings), and daily practice (following the teachings - meditation, selfless service), those same actions will lead you to liberation from the state of bondage. Ignorance of your true Self is the root cause of your bondage to the karmic cycle of life-death-reincarnation-life-death-reincarnation, etc.

No human being can escape from actions.

Actions must be performed by everyone. Even breathing is an action. Therefore, nobody can escape actions. No one can say: "I will go far away from civilization and escape all actions and then my actions will not lead me to a state of ignorance about my true Self." This form of thinking is a fallacy because, as just discussed, breathing, eating, drinking, sleeping, sitting, and walking are actions. The process of liberation requires more than just removing yourself from the field of physical actions. You could go to a quiet cave, temple or church and you would still be plagued by the unruly thoughts of the mind which cause distraction from the Self. Thoughts are subtle forms of actions. Therefore, an action performed in thought can be equally significant and cause as much karmic entanglement as an action performed with the body. An action first originates in the mental field (Astral Plane) of consciousness which is stirred by desires rising from the unconscious mind. This agitation prompts the mind towards thoughts and actions in an attempt to fulfill the desires of the unconscious, but those actions and thoughts create more desires and more future agitation. This is the state of bondage which is experienced by most people and it continues for lifetimes without end. This cycle continues until there is a discovery that desires cannot be fulfilled in this manner. Therefore, the root of desire, ignorance, must be eradicated in order to end the desires of the mind and achieve true peace and balance.

You need to develop subtlety of intellect and profound insight into the nature of the universe and of your innermost Self. The best way to achieve this goal is to practice a blending of wisdom and action in your personal spiritual discipline in order to harmonize your mental and physical qualities.

In this process, you must understand that the ancient Sages-*Rekhat* have given guidelines for which thoughts and actions are in line with the precepts of Maat and which actions and thoughts are not. The 42 precepts of Maat constitute the focus of the *Egyptian Book of Coming Forth By Day*, however, throughout the book, many other injunctions are given. Their purpose is to cleanse the heart of the aspirant.

. The 42 precepts of Maat.

> *"The wise person who acts with Maat is free of falsehood and disorder."*
>
> Ancient Egyptian Proverb

The practice of Maat signifies *wisdom in action*. This is to say that the teachings are to be practiced in ordinary day to day situations, and when the deeper implications of this practice are understood, one will be led to purity in action and thought.

In order to become one with the Divine, you must become the Divine in thought and deed. This means that you must spiritualize your actions and your thoughts at all times and under all conditions. Actions which present themselves to you in the normal course of the day as well as those actions which you have planned for the future should be evaluated by your growing intellectual discriminative quality (Anubis and Saa), and then performed to your best capacity in a selfless manner.

When steadfastness, ⏏, *Djed,* is established the mind, that is, when the mind is firmly rooted in spiritual aspiration, the mind which had been accustomed to being externalized, becomes internalized. It is the externalized state of mind which causes bondage to the world of time and space. This externalized state of mind arises because out of ignorance people believe the external world to be an abiding reality. When the mind becomes internalized the innermost desires of the soul are realized in a way that concentration upon external objects cannot allow. This is the most important teaching of the reflective stage of spiritual discipline. When this idea is perfected (when one's awareness becomes rooted in the source of mind) every moment of the day becomes a meditative state which leads to the purification of the mind and the sublimation of negative energies (egoism, selfishness, anger, hate, greed, vanity, lust, etc.).

Living in harmony with Maat is the art of true spiritual life which must be developed. It leads one to detach from the world even while continuing to live in it and thereby, to discover the hidden inner spiritual dimensions of the unconscious mind and what lies beyond. The doer is always bound to a form of experience which is determined by and bound to the world of time and space, because only in time and space can there manifest the memories of the past and the expectations for the future. The non-doer eventually discovers a transcendental experience of expanding consciousness in the present moment.

The philosophy of Maat

The philosophy of Maat may seem foreign to you at first, but if you reflect upon it you will discover that it holds great truth as well as great potential to assist you in discovering abiding peace and harmony in your life. When you begin to practice and discover how wonderful it is to be in control of your mind instead of being prey to the positive or negative emotions and desires, you will discover an incomparable feeling which goes beyond the ordinary concept of happiness. As with other human endeavors, in order to gain success, you need to study the philosophy intensively with great concentration and then practice it in your day to day life. Do I need to change my situation or just my attitude, the way I deal with it? Even if the situation needs to be changed, you may not be able to physically do so right away for financial reasons. You may need to do some long term planning to be able to change locations, jobs, etc. However, you can change your mental outlook (attitude) towards the situation at this very moment. Realize the positive aspect of the situation, because no situation, no matter how terrible it may appear to be, is without some attributes. In addition, while you continue to put forth effort to better your situation, you can make the current situation into a positive one by seeing it as a divinely ordained situation which has been created in order to allow you to practice developing spiritual qualities such as endurance, patience, compassion, forgiveness, detachment and fortitude. Some people seek to leave the world of human experience by going to some secluded area in order to practice austerities and penances in an effort to purify themselves and gain spiritual merit, but with insight you can discover this opportunity anywhere you may be. Remaining in the world while practicing the spiritual disciplines is in many ways a more intensive spiritual program, requiring greater fortitude and inner strength in order to meet the greater challenges of modern society. Under these conditions the fruits of spiritual practice (patience, detachment, compassion, expansion in consciousness) will be more established in the personality of this individual than in a person who is separated from the world of human experience. Follow the teachings and discover the inner resources you have to discover true happiness and to overcome the obstacles of life. The challenge of spiritual life is not how to separate yourself from the world in order to discover peace. This is an immature view. The real challenge is how to meet and defeat the challenges, temptations and vices which the world presents to everyone. If you are in business, then your challenge is how to use your resources to do business ethically to provide products and services which will improve society and allow more people to find inner peace and harmony. If you are a doctor your duty is to meet the challenges of science and at the same time discovering the mysteries of life while renouncing greed and pride, recognizing that it is the Divine energy to flow through you (in the form of intellect and action) and that it is the true healer of your patients. If you are a garbage person your challenge is to understand and allow others to understand (through your dignity and righteous service) that every job is an integral part of society and no job which allows civilization to move forward is beneath another. How long can a city operate without garbage disposal?. Your challenge is to develop more ways to work efficiently and to promote a healthy environment through recycling and community consciousness with the inner attitude that nature is God's temple. Within every job that is righteous and truly needed by society there is a path to spiritual awakening if the correct understanding is observed.

Spiritual awakening through your job or occupation.

Meskhenet refers to the actions which one has performed during this and previous lifetimes, as well as the destiny that one is creating for oneself based on those actions. Your actions are like extensions of yourself. If you perform positive actions those actions will produce positive effects, feelings and vibrations which will in turn lead to experiences of bliss and peace. If you perform negative actions those actions will lead to negative situations in life and after death they will lead to hellish experiences. Positive actions lead to purity of heart and spiritual realization. Therefore, the idea is to create a positive situation in life through virtuous acts, feelings, speech and thoughts.

Many people feel that once they begin to practice spirituality based on this teaching that they should be spared the past negatives due to the positive in the present. Meskhenet does not work that way. For instance, if you hurt someone ten years ago because you were a negative person then and they held a grudge against you, you cannot expect that if you were to meet that person now that they would no longer hold anger towards you because you turned to spirituality two years ago. Similarly, if you committed a crime and ran away you cannot expect that the authorities will stop looking for you simply because you felt guilty and regretted what you did. The repercussions will follow actions. This is why it is so important to act correctly in the present so as to reap the fruits of peace and harmony in the future. Therefore, you will have to develop a sense of endurance and determination to persistence as you continue your spiritual practice even as you experience the negative results of past actions.

However, in time even these negative repercussions of the past become swept up in the course of time as you strive to act righteously now and in the future. The most important thing at present is to eradicate the negativity within you which causes the negative feelings, thoughts, words and deeds which lead you to hurt others, and commit various sins against your own conscience. This is what will free you from inner unrest and outward experiences of negativity and adversity.

Spiritual vigilance.

Vigilance-*Snehas* at all times as to one's thoughts and actions and remaining selfless are the main ingredients for *"purifying the heart."* The aspirant must watch out for every thought that goes into or comes out of the mind because negative impressions create mental blocks in understanding which hinder spiritual movement. This point is so important that there are no less than two verses dedicated to it in the Gospel of Thomas, an Ancient Egyptian Christian text. By taking up the cross and crucifying the egoistic tendencies of one's behaviors day by day, the thieves of anger, hate, greed, selfishness, etc., are not able to enter the house (unconscious mind) and to cloud the vision of the Soul (oneness).

From the Gospel of Thomas:

> 25. If the master of the house knows that the thief is coming, he will watch before he comes and will not allow him to force an entry into his royal house to carry off its furniture. You then be on the watch against the world. Gird your loins with great energy, so that the brigands (bandits) do not find any way of reaching you; for they find any place you fail to watch.

> 107. Jesus says: "Blessed is the man who knows where the robbers are going to enter, so that he watches, he gathers his belongings and girds his loins before they enter.

The Self, the innermost essence of every human being, "saves" the individual when they turn to the Self as the only reality. This turning towards the Self instead of indulging in the egoism of the mind destroys the possibility of any danger in the realm of time and space or in the Astral

Planes. This is what Jesus referred to when he spoke about guarding against robbers. The robbers are egoism and ignorance, i.e. anger, hate, lust, etc. For one who is watchful, there can be no surprise. For one who is not aware, there is always surprise and unexpected tragedy. By giving importance and primacy to these thieves instead of to the Self, these thieves become the reality of the mind and through identification with the mind, the soul is drawn to experience the fate of karmic entanglements of time and space existence. For they who turn to the Self, even if there were mountainous negative karmic impressions in the mind (heart), self-effort will mitigate those karmas in the same way that soap cleanses impurities. You are the creator of your destiny. Since God is your intrinsic reality, there is no one to look to for redemption other than yourself. You caused your own existence in this time and place and it is you who are responsible for the conditions of your incarnation and the situations in life which you find yourself. Also, since your innermost reality beyond the ego is the Divine Self, you have infinite resources to achieve any goal, transform yourself, and change your entire life. Therefore, through the science of Yoga, you can develop the understanding of the mind which will enable you to effect miraculous changes within yourself. This is the magic of yogic wisdom.

Self-effort will mitigate some negative karmas.

If you are interested in the path of righteous action and the Selfless-Service path of Yoga the books *The Wisdom of Maati* and *Egyptian Proverbs* will be your emphasis in the study and practice of the teachings. Also the book *Healing the Criminal Heart: Introduction to Maat Philosophy, Yoga and Spiritual Redemption Through the Path of Virtue* is good for anyone who would like to gain insight into the nature of sin and how the practice of Maat Philosophy can lead anyone to a complete transformation, forgiveness and spiritual realization regardless of their past.

18. To him belong both eyes and ears, on every path of them whom he loves.

The Self is everywhere at all times because the Self is all that exists. When egoism is prevalent, the eyes and ears seem to belong to individual human beings, animals, etc. When the aspirant consciously comes into awareness of the Self, then His or her eyes, ears and entire being are said to belong to the Self. They become instruments of the Self. In reality, it is the Self who listens, feels, sees, etc., however, through the delusion of egoism born from ignorance of your true deeper nature, you have developed a fictitious character and have become entangled with others who you consider to be part of your family, country, world, etc. in a complex set of relations.

A similar statement to this one appears in the Indian Upanishads. It echoes the same teaching presented here.

> The world existed first as seed a, which as it grew and developed took on names and forms: As a razor in its case, or as fire in wood, so dwells the Self, the Lord of the universe in all forms, even to the tips of the fingers. The ignorant do not know him, for behind the names and forms he remains hidden. When one breathes, one knows him as breath; when one speaks, one knows him as speech; when one sees, one knows him as the eye; when one hears, one knows him as the ear; when one thinks, one knows him as the mind...

> The opening line from the
> *Brihadaranyaka Upanishad*

God is
described
as
"Hidden."

Indeed the Upanishad reiterates the point made in the Hymn of Amun using the same appellations to describe the Self which were used in Ancient Egypt. God is described as "Hidden." God is the true and only entity and the subject who lives through all "living" and "non-living" things. However, human beings, through ignorance, come to believe that they are the ones seeing, hearing and so on. They come to believe themselves to be individuals separate from objects in a world of time and space which is separate from its Creator. In reality, there is no Creator because God or the Self is all. If you paint a tattoo on your skin, your appearance may change, but it is still you. In the same way the objects of the world are nothing but expressions of God according to the combinations of elements which are in themselves composed of God. Thus, human identity is an illusory development based on ignorance. It is a development which is subject to time and space and is therefore subject to birth and death. If you were to discover the "Hidden" divine essence within you, you would discover that which transcends your temporal personality and thus would consciously become aware of your immortality and oneness with all that exists.

19. He hears the petitions of they that appeal to him.
20. To them that call Amun, he comes instantly.

Since the Self is the innermost reality of all human beings, there is no effort made on the path of spirituality that goes unnoticed. Any prayer, any thought of remembrance of God, any positive thought of love-*Merr* and unity brings the mind toward conscious awareness of the Self. Self-effort is the key to drawing the grace of the Self. Since all souls are essentially the Self and therefore, all powerful, each human being has the power to draw infinite energy and create any reality according to his/her will. So through the control of the mind (giving importance and primacy to the Self over the transitory pleasures of the world), the Self is instantaneously present upon its remembrance. The deeper the remembrance of the Self, the deeper presence the experience of the Self will be.

The myriad of thoughts and feelings in the mind cloud the perception of the Self who is always there as your innermost reality. When praying "to" God there is often a feeling, especially at the beginning of studies in spirituality, that God is somewhere and needs to be found. Also, there is a feeling that the Divine is in some far off realm which is almost unattainable. These are great obstacles in the spiritual process because they are ideas based on ignorance and the mind cannot grow spiritually when shrouded in ignorance. From an advanced perspective, God is everywhere and most assuredly in the heart of every individual. However, the outgoing mind and senses direct the attention of the soul away from the inner reality. But when the soul regains control of the mind and senses, through spiritual practices, then it discovers the Self within, like looking in a mirror and seeing the image reflected back. Thus the individual human soul (Ba) is the image of the Universal Soul (God-The Self). Therefore, no prayer goes unheard, and no thought goes unnoticed. Prayers are answered according to the needs of each individual, taking into account their karmic background and present course of action. Thus, the present direction or course you set out on will be supported by the innermost Self in a most mysterious way and according to the wisdom of the cosmic mind.

No prayer goes unheard.

21. He lengthens life, He cuts it short.
22. To them whom He loves, He gives more than hath been decreed for them.

Left up to the fate of the ego, the soul experiences the fleeting, insecure and stressful karma of the mind and its complexes, illusions, imaginations, fears and failings. By securing the love of the Self (applying self-effort and sublimation of the ego), negative karma which would have occurred otherwise is transformed into spiritual discipline which leads to prosperity and enlightenment.

From another perspective, it is the innermost Self of every individual who decides their life span. Many people are baffled by the fact that a person can be alive one day and gone the next or that an innocent child was born into a family where they were abused and killed, etc. All of these occurrences would seem senseless and chaotic if looked at from the perspective of the ordinary spiritually immature philosophy of the masses.

However, the laws of karma or cause and effect prescribes that each individual is always experiencing the fruits of past actions. Therefore, wherever an individual finds himself or herself it is due to their past karmic background, their thoughts, actions, desires and beliefs of the past. Thus, as a spiritual aspirant you should look on the suffering of others with compassion but with the understanding that it is the fulfillment of a karmic plan for their eventual enlightenment. With this vision you should develop detachment and dispassion for others as well as your own karmas which are fructifying in your life. As you begin to dispel the ignorance which compels and drives you into negative actions you begin to eradicate the negative karma (impressions lodged in the unconscious based on ignorance) which would have otherwise led you to experience negative situations in this life and future incarnations as well.

23. When Amun casts a spell on the water, and His name is on the waters, if this name of His be uttered, the crocodile loses power. The winds are driven back, the hurricane is repulsed.

The demons of the mind.

Spells are utterances, hekau, mantra, words which when uttered with meaning and feeling have the power to change consciousness, perception and state of mind. When the Divine name is uttered, the entire being is filled with unshakable power through identification with the true Self which is omnipotent and immortal rather than with the ego which is transient, and therefore, illusory, and subject to birth, death and the fears of human existence. Will I succeed or will I fail? Will I have enough to eat or will I starve? Will he or she accept me or not? All these are concerns of the ego. These thoughts are the demons of the mind, the crocodiles that lurk in the waters, ready to attack the unsuspecting ego of a human being. The mouth is connected to the unconscious. When words are uttered with conscious awareness, they can have a profound effect on the unconscious levels of the mind. Even under the stress of the winds of thoughts in the mind which turn into hurricanes of mental distress, anguish, misery and grief-*Mesqeh,* uttering the words of power-*Hekau,* can have the effect of calming the mind and the distress and anguish can be dissipated or prevented all together. The Self is ever fulfilled, content, and satisfied, therefore, the question of rejection or acceptance, failure or success, life or death, etc., are irrelevant.

*24. At the remembrance of Amun, the wrath of the angry man dies down.
He speaks the gentle word at the moment of strife.*

It will become apparent to anyone who practices introspection, self-examination and self-awareness, that ego sentiments such as anger, hate, lust, greed, etc. cannot exist at the same time in the mind when conscious awareness is present. When egoism exists in the mind, thoughts about the Self cannot enter and likewise when total immersion into the experience (*Sâa*) of the divine presence occurs, egoism (evil, *Set*) and ignorance (*Sâaa*) cannot exist. In a manner of speaking, Jesus implied the same thing with the statement in Matthew 6:24: *No man can serve two masters: for either he will hate the one, and love the other; or else he will hold to the one, and despise the other. Ye cannot serve God and money.* Through continued practice of ego sublimation techniques, the patterns of egoism whereby the thoughts of anger, hate, desire, etc. which used to immediately enter the mind and be accepted are now consciously examined and rejected in favor of remembrance of the Divine Self.

Also, when you remember your true nature, you immediately become aware that the true essence of the person you are angry at is the same Self. This remembrance allows you to replace the anger with compassion and understanding. You will remember that those who have angered you have performed whatever actions they did out of their own ignorance and further, you will realize that your anger is due to your own lingering ignorance. You must strive to be like the sun who shines on all, good or evil, without discrimination or regret, abiding in its own glory and ever detached.

> "The higher the sun rises, the less shadow does he cast;
> even so the greater is the goodness, the less does it covet
> praise; yet cannot avoid its rewards in honors."
> Ancient Egyptian Proverb

> "The Sun is the preserver and the nurse of every group.
> And just as the Intelligible Cosmos, holding the Sensible in
> its embrace, fills it full, distending it with forms of every
> kind and every shape - so, too the Sun distendeth all in
> Cosmos, affording births to all, and strengthen them."
> Ancient Egyptian Proverb

Thus, anger dies down, and even though you are in the midst of strife and conflict, you will utter words of peace and understanding which will bring harmony and stability to yourself and others. This practice of reminding yourself of your true identity allows the illusory ego identification you have built up over many lifetimes to dissolve. When this level of mystical practice takes hold in your unconscious, you will notice a profound transformation in the way you see the world and all those around you.

25. He is a pleasant breeze to him that appeal to him.

When you discover the joy of spiritual practice, you will discover the relieving feeling which occurs upon remembering your divine essence just as a cool breeze is always a welcome refreshment during a hot day. In an instant, at any time, the mind can recall the reality which is forgotten when the automatic Ego-consciousness takes over and bask in the blissful rays of the Self. There is no place on earth which can provide this kind of "breeze." Even the most beautiful scene of nature you could possibly imagine could not compare to the peace and bliss that arises from movement towards the Divine.

26. He delivers the helpless one.

This utterance is strongly related to the previous one. The ego-personality is utterly helpless in the vast realm of the physical world. It cannot control time, the weather or other people. The Self delivers the soul from the identification with the ego and its plight, through enlightenment. In reality, even the most powerful person on earth is indeed weak, feeble and helpless if there is no spiritual knowledge. All things in the phenomenal world are fleeting and illusory. Therefore, any security people think they have in this world is only a fanciful notion of the mind based on ignorance. In fact, while people in trouble feel that they can call on others for help, it is in reality the Self, in the form of family members, police, armies, etc., who answers the call for help. God is working through all activities in the world. Good as well as evil operate in the world according to the divine plan for the karmic evolution of humanity. So deliverance from negative circumstances is based on the level of one's spiritual attainment and not on the situations which arise. This means that those who discover the Self have discovered the source of inner peace and happiness which transcends all past karmic impurities in the mind and all worldly situations which may arise. The only true strength comes from the attainment of spiritual insight and experience. When this occurs, the problems and challenges of human life become like minute particles of dust which can be blown away easily by the breeze of enlightened soul.

. God is working through all activities in the world.

27. He is the wise God whose plans are beneficent.

Creation is set up in such a way that participation in time and space is designed to give the soul experiences as well as lessons which will lead it to enlightenment. The path of every soul is based on its state of consciousness and past experiences. Both of these constitute what is known as Karma. It is your mental state which draws the present situations and objects to yourself. Therefore, every soul produces circumstances which are designed to create certain events, incidents, and occurrences which will produce challenges in life. By successfully meeting the challenges which are presented to you in life, you will be led to spiritual realization. This is the mysterious and compassionate plan set up by the Self which is the essence of your innermost being. A simple example of a challenge in life is stealing. If you are caught, you will be punished. The challenge is, can you resist the temptation to repeat the crime once you are free, or will you once again fall prey to your ignorant desire to acquire the object at all cost? If you meet the challenge, you will not suffer further punishment and eventually, through your understanding that stealing is an expression of your ignorance (you are stealing from God and ultimately from yourself), transcend even the desire to steal and thus experience the peace that comes from having a clear conscience. If you practice yoga, you will experience an even greater expansion of consciousness and bliss, which cannot be experienced by acquiring any object in the world.

The challenges life presents a human being.

28. He is more helpful than millions to the man who hath set Him in His heart.

All complexes of the human being are a result of identification with the body and mind, the belief that one is a finite and limited individual. These complexes (anger, hatred, lust, jealousy, greed, delusions, fanciful notions, etc.) burn in the mind as a never ending bonfire of unfulfilled desires, leading one along a path towards what one believes will bring happiness, but in reality, they lead to pain and suffering in human life. In a mind beset by ignorance, money and other worldly objects only serve to fan the flames of the fire of pain and sorrow. Only the knowledge of one's true nature as the all-encompassing Self can extinguish the flames of pain, grief, upsetness, unrest and sorrow in life by eradicating ignorance in the mind which is the source of all desire and the will to perform negative actions, ignorance of the Self.

There is no way to describe in words, the depth and majesty of the freedom which can be experienced when the Divine Self is "*set*" (the sole object of interest) *in the heart* (psyche). It is not difficult to see that material riches cannot produce abiding happiness. If there is no money there is worry about getting it. If there is wealth, then there is worry about holding onto it. In either case, there is worry about worldly concerns and this worry agitates the *waters* of the mind. It is this agitation that creates more intensification of the illusions and fears of the mind. Physical, mental and emotional peace are the blessings given to those who set the Divine in their hearts. When you "die," all of your accumulated wealth stays behind. If you believe yourself to be the body and fear death, even if you had millions of dollars, it could not bring peace to your heart when you die, the only thing you take with you is your psyche, the unconscious impressions of desires, feelings, concepts and inclinations from this and previous lifetimes. If it is filled with greed, anger, hatred and egoistic desires you will be lead to after-death experiences which reflect this state of consciousness and you will not be able to discover peace.

29. One warrior (who fights) under His name is better than hundreds of thousands.
30. Indeed He is the beneficent strong one.

Thoughts as warriors.

The thoughts in one's mind can be seen as warriors. If your thoughts are dispersed and distracted among worldly objects and desires one's will power will be diluted and weak. If however, through intuitional awareness of your divine nature, you can withdraw your thoughts from the delusions and entanglements of the world in the form of objects, people, relationships and other involvements. You would develop immense will power and a mind that would become the *one warrior who fights better than hundreds of thousands.* This is the battle which every human being fights, knowingly or not.

Every human being is a warrior. The true war is between the Higher Self and the lower. When the Self is called upon (through spiritual discipline and self-effort), the omnipotence of the Higher Self becomes awakened. The power of the Self is the strongest ally in the battle of life. Therefore, any accomplishment, be it spiritual or worldly, has a greater chance of success when done in the name of the Self rather than for the ego.

31. He is perfect and seizes His moment; He is irresistible.

Enlightenment occurs in degrees and it is the Divine that chooses the moment to illumine those who are on the path. The experience of glimpsing the Divine (mystical experiences) leaves an indelible and irresistible impression on the mind. It is far beyond any worldly experience of the senses. After these experiences, the mind will never be the same. These experiences enable the mind to turn away from the experiences of the world and to focus on the transcendental Self.

Imagine for a moment that you are asleep and that you are having a dream. Suddenly, you wake up within your dream and realize "I am dreaming." You see all of the things that are going on and have an internal awareness that it is all a "dream." You "KNOW" that you transcend the dream, that it cannot affect you in any way, and that you will continue to exist even after the dream is over. Now, imagine that you are awake and all of a sudden you realize that you are not the body, nor are any of the memories you have experienced in your life really yours. They are experiences which have happened to the body but not to you. See yourself as one with the universe and know yourself to be immortal and eternal. Also, look around and see all objects in nature, all animals, all people as having the same reality as the one you have discovered. This is only to begin to give you an idea of the glory of Enlightenment. The flashes of awareness grow through increasing self-discovery and culminate in a perennial awareness of *Nuk Pu Neter,* "I Am God." Therefore, seek the Divine in earnestness and with continuous self-effort through the practices of yoga (health of mind and body, study of teachings, reflection on the teachings, meditation, control of the senses and emotions, etc.) and discover your divine nature in this lifetime.

The waking dream.

This hekau is similar to one which occurs in the *Katha Upanishad* of India:

> The Self is attained by the one whom it chooses. This Self reveals
> its own form. (II.23)

These teachings refer to the understanding that the Self manifests to those who seek him/her through the practices of mystical spirituality. This is true because the desire to practice the various yogic techniques is itself an expression of Divine Grace operating through your good meskhenet of this life and from past lifetimes. Therefore, those whom the Self chooses are those who practice mystical spirituality and to whom the Self will reveal him/herself to in the course of time.

Freedom
from
contradiction.

One of the most important teachings about meskhenet is that activities in the world of human experience and the activities of a spiritual initiate do not contradict each other. This means that a spiritually inclined person does not have to feel burdened by the world nor should he or she feel that they cannot progress spiritually unless they "get away from the sinful world." The important factor here is to base your actions on the principles of Maat. When you perform actions with a sense of divine duty your actions become purified and in so doing you are also purifying your thoughts and speech and turning towards the Divine even as you live in society. Along with this when you perform actions based on righteousness, self-control, non-violence and harmony you are benefiting humanity in ways you cannot even begin to appreciate. This is the sagely form of lifestyle which a spiritual aspirant must pursue in order to grow spiritually while living in modern times.

32. All the gods are three, Amun, Ra and Ptah, and there are none other like unto them.

This utterance commences the most important teaching of the hymn which will be elaborated in the next four utterances. Here you begin to discover *The Secrets of Sheti*. Sheti means: *Spiritual discipline or program, to go deeply into the mysteries, to study the mystery teachings and literature profoundly, to penetrate the mysteries.* Recall the teaching:

"I became from God one gods three."

The Sheti which will be revealed here refers to the nature of the Trinity itself and the nature and origin of the neteru who compose Creation. This utterance points to the fact that all of the various Gods and Goddesses that are described in the varied religious scriptures are in reality manifestations of the same Trinity principle, which is of course, a manifestation of the One and Absolute Supreme Being. There is no other being besides the Supreme Divinity. Also, since everything is a manifestation of the Self, all things, including Gods and Goddesses (neteru), planets, animals, stars, etc., are manifestations of the Trinity. This teaching emulates the one which is given in Memphite Theology (based on the God Ptah) as well as Anunian Theology (based on the God Ra) and closely follows another utterance from the *Egyptian Book of Coming Forth By Day*, Chap. 83 Lines 1-3:

> *I came into being from unformed matter, I came into existence as Khepera, I grew in the form of plants, I am hidden in the Tortoise. I am the essence of every god. I am yesterday...*

33. He whose name is hidden is Amun, Ra belongeth to him as His face, and the body is Ptah.
34. Their cities are established on earth forever, Waset, Anu, Hetkaptah.

Amun, the Self, is the "hidden" essence of all things. The Sun (Ra) is the radiant and dynamic outward appearance of the hidden made manifest and also the light of cosmic consciousness, the cosmic mind or that through which consciousness projects. In this aspect, Ptah represents the physical world, the solidification or coagulation of the projection of consciousness (Amun) made manifest. These manifestations are reproduced symbolically on earth in the cities of *KMT* (Egypt) and *Waset* (Weset) or *Newt* (Greek - Thebes). Waset was named Thebes by the Greeks, who knew it also as *Diospolis* (heavenly city). Thebes is the city identified in the Old Testament of the Christian Bible as *No* (city), *No-Amon* (city of Amon), *Anu* (city of Ra) and *Hetkaptah* (city of Ptah).

35. When a message is sent in heaven, it is heard in Anu, and is repeated in Hetkaptah to the Beautiful Face. It is done into writing in the letters of Djehuti, and dispatched to the city of Amun with their things. The matters are answered in Waset (Thebes, the city of Amun).

Hekau-utterances 32-35, as well as 13, are of paramount importance to the understanding of the human mind and its relation to the soul or the *witnessing consciousness*, the *senses* and the *phenomenal universe* (physical world). Accordingly there are many levels of spiritual teaching which can be derived from these verses. Metaphorically, these hekau speak about Amun and the cities of Ancient Egypt as they relate to the Ancient Egyptian Trinity of Amun-Ra-Ptah, however, these are symbols which represent keys to the understanding of the human consciousness and of creation.

When a thought arises in the mind it is only a surface manifestation of a very involved process of cognition. The mind is composed of the unconscious, subconscious and conscious. These three aspects relate to awareness. Then there is also a process of reasoning and this is called the intellect. Thus, in mystical terms when a thought arises it is heard in the subconscious (Anu) and then it is repeated in the conscious mind (Ptah). Then it is approved by the intellect (Djehuti, an aspect of Ra) and finally it is sanctioned by the Higher Self (Amun). There is a very profound teaching being expressed in the last line of this utterance. The statement, "The matters are answered in Waset (Thebes)," refers to the idea that the Soul,

The process of cognition in the human mind.

The teaching of the *Was* scepter.

Amun, is the ultimate and supreme director of that which occurs in creation just as the Soul of an enlightened person governs the thoughts of the intellect (Ra) as well as actions of the mind and body (Ptah). This symbolism is inherent in the "*Was*" or "*Uas*" scepter. The *Was* scepter, ⌙ , is a symbol of "power" and "dominion" which many of the Ancient Egyptian gods, goddesses and Pharaohs may be seen holding. It is composed of a straight shaft with the head of a mythical animal associated with the god *Set* (Seth), who represents egoism, evil and ignorance as well as raw power and brute strength.

Set is the neter who symbolizes the egoistic tendencies of a human being. Set is the aspect of the human mind with impulses of selfishness, greed, mischievousness, lust, boastfulness, arrogance, vanity, anger, indulgence in sense pleasures, undisciplined, impulsiveness, rudeness, etc. The definition of the name Set includes *extroverted, emitting nature, pride and insolence.* According to Plutarch, Set is the name of *one who, full of ignorance and error, tears in pieces and conceals that holy doctrine which the goddess (Aset) collects, compiles, and delivers to those who aspire after the most perfect participation in divine nature.* Egoism produces ignorance and error which block wisdom and experience of the Divine.

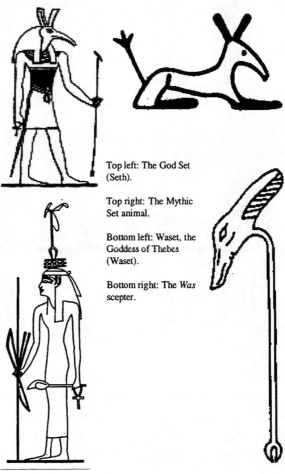

Top left: The God Set (Seth).

Top right: The Mythic Set animal.

Bottom left: Waset, the Goddess of Thebes (Waset).

Bottom right: The *Was* scepter.

The task of sublimating the ego is embodied in the Egyptian story of the battle between Horus and Set, which is a part of the Ausarian Resurrection Mystery (see the book *The Ausarian Resurrection: The Ancient Egyptian Bible*). In the myth, Set, who represents egoism in a human being, acting out of greed and jealousy, killed his brother Ausar (Asar) who represents the human soul, and then tore his body to pieces. Due to this act, Horus, the son of Ausar who represents spiritual aspiration and righteous action (Maat), engages in a struggle against Set to redeem his father. He must redeem the *Eye*, the center of his power, which Set has stolen. Set as the lower self (ego) is in continuous conflict with Horus, who also represents the rebirth of the soul or Higher Self as an incarnation of his father (Ausar). After a long conflict, Horus succeeds in controlling Set by reconstructing the damaged Eye and controlling Set's sexual energy. When this occurs, Horus becomes the ithyphallic *Amsu-Min* or Horus in the aspect of *overthrower of the enemies of his father*.

The battle between Horus and Set.

Above from left to right: Isis, Osiris, Nephthys, Horus and Set.

Below from left to right: Anubis, Ra, Tehuti, Hathor and Sebek.

After the struggle, Set ends up in the service of the Soul. This is symbolized by the depiction of Set assisting the voyage of the sacred barque of Ra as it traverses the heavens and is attacked by fiends (chaos, negative thoughts and feelings, unrighteousness) who were previously Set's accomplices. Set's energy is transformed from raw sexuality to spiritual ecstasy and placed at the service of the Soul. Set becomes a champion who fights against the forces of evil (anger, hate, greed, etc.), which in the past, he himself represented. There are several pictures showing that Horus and Set are aspects of the same being, both represent the conflicting aspects of the human mind. When the lower self (Set) is mastered and placed in the service of the Higher Self (Horus), then spiritual realization is assured. The same idea is conveyed in the *Sphinx*. It represents the embodiment of the initiatic ideal, the infinite energy and Life Force of nature, symbolized by the animal body, commanded by the intuitive intellect, symbolized by the human head.

Sebek and Anubis.

Another deity which symbolizes the idea of the sublimated animal energies in man is the neter *Sebek (Sbk, Sobk)* ⌐⌐. Sebek is a crocodile god who, like Set, symbolizes the forces of nature. In the uncontrolled state, Sebek is a dangerous beast who kills all who cross his path. In this aspect, he is an associate of Set as the one who fetters humans. In the tamed (sublimated) state, Sebek is a formidable ally to Asar in repulsing the forces of evil. In the Pyramid Texts, Sebek assists in the overthrow of Set, and like Anubis, he assists the initiate along the spiritual path and restore the spiritual *Eye* (intuitional vision of the Divine) to the deceased (initiate). Sebek represents spiritual energy which when sublimated, allows an initiate to succeed in the trials and tribulations of life. Thus, Sebek can be seen carrying the mummy of Asar and at other times guarding his tomb (see picture above).

The *Was* represents the energy which engenders life. When this energy is controlled by the ignorant ego, evil and negative activity, restlessness, agitation and unrest are the result. When the same energy is sublimated and controlled by the purified intellect, divine work can be accomplished in a most effective and exalted manner. Thus, any being who holds the *Was* is in control of the source and power of the soul. For the spiritually advanced personality this means having dominion over one's desires and passions and being free from delusion and ignorance. In a historical, political or exoteric sense, this implies being the Pharaoh who resides in Waset. However, the esoteric symbolism implies that the possessor of the *Was* is in communion with the Supreme Ruler of *Waset*, who is none other than Amun, the Divine Self. Thus, the Was scepter was the emblem of Waset as well as the head ornament of the goddess of the city itself, who was also known as *Waset*.

This hekau also relates to the nature of time and space. As we discussed earlier in commentary seven, time and space are not real. They are in reality projections of the mind in and through the Trinity which is a metaphor to explain the triad of consciousness as previously discussed. However, it must be clearly understood that the entire creation, that is, every element of the triad of seer (Amun), seen (Ptah) and sight-mind (Ra), are in reality projections or emanations of the transcendental Self (Neberdjer). This projection is at all times existing in and supported by the Self; it has no independent reality or existence. Just as the projection of a dream world in the human mind is supported by the individual, the projection of the universe is supported by the cosmic mind (God). Thus, the world expresses as a triad (The Self or Spirit-Mind-Creation) which is a product of the underlying principle of duality (The Self and Creation-multiplicity of objects).

The
projection
of the
universe.

The Principle of Duality

The Self →→→→→ Creation

The Trinity of Creation

The Self

Mind →→→→→→→→→→ Physical Universe

Divine consciousness, which is Divine Will, originates in the transcendental realms (Higher Self-heaven-Amun), symbolized by Thebes. It is transmitted through the bright intellect (the light of consciousness- the sun) symbolized by Anu, and then it is transmitted through the faculty of mental thought, symbolized by Djehuti, to the mind, senses and body (Ptah). Any questions or conflicts are to be resolved-*Menab* in the heart of hearts, the soul, symbolized by Thebes where Amun, the "Hidden" essence, resides and not in the mind which is governed by the senses, desires and ignorance.

Firm of heart,
resolute- *Men- ab*.
(See glossary)

Thus, the Spirit, God, manifests in three forms of consciousness. This is true of human consciousness or the individual human being as well as the cosmos or Cosmic Self. In other words, the same spirit that underlies the human being is the same spirit which underlies the entire universe. Every human being has three subjects or identifications. While awake you identify with the waking, day to day, subject or the person who you think you are including the memories of your present lifetime. While having a dream you identify with the sleep subject or the personality who is having the experiences in your dream. While in the dreamless Sleep State you identify with the absence of all subjects and there is existence but not of awareness, you are blanketed by dullness- *Wmet htp ab*. Nevertheless, there is existence in this state because when you wake up you remember that you experienced deep rest but no specific memory as in a dream.

Ptah
(Waking and Physical Subject, conscious mind and sense organs)

↑

Ra
(Intellect and Dream Subject, subtle senses)

↑

Amun
(witnessing and sleep subject)

↑

Pa-Neter-Neberdjer
(Pure Consciousness - The Absolute Self)

The same spirit expresses as the waking subject, the dream subject and the sleep subject. Therefore, the spirit, when involved with subjectivity, manifests as the different levels of awareness or consciousness. However, when not involved with subjectivity the spirit is free from all associations with personality or ego (waking, dream and sleep). So, from another perspective, the same spirit in you, the pure Self (Pa-Neter-Neberdjer), devoid of all subjectivity, expresses as the witnessing and sleep consciousness (Amun), the dream consciousness (Ra), the waking and physical consciousness (Ptah).

The senses and the sense organs.

This teaching also relates to the kind of experience which a human being has depending on the manner in which consciousness is expressing. In this respect there are three modes of experience, the Waking State, the Dream State and the Sleep State. In each of these the spirit identifies itself with a different subject. The waking subject experiences gross physical objects with the conscious mind and the sense organs (hearing, sight, smell, touch, and taste). The dream subject experiences the subtle mental world of thoughts, ideas, imagination, etc. with the mind and subtle senses. The senses and the sense organs are distinct operations. This is why there can be experiences in a dream while there is no outward sign in the physical body when a person sleeps. The subtle senses are used in a dream instead of the gross physical sense organs. In actuality the sense organs are an emanation of the senses and the senses are emanations of the mind and the mind is an emanation of consciousness. Thus, the mind, the physical objects of Creation as well as the senses which are used to perceive those objects and the subject who is said to experience them are all emanations from the one, pure and undifferentiated consciousness, God.

This wisdom leads to the understanding that the multiplicity of Creation, the triad of consciousness, is in reality one all-encompassing existence, non-dual and in fact devoid of subjectivity and differentiation. The witnessing subject (dreamless Sleep State) experiences the subtlest form of awareness in the form of intuition and insight which transcends the mind and intellect. These states have positive and negative aspects. In your own life you are most familiar with the waking subject and the gratification that comes from contacting physical objects you desire. This is the negative aspect of the waking subject. The positive aspect is when you experience the waking world but without attachment and desire. When you experience the joy of understanding a problem or some subject you had difficulty with this is the experience at the level of the intellect. This is the positive aspect of the dream subject. The negative aspect of the dream subject is when the mind is caught in the illusion of thinking that its present situation is an abiding and pressing reality. In a dream, as in waking life, the situations which occur take hold of a person and seem compelling and real. However, upon waking up from the dream the dream situation was found to be unreal and similarly when the waking subject goes to sleep the waking situation is found to be unreal. Therefore, if there is delusion, that is, if you believe the situation you are caught up in ignorance and delusion; this is the negative aspect. If you are rationalizing that your situations are illusory and that you are not caught up in any of those situations then your intellect is lucid *Beq*. This is the positive aspect. When you experience a feeling of joy for no reason, that you cannot describe or rationalize, this is at the level of the witnessing self, which is beyond the intellect. When you achieve the awareness of infinite peace (Hetep), infinite joy, infinite awareness, etc., through spiritual practice, this level of awareness is transcendental of all three relative states of consciousness.

Lucid, to be bright to see-
Beq.
(see glossary)

An enlightened Sage experiences the transcendental level as well as the relative levels. However, the Sage is never caught up in the delusion caused by ignorance because the Sage has discovered and is constantly aware of his or her true identity. Just as an ordinary person sees himself as a human being with a definite history of birth, family and other relations a Sage sees that he or she is a spirit and that the entire universe is their family. Sages do not hold onto fanciful notions or expectations because they know that the world of human experience is full of uncertainty and limitation. They have already discovered what is abiding, limitless, eternal, immortal, pure and true within their own heart and thus have no desire or need for any worldly activity, object or personality. Thus, a Sage operates in the world without attachments or hindrances of any kind. So there is the experience of freedom and a sense that nothing is impossible. This is the kind of mind which a spiritual aspirant needs to develop. When a spiritual aspirant is struggling to maintain these ideals he or she is considered to be in the striving stage of spiritual practice. When a spiritual aspirant reaches the level where this form of consciousness is spontaneous and without effort they are said to be enlightened Sages. The Sage is always in control of the ego-personality and uses it to serve humanity in various ways. The three levels of relative consciousness (waking, dream, sleep) constitute the ego-personality of a human being. In this sense the cosmic ego is composed of Amun-Ra-Ptah and the real Self is Pa-Neter or Neberdjer, the Absolute Self.

Body and Sense Organs

↑

Conscious Mind and Senses
Intellect

↑

Subconscious

↑

Unconscious - ego

↑

Soul

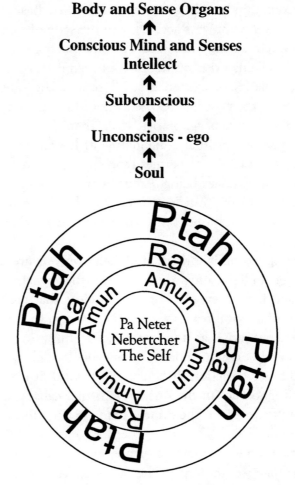

Above: A two dimensional depiction of Creation as symbolized by the Trinity of Amun-Ra-Ptah and the Transcendental Self.

In this manner it is understood that creation is an emanation from the Divine and further, that the emanation is itself the Divine. There is no separation between God and Creation.

That which is relative is transient and illusory. This is why outwardly the world is constantly changing its form. However, the underlying essence never changes. It is eternal and unlimited. So that which is relative, limited and transient arises or emanates from that which is absolute, unlimited and eternal. Therefore, the task of spiritual practice is to discover the innermost essence which underlies consciousness as well as all Creation, to go beyond the relativity of the ego to discover the eternity of the Innermost Self.

This utterance relates to the understanding of the correct relationship between the soul, mind, body and senses. The mind has many levels. These levels express in different ways according to the state of mind and the realm of existence which is being discussed. A human being is not just a physical entity. A human being exists on the physical, astral and causal as well as the transcendental planes of existence at all times. The question is, is that person aware of their deeper existence or not? If not, that person is considered to be a state of ignorance. If so, then that person is considered to be in the state of spiritual enlightenment, liberation, resurrection, etc. According to this teaching Neberdjer represents the transcendental level or Innermost Self in a human being, Amun represents the causal-unconscious level, Ra represents the intellect, senses and subconscious mind, Ptah represents the conscious mind, sense organs and physical body.

When we speak of ignorance and delusion we are referring to the impressions of individuality, duality, and the negative emotions and qualities (anger, hatred, greed, etc.) and all ideas that are in contradiction with the truth of mystical reality which are lodged in the unconscious mind. These impressions arise as thoughts and feelings in the intellect and subconscious and conscious mind and are manifested as desires, longings, concepts and finally as actions in the physical world. It is the impressions of negativity and ignorance in the unconscious that causes the notion egoism to arise as a self concept in the mind: "I am a mortal individual" instead of "I am one with God." Therefore, these erroneous notions need to be corrected or cleansed through enlightenment. This process is what is referred to as *"purifying the heart."* The causal plane of existence is named as such because the notions lodged in it are the "cause" of either the bondage or freedom of the soul as well as the cause of a persons thoughts, actions and desires which impel him or her to seek experiences through many lifetimes through the process of reincarnation.

The human being is in reality a reflection of the Divine Trinity. Amun is the soul of an individual. Ra is the aspect which reflects as the mind in a human being and Ptah is the aspect which manifests as the physical body of a person.

Neberdjer ➜ Innermost Self

Amun ➜ Soul

Ra ➜ Mind

Ptah ➜ Body

The correct relationship between the soul, intellect, mind and body is as follows. The sense organs and body (Hetkaptah) must be under the control of the mind (Anu), the mind must be under the control of the intellect or reason (Djehuti), the intellect or reason must be under the control of the Soul (Thebes). If this movement of the mind is accomplished, the ignorance which leads to delusion and bondage to the world of time and space, the development of the illusory ego-personality, and the forgetfulness of your true nature will not occur. The soul should be the supreme ruler and sole monarch of all actions which are performed in the life of a human being.

Those people who are beset with ignorance of their true nature are led by their ignorant notions and cannot control their desires, feelings, attachments and cravings. Thus they run here and there in search of money, human relationships and the pleasures of the senses, because this is their understanding of what can bring them happiness and fulfillment. They don't stop to think about the fact that the desires in the mind arise endlessly and can never be fulfilled through worldly means and so they are caught, trapped in the miseries of human existence, which they have led themselves to experience. These may be in the form of loss of relatives, loss of possessions, inability to fulfill desires, lack of health, and ultimately, the supreme loss which occurs at the time of death wherein all objects and loved ones must be left behind.

A very similar illustration of this same wisdom teaching is given in the *Katha Upanishad* from India and was also later used in the great *Bhagavad Gita* scripture. The illustration is given of a chariot rider, a chariot driver, the reins used by the driver and the horses which pull the chariot around.

> Know that the Self is the rider, and the body the chariot; that the intellect is the charioteer, and the mind, the reins.

> The senses, say the wise, are the horses; the roads they travel are the mazes of desire. The wise call the Self the enjoyer when he is united with the body, the senses, and the mind.

When a man lacks discrimination and is mind is uncontrolled, his senses are unmanageable, like the restive horses of a charioteer. But when a man has discrimination and his mind is controlled, his senses, like the well-broken horses of a charioteer, lightly obey the rein.

He who lacks discrimination, whose mind is unsteady and whose heart is impure, never reaches the goal, but is born again and again. But he who has, discrimination, whose mind is steady and whose heart is pure, reaches the goal, and having reached it is born no more.

The man who has a sound understanding for charioteer, a controlled mind for reins, he it is that reaches the end of the journey, the supreme abode of Vishnu (God-Brahman-The Self), the all pervading.

Katha Upanishad

In much the same way as hekau-utterance 35 from the Hymns of Amun has done, the segment from the Katha Upanishad stresses the need to have the proper "chain of command" wherein one trains one's senses, intellect and mind to obey the dictates of the Soul and thus achieve self-knowledge or enlightenment.

The mind is a higher reality than the waking world. Consider that without the mind there can be no experience and the most healthy body as well as the most enjoyable objects a person can desire are of no use. Therefore, mind is a higher reality. This is why mental experiences are more intense than experiences in the waking world. However, the witnessing consciousness is higher than the mind because the mind emanates from it. Through spiritual practices and meditation it is possible to discover the witnessing Self and then to transcend the mind. Therefore, the Self is highest of all and at this level there is absence of desire, pain ignorance, etc. This is because enlightenment to the true Self has eradicated all ignorance. Without ignorance there cannot be delusion or desire, but only fulfillment-*Si*, contentment-*Meht* and peace-*Hetep*. Without desire and delusion there cannot be frustration, anger, hatred greed, etc. Thus an enlightened Sage lives internally on a transcendental plane while his or her body continues to exist in the Physical Plane.

In essence the dreamless Sleep State is a negative experience because while there is non-duality there is also absence of lucidity. The difference between the enlightened Sage state and dreamless sleep is that when your are in the dreamless Sleep State, you are not aware of the non-duality and the vast expansion of consciousness. While there is no mentation, there is also no wisdom. But when the transcendental experience of Enlightenment occurs, there is an experience and conscious awareness of the oneness of existence. The illusion of the mind, the dream of the world, dissolves back into the primordial ocean of infinite being from which creation arose. This is the conscious perception of a liberated Sage endowed with enlightenment. The enlightened Sage perceives himself/herself as that primordial God who arose out of the primeval waters with the original thought, and the entire creation as that same Primeval Ocean. He/she understands that though the primordial ocean appears to have changed into the multiplicity of the various objects of creation, it never did truly undergo an irreversible transformation. What is seen as "the world," to the un-enlightened mind, is viewed as the movement of Ra as he traverses through the ocean of consciousness as well as the manifestation of the "Hidden" essence, "Amun," which underlies all existence.

36. *His heart is understanding, His lips are Taste, His Kau are all the things that are in His mouth.*
37. *He enters, the two caverns are beneath His feet. The Nile appears from the hollow beneath His sandals. His soul is Shu, His heart is Tefnut. He is Horus of the two horizons in the upper heaven.*

The heart of the Self is all knowing and compassionate. The *Kau* (images, reflections - creation) of the divine are in His consciousness. The Self is the source of the life giving Nile river, the breath of life (Shu - male spirit) and the fertile moistness (Tefnut-female creation) are its essence.

38. *His right eye is day. His left eye is night. He is the leader of faces on every path. His body is Nu. The dweller in it is the Nile, producing everything that is, nourishing all that is.*
39. *He breaths breath into all nostrils.*

The day and night are prime examples of the principle of the pairs of opposites. They also refer to the Sun and Moon, which are the cosmic symbols, used throughout the world to convey the idea of totality and all-encompassingness of the Supreme Divinity. In this aspect, the sun represents the Spirit, God, the Cosmic Mind, who is the originator and sustainer of creation. The moon symbolizes the lower mind which is a reflection of the light of consciousness. Thus, in saying that Amun contains both day and night, is to say that the non-dual Self is the source of the pairs of opposites.

The Self is the true identity of all beings in every walk of life. The body of the Self is the waters of consciousness, Nu, and everything is a manifestation of consciousness. It is the same Self who enlivens the Self in the form of creation (breaths breath into all nostrils), just as water is wet and moistens everything it touches. The Self is creation and gives life to everything in it.

40. The luck and destiny of every man and woman are with Him.

Many people believe that karma is equal to fate or destiny, however, this interpretation could not be further from the original understanding of the ancient Sages. The etymology of the word, karma, comes from the Sanskrit "karman," deed or action. In Yoga philosophy, karma also refers to one's actions and these same actions lead to certain experiences and consequences. In Ancient Egyptian philosophy the word meskhenet comes from the goddess who goes by the same name. She presides over the birth circumstances and life experiences of every individual. She is the one who carries out the decree which has been ordained by Djehuti after the judgment of the heart in the hall of Maat. It is Djehuti who records the deeds (actions) or karmas of every individual and then decrees the Shai and Rennenet which are fitting for that particular individual. Then with the help of Shai and Rennenet, Meskhenet causes the individual to experience the proper circumstances based on their previous deeds.

The teachings drawn from the symbolism of *Shai, Rennenet, Meskhenet* and *Djehuti* which were introduced earlier in the commentary to hekaus 15-16, bring our attention to the intellect. Your fate is determined by your actions, feelings, desires and thoughts and these are determined by your understanding. Those who have cultivated an intuitive intellect which understands the nature of creation and the oneness of all things in the one Hidden God (has experience of virtue, has controlled the senses, and has upheld Maat), will achieve *Saa-Amenti-Ra,* the intelligence or knowledge of the Amenti of Ra, the hidden world (God). *Sa* or *Såa,* is wisdom deified, wisdom which has progressed to the level of experience, to know something not only intellectually but by experience. Therefore, wisdom, knowledge and learning are *Sa-t,* and a wise person or Sage *Sau,* or *Saåu*[18]. *Såa,* , is also a form of Djehuti. The sound of the word *Sa-t* is also used to signify moral weakness or evil when used with the symbols ( ) "in back of" and "small" ( )

---

[18] Incidentally, the Sanskrit word, Sat, in Indian Yoga-Vedanta philosophy means that which is real and true.

as in reduced intellectual development. Therefore, evil is associated with moral and mental weakness or constriction of the mind and that which is divine is associated with intuitional realization of truth.

Nature herself offers one path to spiritual realization. The path of nature, learning through mistakes, suffering, and the process of trial and error, is arduous, requiring many reincarnations. Therefore, the path of nature is to be avoided because it requires repeated embodiments wherein one learns the lessons of life by experiencing pain and suffering along with the pleasures. Yoga disciplines do not rely on fate, or reincarnation, but on the science which is directed towards psycho-spiritual transformation. Advancement in Yoga is therefore dependent on the desire of the individual to put forth his/her effort in the direction towards self-improvement under the proper guidance. In this way, the negative karma (mental state) of the past which has created the present conditions can be changed, leading one to prosperity and spiritual emancipation. Further, even without knowing it, the actions, thoughts and aspirations of all people occur within creation and the Self is creation. Therefore, any fortune and destiny lies with the Self. There is no other fate since all else is an illusion.

41. His wife is the Earth; He united with her.
42. His seed is the wheat plant; His effluxes are the grain.

From this point of view, the Self is seen as the male aspect and creation is the female. The Self is the spirit that imbues creation with life (*Ka-mut-f* - Bull of its Mother). This is the reason why all divinities, the neteru, are presented as pairs of male and female beings. This verse points to a dualistic point of view and as we have seen, the duality of Creation originates in the singularity of the Primeval Ocean and the essence of that ocean is the Supreme Being. Therefore, from a higher perspective, it is the Self which is the cause and effect of all things, the seed as well as the land which is cultivated and the fruits which come forth thereof.

43. Thou art Temu, who did create beings endowed with reason; Thou make the color of the skin of one race to be different from that of another, but, however many may be the varieties of mankind, it is Thou that make them all to live.

This line is important because it establishes a relationship between Amun and Tem. We are not talking about different deities, but about one and the same. Memphite Theology also makes this same point. Amun, Tem and Ptah are different names for the same principle. This passage once again proclaims that all names and forms, and all human beings, regardless of their skin coloration, are in reality expressions of the divine force which causes them to live. This verse is referring to Amun in the aspect of Khnum, the Potter, who is a deity who fashions the forms of an individual's body. Therefore, this statement acknowledges the divine essence of all human beings. Thus, although it appears that there are different races or ethnicities of human beings, the source and underlying essence of all human beings is one and the same: The Supreme Self.

44. Thou art the lord of intelligence, and knowledge is that which proceed from Thy mouth.

God is the Supreme Preceptor, the source of all knowledge and the force behind the intelligence (*Saa*) which is capable of comprehending it. This same knowledge is what proceeds from the Supreme Being in the form of *Hekau*. The *Eye of Horus* also embodies the same idea of the divine essence moving into creation and enlivening it. It is knowledge, through the medium of sound, which penetrates the ocean of pure undifferentiated consciousness and causes it to assume different names and forms. However, this modification into forms is only a temporary development in cosmic terms and is not a permanent transformation.

This idea of the sound which engenders creation is known as *Heka* in the Ancient Egyptian tradition, the *Word* of the Christian faith, *AUM* in Vedanta Philosophy and *Logos* in Greek-Gnostic philosophy.

In Hermetic philosophy, Logos means reason or intellect. In a larger sense or context, Logos is the rational principle that orders the universe, also known as Maat in Egypt. The Stoic philosophers thought of this principle as the soul of the world. There have been many debates in theology about the meaning of the Greek word "Logos" as used in the Gospel of John. The writers of the Bible translated the term as *"Word"* in John 1:1: *"In the beginning was the Word and the Word was with God, and the Word was God."* "Word" can be taken to mean *God* or *wisdom*. However, these principles were first established in the Ancient Egyptian theology of Amun-Ra-Ptah. This *Word* itself is God, the source of all wisdom and creation; all are indeed one and the same. The use of the term "Word" in this context, along with the following verses from the Bible, reveals a concordance and kinship to the Amunian theology, denoting its origin in Ancient Egyptian mystical and metaphysical philosophy. The object of mystical philosophy is to assist the initiate in unlocking the divine energy (word) of his/her consciousness which has incarnated itself and has become associated with gross matter. The unlocking process of enlightenment leads to the soul's regaining its subtle form once again.

John 1

1 In the beginning was the Word and the Word was with God, and the Word was God.

2 The same was in the beginning with God.

3 All things were made by him; and without him was not any thing made that was made.

4 In him was life; and the life was the light of men.

5. And the light Shines in darkness; and the darkness comprehended it not.

Lines 4 and 5 above is essentially the same as the line in line 1 of the Hymns of Amun which states: *He is self-created and as He fashioned Himself none knows His forms.* Compare John 3 to verses 45, 47 and 48 of the Hymns of Amun.

Certain sounds are recurrent in nature and this reflects in human languages. One example of this is the sound "ma." This sound ma is the same in the Sanskrit, Spanish English, as well as Ancient Egyptian. Astoundingly, it caries the same general meaning, mother. The important factor about sound, from a mystical point of view, is that when it is tied to a mystical understanding, the meditation upon that sound can lead to deeper and deeper levels of self discovery leading to enlightenment. This is because sound emanates from the subtle levels of consciousness. This is why a mindless person will utter things he or she did not want to say. The faculty of speech is linked to the unconscious levels of the mind and this level is closest to the innermost Self. Therefore, if a sound along with a mystical meditative principle are used in the form of a chant or prayer it can be as a vehicle to divine realization. This is the basis of what are known as *words of power* or *hekau*. In this respect the verses of the Hymns of Amun are hekau or Words of Power. Along with the individual verses we have also discussed hekau related to the Divine Trinity. Thus, *Amun-Ra-Ptah* as well as the individual Divine Names: *Pa-Neter, Neberdjer, Om, Amun, Ra, Ptah, Asar, Nu, Aset and Mehurt* can be effective words of power if used in conjunction with the spiritual understanding as presented herein.

45. *Thou make every work to proceed, Thou work in the sky and Thou make to come into being the beauties of the daylight; the gods rejoice in Thy beauties, and their hearts live when they see Thee.*

The Self (God) is the mover behind all movements, all beauty, and even the gods (advanced beings) are in awe at the sight of the Supreme Self, so much so that they themselves find true life in the Self.

The deeper implication here is that the Self is the ultimate cause of everything that happens in creation. As discussed earlier, there are three realms of existence: Heaven, Duat and the Physical world. However, the *Ancient Egyptian Book of Coming Forth By Day* states that there is a realm within the Duat *"where the cedar tree existeth not, where the acacia tree does not put forth shoots, and where the ground neither produces grass nor herbs."*

MAUI
"to think, to ponder, to fix attention, concentration"

This is the transcendental realm which is beyond time and space, the mind and its thoughts and concepts, and physicality. It is a realm wherein there is no thought and no duality. This is the Supreme Abode of the Self and it is the source of all Creation, which itself appears as duality and multiplicity. With this understanding we can gain greater insight into the mind and its movements. Think of the mind and all existence as an ocean. When there is no vibration in the mind, consciousness is pure, without form. This is what the teaching above is referring to as the realm where "the cedar tree existeth not, where the acacia tree does not put forth shoots, and where the ground neither produces grass nor herbs." When consciousness is in the state of movement, vibration (*Neshsh-*agitation), then it takes on the various forms of nature. When you think your mind is actually taking on a form. When there is no thought there is no awareness of forms, time and space or duality. This is the objective of the practice of meditation and spiritual discipline, to discover the realm of consciousness which is beyond the level of ordinary human awareness. Ordinary human awareness, beset with delusion, ignorance, and distraction, becomes caught in the waves of emotion, elation and depression, etc. In the transcendental realm however, it there is an incomparable experience of bliss and peace which cannot be described; it can only be experienced in order to be understood.

The ability to control the mind is possible to the extent that there is awareness of one's separation from and control over the ego. The ego itself is like a vibration, a ripple in the vastness of your consciousness. Therefore, by gaining insight into your true identity as the Self you can gain control over every aspect of your personality (mind, body and sense organs). The essential teachings of the Ancient Egyptian Kybalion in reference to the mind are presented below.

"To change your mood or mental state, change your vibration."

"Mastery of self consists not in abnormal dreams, visions and fantastic imaginings or living, but in using the higher forces against the lower thus escaping the pains of the lower by vibrating on the higher."

"Mind, as matter, may be transmuted from state to state, degree to degree, condition to condition, pole to pole, and vibration to vibration. Transmutation is a mental art."

"To destroy an undesirable rate of mental vibration, concentrate on the opposite vibration to the one to be suppressed."

"The wise ones serve the higher planes and rule the lower. In this way one operates the laws instead being a slave to them."

"Those who may come to understand the law of vibrations will hold the scepter of power in their hand."

"Nothing rests, everything moves; everything vibrates."

"Gender is in everything; everything has its masculine and feminine principles; gender manifests on all planes."

"Everything is dual; everything has poles; everything has its pair of opposites; like and unlike are the same; opposites are identical in nature, but different in degree; extremes meet; all truths are but half- truths; all paradoxes may be reconciled."

"Everything flows out and in; everything has its tides; all things rise and fall; the pendulum-swing manifests in everything; the measure of the swing to the right is the measure to the left; rhythm compensates."

"Every cause has its effect; every effect has its cause; everything happens according to law; chance is a name for law unrecognized; there are many planes of causation, but nothing escapes the law."

In the Kybalion, the universe is explained as a vibration. Also the mind and the mental substance from which thoughts are made are also composed of vibrations. In the realm described above, where Asar abides, there is no vibration; "nothing happens" from the point of view of a human being because this realm does not exist as a factor of mentation. Think about it. Everything you know or have experienced in your life has been a factor of your thinking process. In fact, without this thinking process the mind cannot function; it will stand still. When the mind operates it vibrates and this vibration stirs up the ocean of consciousness. This stirring or vibratory process is what people perceive as life experiences, sense perceptions, the awareness of the passage of time, the awareness of space between objects and their thoughts. Upon closer reflection you should realize that throughout all of your experiences, being born, growing to adulthood and middle age throughout the entire aging process, you have been the same all the time. It has always been the same "you" but the experiences have been different. The experiences of your waking life are not really different from those of your dreams. They are all just vibrations in the mental pool of water which is a fraction of the vast ocean of consciousness.

Thus, all experiences occur either in the Duat (Astral Plane composed of the subtle mind and senses) or in the Physical Plane (the conscious mind, sense organs and body), which are creations of the mind of God (The Self) in which the mind and senses of the individual human being interact. Once again, this interaction process in which you see yourself as an individual having experiences in time and space is composed of the Triad. In the Triad there is an object, a subject and interaction between the two. As a soul you are a special reflection of the light of Supreme Consciousness which emanates from the Self (Asar). This is why you have consciousness and awareness of being alive. However, due to your ignorance you are wandering in the vast realm of the mind which can only operate in the Duat or in the physical world. You have forgotten your Higher Self which is needed in order to perceive that which transcends the vibrations of the mind and senses.

Also, human emotions and desires such as falling in love or desiring to possess an object in order to experience pleasure all occur in the mind and are in reality projections in the mind based on the person's understanding of reality, just as an entire world is created in a dream out of one's consciousness. Those people and objects which you desired are composed of mental substance and your body and thoughts are also composed of the same substance. Everything is composed of atoms, and atoms are composed of energy, and energy is composed of the Self. In reality, that which you desire is a reflection of God in the mental pool of consciousness (your mind), but through the deluded state of mind, you have come to believe that personalities and physical objects in the world are abiding realities. Just as the dream world appears to be "real" and "tangible" during the dream, the physical world also appears to be real and tangible, and yet they are composed of the same stuff. In reality the only truth behind all things in creation is the Self, and it is this Self which supports all of the vibrations in all planes of existence. Thus, if you desire an object or a person to make you feel "good", you are in reality desiring to experience the bliss of the Self, but you are doing so in a most indirect manner. Instead of going after the Self you are trying to grasp the reflection of the Self. This would be like seeking to experience the warmth of the sun by jumping into a lake where the sun is reflecting instead of just sitting in the sun.

Therefore, the mystics and Sages who have discovered the Self have enjoined the practices of dispassion and detachment. These disciplines involve living life but not holding on to it as a source of abiding happiness. They are dynamic qualities, which when developed, allow you to experience life while not being bound to it or affected by it. Since both good situations and bad situations in life are both illusory, then it follows that positive developments in life should not become the cause of elation while at the same time negative developments should not be viewed as a motive for depression and sorrow. All situations, good or bad, are determined by the concept of the person who is experiencing them. They are therefore dependent on the attitude or frame of mind of that person. For those who have discovered the reality beyond the illusoriness of the mind and time and space, there is neither good nor bad, happy or sad, only the knowledge of peace and immortality. From the standpoint of those who are unenlightened all events which occur in life seem real, but from the standpoint of one who has discovered the absolute reality, all of this is illusory as a passing cloud or a dream. Thus, any experience which depends on the mind and senses occurs either in the Astral or Physical Planes and therefore, these planes are also illusory and unreal.

Understanding the Planes of Consciousness

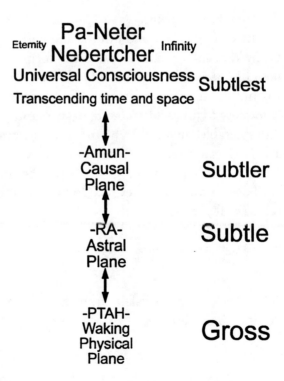

The diagram above depicts how the phenomenal universe emanates from the Self in the following manner. The Self, which is the subtlest essence, projects itself into time and space. Then the consciousness itself vibrates, like waves in an ocean, at varied rates. These vibrations constitute thoughts. The more congealed consciousness becomes with form, the more concrete, solid and tangible it becomes. These constitute physicality. A human being is a blend of subtle and gross essence. However both the subtle and gross are essentially emanations from the same Divine Self, who is the subtlest essence.

When the mind and senses are transcended through the process of meditation it is possible to discover that special realm wherein there is no vibration, no time, no space. There is no existence or non-existence and no being or non-being. It is the realm that is beyond all concepts of the mind and it is the realm from which time and space emanates.

This beautiful and supremely poetic verse also points to another important mystical teaching. How is it possible to see God? We have been told elsewhere that no mortal person has seen or can ever see God. Therefore, it would seem that the verse is contradicting other Ancient Egyptian teachings. The following are Ancient Egyptian teachings on the nature of God.

Aset says: "I Aset, am all that has been, all that is, or shall be; and no mortal man has ever unveiled me."

"God is the father of beings.
God is the eternal One... and infinite and endures forever.
God is hidden and no man knows God's form.
No man has been able to seek out God's likeness.
God is hidden to gods and men... God's name remains hidden...
It is a mystery to his children, men, women and gods. God's names are innumerable, manifold and no one knows their number... though God can be seen in form and observation of God can be made at God's appearance, God cannot be understood... God cannot be seen with mortal eyes... God is invisible and inscrutable to gods as well as men."

Portions from the Egyptian Book of Coming forth by Day and the papyrus of Nesi-Khensu

The following passage is taken from a passage where princess Nesi-Khensu glorifies Amen-Ra.

"August Soul which came into being in primeval time, the great god living in truth, the first "Nine Gods" who gave birth to the other two "Nine Gods," the being in whom every god existeth, One One, ⤸⟶◻⤸⟶◻ℓ⟍𓀀, the creator of the kings who appeared when the earth took form in the beginning, whose birth is hidden, whose forms are manifold, whose germination cannot be known."

The process of reflection on the teachings referring to the Trinity and the Triad of human consciousness reveals a method by which God can be discovered and viewed. However, this viewing is no ordinary sight. It is an experience which is at once astounding and transformative. In essence, the sight of God is an experience which transforms an ordinary human being into a divine vessel, a neter.

How is it possible to achieve this divine sight? As we have discussed throughout this text, spiritual transformation requires a change in one's lifestyle, the way in which life is understood and lived. Then it is necessary to reflect upon the teachings of mystical spirituality. Along with the disciplines discussed so far meditation is the next most important spiritual exercise. Meditation is the discipline which allows direct access to divine awareness, in essence, to see God directly, without forms or modifications.

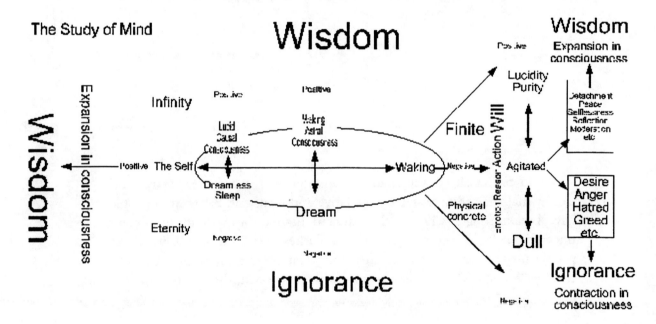

We have seen how God manifests as Creation through the medium of the Trinity which in turn refers to a triad of consciousness. In order to understand how to make use of this mystical understanding we will need to discover more about the nature of the mind and its inner workings. The depths of human consciousness can best be understood through the study of waking, dream and the dreamless Sleep States of consciousness in conjunction with the wisdom of the fourth or transcendental state. Most people are familiar with the three primary states mentioned above but not with the fourth or transcendental state, otherwise they would be enlightened already and would not require any philosophy or spiritual instruction. Each of the ordinary states of consciousness has a counterpart which can be discovered through correct understanding and spiritual practice. Actually, the ordinary states (waking, dream and dreamless sleep) are negative states. The basis of their very existence is rooted in ignorance. They are opposite to true awakening and real illumination of the inner reality. However, if the positive states were discovered and explored, that exploration would lead to an expansion in consciousness which would lead to spiritual enlightenment. In order to discover the positive states of consciousness we will make use of the Trinity (triad) model and the wisdom of the three ordinary states. The mystical wisdom we will explore in the following section based on the Hymns of Amun and the Trinity of Amun-Ra-Ptah is of a very highly advanced order.

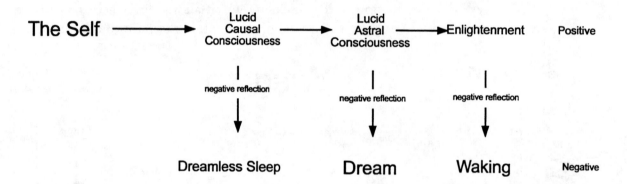

Upon reflection on the triad of consciousness it becomes clearer and clearer that the ordinary states are relative and transient. Sometimes people have breakthroughs wherein they discern higher forms of intuition and understanding. However, these come as flashes and soon fade. Oftentimes people shrug it off as a coincidence or in fear of going insane or the idea that an "evil spirit" is messing around with their head, they try to deny the occurrence altogether.

In reality, the three states are merely reflections of the positive states. Thus, the dreamless Sleep State has its counterpart in the Lucid Causal Consciousness state wherein there are is awareness but no thoughts or desires. The Dream State has its counterpart in the Waking (Lucid) Astral Consciousness state. The ordinary Waking State has its opposite or positive in the Transcendental Self or enlightened state.

The personality of every human being is somewhat different from every other. However the Sages of Yoga have identified four basic factors which are common to all human personalities. These factors are: Emotion, Reason, Action and Will. Also, the human personality expresses in three basic formats. These are *Dullness, Agitation* and *Lucidity (Harmony and Purity)*. This means that in order for a human being to properly evolve, all aspects of the personality must develop in an integral fashion. Therefore, four major forms of Yoga disciplines have evolved and each is specifically designed to promote a positive movement in one of the areas of personality. The Yoga of Devotional Love enhances and harnesses the emotional aspect in a human personality and directs it towards the Higher Self. The Yoga of Wisdom enhances and harnesses the reasoning aspect in a human personality and directs it towards the Higher Self. The Yoga of Action enhances and harnesses the movement and behavior aspect in a human personality and directs it towards the Higher Self. The Yoga of Meditation enhances and harnesses the willing aspect in a human personality and directs it towards the Higher Self. The willing aspect of human personality may be defined as that which involves resolution, determination, resolve, choice and volition.

Lucid, to be bright to see- *Beq*

Agitated, disturbed- *Neshsh.*

Dense Dull of heart- *Wmet htp ab.*

(see glossary)

The process of spiritual life means turning away from the negative aspects of consciousness and turning towards the positive or lucid aspects which lead to enlightenment. The Waking State is the most concrete state and as such, it acts to anchor the soul to a physical form (human body) over an extended period of time, and through it the soul encounters various experiences which will provide pleasure and pain. It is not possible to practice the spiritual disciplines of yoga and mystical religion in the Dream State or the Sleep State. Thus, the waking - physical state is the field in which the *Emotion, Reason, Action* and *Will* of a human being can be played out in an extended format of time and space, unlike the dream plane in which an entire world can come into existence and vanish in a flash. So the task of spiritual disciplines is to engage in practices (virtues) which will promote a movement towards lucidity (wisdom-enlightenment) and move away from the activities, thoughts and feelings which promote agitation, distraction, discontent and ultimately lead to the state of *Dullness* and ignorance of the intellect. This process entails controlling anger, hatred, greed, etc., and promoting effacement of the ego through righteous actions, simplicity, truthfulness, patience and other virtues.

Once a spiritual aspirant has worked on promoting *Lucidity* in the Waking State by controlling the agitating factors which lead to the state of *Agitation* such as distraction, desire, longing, anger, hatred, greed, lust, etc., it is possible, with a mind that is calm, lucid and strong willed, to practice formal meditation on the innermost Self. When this level of spiritual practice is reached such a person is considered to be advanced on the spiritual path. Their powers of concentration, fortitude and inner peace they have gained through intellectual knowledge has allowed them to develop real faith in which they can understand the goal of spirituality and exert the necessary self-effort needed to realize the objective. Already they are far elevated from the masses of people who live to satisfy their desires for the limited enjoyments which the world seems to bring. Their constantly agitated state of mind precludes reflectiveness and inner peace, without which it is not possible to discover the inner meaning of spirituality. Their understanding is shallow, intellectual, theoretical and their will power is weak, so they do not desire for spiritual emancipation. As a result they are caught up in the activities, desires and longings of modern society. This process of self-control and inner development which leads to divine realization is described in Chapter 77 of the *Ancient Egyptian Book of Coming Forth By Day*. Some excerpts are included below.

The need for Self-control.

> I have risen, I have gathered myself together like a beautiful golden hawk, with the head of the Benu, and Ra hath entered in [to hear my speech]. I have taken my seat among the great gods, [the children of] Nut. I have settled myself, the Sekhet-hetepet (the Field of Offerings) is before me. I eat therein, I become a Spirit-soul therein, I am supplied with food in abundance therein, as much as I desire. The Grain-god (Nepra) hath given unto me food for my throat, and I am master over myself and over the attributes of my head.

In Chapter 78 the litany of purity and righteous action continues:

> I have bound up and I have gathered together your Powers. I have directed the Powers of the ways, the wardens of the horizon, and of the Hemat House of heaven. I have established their fortresses for Asar. I have prepared the ways for him. I have performed the things which [he] hath commanded. I come forth to Djedu.

For those who have developed self-control and who have intellectually understood that the world does not hold abiding peace and happiness for them, formal meditation is the next important step on the spiritual path. Through the practice of meditation it is possible to transcend the Waking State of consciousness and to discover the Waking (Lucid) Astral Consciousness state. This state appears like the dream world but, unlike a dream, you are completely awake or "Lucid." Essentially, the Astral Plane is a higher reality than the physical. Within the Astral Plane it is possible to experience that you are separate from your physical body, and that the physical world and your body are only projections on the screen of Cosmic (astral) Consciousness in much the way as a movie is only a projection on a blank screen. From here it is possible to actually experience what is meant by detachment since you can actually see that you are not the psycho-physical personality you thought you were. This is why the Sages exhort the practice detachment and dispassion in your day to day waking existence.

From the Astral Plane it is possible to discover the Causal Plane. However this requires a high degree of purity. This is why the teachings urge the practice of controlling the thoughts, longings and desires to the point of indifference, equanimity and balance. These qualities will allow you to develop sufficient serenity in the mind to experience the ocean of quietude that is the mass of consciousness which you are essentially, like an ocean after the winds have died down and the waves cease to rise. Here there is awareness without thoughts and desires, existence without form or objectification... an expanding stretch of existence without end. Therefore, having experienced yourself as a personality in the Waking State in the physical world and as an astral personality in the astral world and as a subject in the causal world, you can gain intuitive wisdom of the fact that you are none of these relative states. The practice of these reflections and meditations leads to the discovery of absolute existence which transcends all states. This is the absolute reality which you are. In it there is no awareness of the world, your personality or any relativity or duality. There is only you, as the source of all. This is referred to in Ancient Egyptian Mystical teaching as the inner shrine, the abode of God, and having entered in to the innermost room, after successfully meeting the challenges of demons in the form of your own negative emotions, desires and concepts, you can exclaim with joy that you have arrived and that you have seen what is inside the mysterious abode of the innermost Self.

The mystical significance of the inner shrine.

This process is described in Chapters 77 and 78 of the *Ancient Egyptian Book of Coming Forth By Day*. Some exerts are included below.

> I come daily into the House of the twin Lion-gods. I come forth therefrom into the House of Aset. I look upon the holy things which are hidden. I see the being who is therein (Asar-The Self).

The practice of meditation is two-fold. Just as a bird needs two wings in order to fly, a spiritual aspirant needs to practice two forms of meditation. This first entails a constant reflection of the truth provided by the wisdom teachings. The second involves the practice of formal meditation exercises. This involves the practice of concentration. Concentration on any object will lead to the focusing of the mental rays of consciousness instead of their scattering into the relative states (waking, Dream and dreamless sleep). This will allow consciousness to focus and thereby allow the mind to peer into the depths of higher consciousness (Astral and Causal Planes). Having begun the process of expanding in consciousness, the practitioner can then experience, first hand, the depths of his/her own true Self. When a spiritual aspirant enters into these practices with the correct guidance and understanding, the Self, which is consciousness itself, acts as the guide and in so doing, an initiate discovers the he or she is that very same Self, the transcendental being from which all of the planes arise and into which they all subside. Within this experience there is indescribable peace and joy, true fulfillment of all desires and the knowledge of the Absolute, knowing which there is nothing else to be known. The inner Self moves towards those who exert self effort towards spiritual realization. This is why Jesus said: *Ask, and it shall be given you; seek, and ye shall find; knock, and the door shall be opened to you...* (Matthew 7:7) Your spiritual practices are the asking and the result of asking is inner discovery and unity with God. This teaching is what is referred to as *Divine Grace*. The Self, God, moves towards those who move towards the Self and also the Self denies those who deny the Self. Denial occurs in many ways. A person denies the Higher Self by acting out of egoism when they know better. This process of denial and ignorance is like reading the wisdom teachings and not going beyond the superficial level of their teachings. If you know how to understand mythology, the teachings come to you unhampered. This is an example of the mutual movement; the spiritual aspirant (reader) and the Self (meaning) move towards each other. If a person does not apply concentration and study, they can read even the most an miss the entire moral of the story and thus negate their higher power of understanding. So the wisdom which could have led them to divine inspiration is denied to them. The experience of inner fulfillment is more profound than the outer forms of happiness. This is because as you move within, you are moving closer to what is true and abiding. It is this greater enjoyment which will allow you to leave behind the lesser pleasures, vices and negativity that hold onto you and degrade your ability to discover true peace and contentment.

> The Self denies those who deny the Self.

uaa
"Meditation"

Meditation can be practiced by many methods. Some people prefer to concentrate on a religious icon or a Divine form while others choose to allow their mind to flow with an unbroken succession of thoughts directed towards the Absolute. Whichever form you choose observe the following general guidelines.

If you reflect upon your own situation you must realize that you have three personalities, the waking personality, the dream personality and the dreamless-sleep personality. Philosophically you can now understand that each of these personalities are relative and therefore illusory, otherwise you would remain the same personality as you go into the different states of mind (waking, dream and dreamless-sleep) and you would take with you the same clothing, the same problems, the same memories, the same possessions, etc. Since this does not occur, one must conclude that they are all variable, depending on the concepts, fancies and desires of the mind of the individual. This points to the wisdom that you do not belong to any of the relative states. You are in reality like a traveler who is going to different train stops at the same familiar locations every day. However, you are traveling without any luggage, ticket or control over your destination through worlds that are not abiding. They are only real in a relative sense when you are caught up in them. Understanding this you should now be able to maintain a certain level of detachment and dispassion toward your life just as you become detached from your dream when you wake up, even though it seemed quite real while you were dreaming. The pride, vanity and egoism related to the body, how good or bad it looks, how attractive it is to others, how famous you are, how wealthy your are, etc., must now begin to seem amusing, if nor ridiculous. Also, the pressing desires of life, the problems with relationships and the general struggles of life should now be coming into a perspective based on a larger picture wherein they are all viewed as only a small part of who you are essentially. Your attachments and desires are what is holding you tight and fast to the limited waking reality. Therefore, as you loosen the ties of passion and attachment, you will grow in expansion of consciousness.

The pride, vanity and egoism related to the body.

In order to practice the disciplines of detachment and dispassion there must be a higher understanding of these virtues beyond the ordinary sense given by society. In mystical terms, the practice of detachment and dispassion do not signify a morbid sense of loneliness or lack of caring. Rather, they imply a higher understanding as to what is truly worth caring for in this world and to what one should become attached. Detachment and dispassion do not imply seclusion from the world, separation from loved ones or an attitude of cold indifference. In other words, this practice does not mean a literal giving up of possessions, friends and family. It does mean that you should not hold onto the relative, transient appearances of the world because even your own body, your life, memories and possessions do not belong to the real you. You must now look at your physical existence, its circumstances and relations from an objective manner, and this point of view will allow you to care for others better because you will not harbor egoistic desires, preferences for certain people over others, expectations or prejudices that might hamper your ability to feel universal love for all. You will be able to draw on higher sources of spiritual energy which will allow you to serve humanity in more ways than you can imagine.

Is there a better way to serve and care for others? True love and caring is unconditional. It can only be felt when there is an understanding of the universality of life. Yoga and mystical religion lead to that understanding, and in so doing, the world is made a better place for all.

So if the states are illusory and relative what is abiding and real in all of this? To find the answer, reflect upon what element is present in all levels of experience. There is only one element which is common to all the states of consciousness. That element is Consciousness itself. Consciousness is present at all levels of your experience (in all of the relative states - waking, dream and dreamless sleep), otherwise there would be no experience at all. However, if consciousness is beset with ignorance, agitation and/or dullness it will not experience itself as a detached traveler, eternal and unlimited, it will fall into the delusion of seeing itself as limited, finite and mortal. This is the predicament of people who are ignorant of the higher spiritual realities. Therefore, in order to dispel the ignorance of the mind the spiritual disciplines as well as the practice of meditation are enjoined by the spiritual scriptures and Sages from all over the world.

A meditator who is successful in discovering the Astral Plane of Consciousness finds that the physical body, the Waking State and the phenomenal world of time and space are projections of the Astral Plane, and from that vantage point the physical world and the physical body are merged into a mass of subtle elements. In other words, your personality or waking subject is discovered to be "not the real you." A meditator who is successful in discovering the Causal Plane realizes that the astral personality, who was looking at the physical world, is also a projection. A meditator who is successful in discovering the transcendental realms of consciousness beyond the Physical, Astral and Causal Planes, realizes that he or she is one with the Divine Self, from which all of the planes emanate. This discovery is the end of the road, the Self of all selves, the Supreme Being, the source of all peace and abiding happiness, the eternal, unlimited expansion in consciousness and the reality behind all projections or phenomena of nature. The result of this practice is the intuitional experience and understanding that the physical world, which seems so solid and concrete, is in reality composed of a subtle essence; there is no physicality in Creation. Sometimes a person can become intensely deluded because of the strong belief in the waking or dream world. The more attached you are to the idea of physicality and the more you rely on the sense organs of the body and cling to the grosser aspects of the human experience (desire, anger, hatred, greed, vanity, pride, lust, expectations, passion, etc.), the more concrete, solid and inescapable the world seems to become. Also, the more intense the delusion of the mind becomes, the more insane a person becomes. This delusion can become so severe as to render a person

What the successful practitioner of meditation discovers.

incapable of holding onto the day to day realities of ordinary human life. They become psychotic and sometimes so insane as to enter into a deep state of dullness, as in the dreamless Sleep State. The mind itself is therefore the instrument which enslaves the soul as it were, but when it is enlightened through the mystical teachings, it becomes the instrument which frees the soul, the liberator, the savior, the messiah. The liberating forces which free the mind are the lucidity, righteousness and purity of heart which allows intuitional vision to dawn in the mind. This understanding brings us back to the teaching in reference to the Primeval Ocean which began this discussion. Creation is not an ocean that existed in the beginning and from which God emerged to create the first solid object. There are no solid objects in Creation. Modern physics has already proven this point. Creation is and always has been the same ocean of consciousness which is sustained at all times by the consciousness of God. Though expressing in different degrees of subtlety, all forms are composed of the same essence. The other important realization is that this consciousness is the same one which is sustaining your existence and which is the very essence of your own being. This is why the Ancient Egyptian Initiates would chant: *Nuk pu Amun (I am Amun), Nuk pu Asar (I am Asar), Nuk pu Ra (I am Ra), Nuk pu Ptah (I am Ptah), Nuk pu Aset (I am Aset), Nuk Pu Nuk. ("I Am That I Am."), Ntef änuk änuk Ntef. ("He is I and I am He.")*, etc.

The mind enslaves the soul.

Success in meditation comes in degrees over time. It is important to maintain an integral schedule of spiritual practices including study of the teachings, chanting, exercise, righteous work, etc. along with the regular practice of meditation in order to obtain effective results.

Understanding the process of meditation.

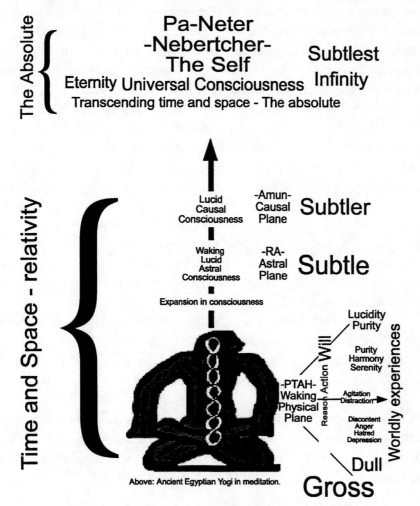

Above: Ancient Egyptian Yogi in meditation.

Above: The relative states of consciousness and the path of meditation. An initiate from Ancient Egypt is shown sitting in the yoga lotus posture. Superimposed on him are the seven rings symbolizing the seven centers of psycho-spiritual energy consciousness known as Arat in Ancient Egypt or Kundalini in Indian Yoga mystical philosophy. Through the process of meditation, a meditator lifts him/her self up beyond ordinary consciousness and discovers the transcendental realms and finally the Absolute Self.

Tips for Formal Meditation Practice

Begin by meditating for 5 minutes each day, gradually building up the time. The key is consistency in time and place. Nature inspires us to establish a set routine to perform our activities; the sun rises in the east and sets in the west every day; the moon's cycle is every 28 days and the seasons change approximately at the same times of the year, every year. It is better to practice for 5 minutes each day than 20 minutes one day and 0 minutes the next. Do a formal sit down meditation whenever the feeling comes to you but try to do it at least once a day, preferably between 4-6 am or 6-8 pm.

Do not eat for at least 2 hours before meditation. It is even more preferable to not eat 12 hours before. For example: eat nothing (except only water or tea) after 6 p.m. until after meditation at 6 a.m. the following morning. Do not meditate within 24 hours of having sexual intercourse. Meditate alone in a quiet area, in a dimly lit room (candle light is adequate). Do some light exercise (example: Chi Kung or Yoga exercise) before meditating, then say Hekau (affirmations, prayers, mantras, etc.) for a few minutes to set up positive vibrations in the mind. Burning your favorite incense is a good way to set the mood. Keep a ritualistic procedure about the meditation time. Do things in a slow, deliberate manner, concentrating on every motion and every thought you perform.

When ready, try to focus the mind on one object, symbol or idea such as the heart or Hetep (Supreme Peace). If the mind strays, bring it back gently. Patience, self-love and self-forgiveness are the keys here. Gradually, the mind will not drift towards thoughts or objects of the world. It will move towards subtler levels of consciousness until it reaches the source of the thoughts and there commune with that source, the Self. This is the desired positive movement of the practice of meditation because it is from the Self that all inspiration, creativity and altruistic feelings of love come. The Self is the source of peace and love and is who you really are.

46. Thy beauties take possession of and carry away all hearts, and love for Thee make all arms to relax; Thy beautiful form make the hands to tremble, and all hearts melt at the sight of Thee.

Glimpses of the Divine are transformative experiences.

This verse is related to verses 24 and 31 above wherein the Self, when turned to, is the source of all fulfillment, all peace and all contentment. When a spiritual aspirant attains even a small glimpse of the Divine (God) it is a transformative experience. The mind which has been previously interested in worldly things is now captivated by the wonders of the Divine Self. This verse is pointing to a specific form of spiritual practice called the Yoga of Devotional Love. It consists of understanding and directing the feelings and emotions towards the Divine Self who abides in all Creation. When you love something, you put that object first, even before your own desires. Through this process of sublimating your own desires and directing the mind towards the Divine, the ego begins to diminish, and this process allows the mind to soar high among the sublime feelings and thoughts. Devotion leads to wisdom and like two wings of a bird, the spiritual aspirant is led from faith to knowledge and then to experience the Divine.

Spiritual Realization
(Merging with the Divine - experiencing the Self)

Devotional Meditation
(I am one with God.)

Worship
(Seeing God in everything; practicing spiritual
disciplines - prayer, meditation, selfless service, etc.)

Learning
(Learning about the Divine through
myths and mystical philosophy.)

It is important to understand that devotional yoga involves more than simply mindlessly or fanatically praising God and praying or singing devotional songs with emotional force. An integrated process of Devotional Yoga involves an understanding of the metaphysical teachings of wisdom and a blending of all of the other Yogic systems. This integrated process which involves wisdom or intuitional understanding of the metaphysical realities behind Creation serves to close any gaps in the mind of the aspirant as to the existence of the Divine. The main disciplines in the practice of the Yoga of Devotional Love has been outlined below.

The *melting hearts,* being referred to in verse 46 above, is in fact the dissolution of the individual mind (egoism) when it dissolves into the ocean of pure consciousness upon attuning to the cosmic ocean of consciousness (Amun). When this movement in devotion reaches its height there is a realization that the ego does not exist, and the "I" which was previously used to refer to the ego-personality is in reality the Self. Thus a spiritual aspirant on the devotional path transcends the individual ego and discovers the Higher Self within.

Out of ignorance of the deeper Self, most people (the masses) become caught up in the dualistic thoughts of their mind. They have not discovered the transcendental peace, being caught up in the waves of positive and negative emotions and the desires for acquiring something that they perceive will bring happiness. They live life in a state of delusion, There is a constant belief that the world will somehow bring them happiness, despite the relentless disappointments and frustrations. It is like gambling. There is a constant expectation that one will win, even though the odds are stacked against it. Even if there is a win, it is not really a win because the winnings will be used to strengthen the belief in the game and will set up the winner for an even bigger loss later on. Spiritual life does not mean that there is no fun or experience of pleasure due to objects of the world. It means that

Living in a state of delusion.

there is no dependence on the world for happiness, instead there is indifference. If pleasure is experienced a Sage accepts it. If pleasure is not experienced a Sage also accepts this. At no time does the absence or presence of pleasure due to worldly objects or situations affect the deeper experience of peace and joy which comes from the inner Self. Therefore, the experiences of pleasure and pain remain in the enlightened state, but they are transcended with the ever-present knowledge of the innermost Self within. It is like standing on the shore and looking at the ocean. Even though the different waves are there, the ocean cannot be missed. Likewise, a Sage looks at the pain and sorrow of life as waves, but never looses sight of the Self which surges like an ocean in every corner of Creation. Thus, the awareness in the mind of the abiding presence of Divine wisdom overpowers all disturbances from the outside world even as those movements, changes, sounds, situations, the passage of time, emotions, waking, dream, dreamless sleep, etc. may continue after the divine awareness has dawned in the mind. For the enlightened Sage such disturbances are seen as transient wave-like forms which will pass. So there is no mourning over, attachment to, or leaning upon the past, present or future for anything that is fleeting, uncertain and unstable. Of course, a Sage harbors no desire or longing for anything and so experiences constant peace, contentment and bliss internally, even while carrying out the various duties of life or performing the most dynamic work in the service of humanity. The ability to sidestep the pitfalls of human existence in the forms of anger, hatred, greed, pain, sorrow, egoistic desires, etc., allows a Sage to conserve energy and attune the mind to the heavenly realms where it is possible to gain intuitive communion with the Higher Self (God) and, in so doing, bring the marvels of spiritual wisdom to humanity. This is the art of living which Sages live by and which he or she teaches to spiritual aspirants for the purpose of leading them to spiritual realization and to promote peace and harmony in the world.

The ability to sidestep the pitfalls of human existence.

In the unenlightened state there is constant unrest in the mind and you feel yourself to be in the center of that unrest. You flow along with the feelings and believe yourself to be happy when there are favorable conditions or sad when there are unfavorable conditions (meaning that you cannot get what you want). In reality, your Soul, your innermost Self, is beyond the opposites of the world which are experienced on the Physical and Astral Planes, but since it has associated itself with the astral body (mind and senses) and the physical body, it has become identified with them and has forgotten its true identity, like a person who has contracted amnesia. This identification with the body has caused you to believe that you are a human personality and thus, are subject to the karmic fate of your physical personality. If the body suffers, you believe "I am suffering." If the body experiences pleasure, you believe "I am feeling pleasure." With these thoughts of "body identification" in your mind, you are constantly in a search of conditions which will provide the greatest pleasures and the least sufferings. This is the illusion of duality. You are never at rest or truly at peace because, consciously or unconsciously, you are always preoccupied with what you can do to promote pleasurable conditions and circumstances. This mental unrest does not end at the time of death. The unconscious impressions impel the soul to have after-death experiences in the Astral Plane (Duat) and thus, it is even then unable to discover abiding peace and happiness. After spending some time in the Duat, it then takes on a new physical body, once again in search of happy conditions. This is known as the cycle of birth and death or reincarnation.

The search for happiness is not incompatible with spiritual practice. In fact, the true definition of the state of enlightenment is abiding peace and happiness (bliss). The problem is that human ignorance leads people to search for happiness through objects and conditions that are fleeting and therefore, incapable of providing peace or happiness. Abiding peace cannot be found through activities in the realm of duality (Astral and Physical Planes). In fact, any activity you perform and any achievement you attain, no matter how grand, will someday perish in the vastness of time. Something that brings happiness today becomes boring tomorrow. Even the greatest conquerors of the world, such as Alexander the Great and Julius Caesar, have been forgotten and their conquests lost and dispersed, even though at their height they were considered almost as gods. No matter how vast your worldly accomplishments may be, they will always be perishable and incapable providing you with lasting peace. From a higher point of view, all accomplishments in the world of time and space are like accomplishments in a dream. After all of the activity in a dream, in the end nothing has really occurred. No matter how real it might have appeared to be, upon waking up the dream world vanishes and all of the attainments and activities of the dream also vanish. In essence, the dream world that you experience while asleep and the phenomenal world you experience when awake are not real. Reality is defined as *that which is the same in the beginning, middle and end.* Reality is unchanging, abiding and self-existent. Is there any dream world which has these qualities? Is there anything in the universe that does not go through the change from birth, to maturity, and then to death? Therefore, what the senses experience in the time between the birth and death of something is an illusion. It is not a real perception. It is a manifestation of the infinite variety which consciousness is capable of projecting in the mind. Thus, at no time can the dream be considered to be "real," not in the beginning, middle or in the end. It is only a relative reality without real substance although it is sustained by "The Reality," the Self. A Sage looks on the phenomenal world as a dream or mirage and does not fall

The search for happiness.

into the illusion of believing that the world is real and that what happens in the world is important to his/her peace and happiness.

People dupe themselves into believing that they are happy because they have been able to purchase some expensive item or have achieved some name and fame, but this happiness is not real. It is full of stress. In addition, if the object is lost the happiness that was derived from it dissolves like a cube of ice placed in warm water. Therefore, in reality, this type of happiness must be considered to be a form of pain disguised as pleasure and happiness.

Due to ignorance, the human mind is carried away with the "beauties" of creation because these excite the senses and the delusion of the mind gives rise to the promise that the world of time and space holds abiding happiness. Thus, the mind constantly swings between happiness and displeasure, like a wave in the ocean rises and recedes. However, a Sage, having discovered the steadfast point within, looks on the various forms of multiplicity in the world and the various conditions of prosperity and adversity as passing waves in the ocean. In a real sense a Sage never loses sight of the fact that the ocean is there no matter how many waves may stir up or how many storms may arise. A person with ordinary understanding becomes fascinated with the sizes, forms and appearances of waves, forgetting that it is all ocean. Having discovered that stable point which is supremely fulfilled and unchanging, a Sage looks on human experiences with a detached eye and is thus, never caught up in the waves of emotion which most people experience and cannot control. A Sage is ever aware of the Absolute Reality which transcends duality and therefore, experiences peace in any and every condition, while at the same time being aware of the relative world of time and space. A Sage does not fear death, having discovered his/her own immortality. A Sage is one with the universe, having discovered the innermost source of the cosmos within him/herself. Even while engaged in various works which uplift humanity such as teaching, writing books, healing, and encouraging others to develop virtuous qualities which lead to self-knowledge, the Sage looks upon all of these activities with the same type of detachment that an actor looks upon performances on the stage of a theater. The Sage "identifies" him/herself with the Self and not with the body. Therefore, any activities of the body are like activities in a dream world. Just as activities seem to have a purpose while in the dream but once you wake up there is no purpose, the Sage has woken up to the reality which transcends ordinary human experience in the phenomenal world of time and space, while unenlightened human beings continue to believe the world and their bodies to be "real" and abiding.

How a Sage experiences the world.

How can these teachings be of use in the practical world? Obviously, knowing that the universe is energy and that your body is also energy does not change their appearance or allow you do walk though walls or fly in the air, so of what use is it? While most people are so caught up in the day to day realities of life which seem so real and pressing, a practitioner of yoga (yogi) deals with life from the standpoint of the wisdom teachings. Instead of trying to acquire worldly objects and becoming more involved with the world in an effort to feel happy, a yogi seeks to fulfill his/her desire to experience happiness by working to discover that boundless source of happiness within. A practitioner of yoga should seek to satisfy the practical needs of life while maintaining a balanced state of mind during both prosperous conditions as well as during negative ones. A yogi should not indulge in the pleasures of the world or seek to experience pain either. A yogi should seek balance and promote peace and harmony for the purpose of attaining enlightenment. A yogi should constantly reflect on the wisdom that this world, as well as the thoughts in the mind and the experiences during a dream, are nothing but vibrations in consciousness which come into existence and disappear as clouds in the sky or waves in the ocean. Therefore, there should be no need to hold onto the notions of the mind or the desires of the body. A yogi should practice keeping a close watch on the thoughts of the mind and the feelings of the body so as to always remain separate from them and not to get caught up in them. When this discipline is practiced, along with meditation and other yoga disciplines, there is a gradual awakening process which occurs wherein the light of intellectual reasoning grows and blossoms into intuitional realization of the transcendental truth. This is the process of becoming a Sage.

An enlightened Sage cannot suffer or feel elated over any development in the Physical or Astral Planes since a Sage has discovered and experienced that these two planes are both emanations from the Self which is the absolute and transcendental reality. Knowing this and having experience of this, a Sage cannot fall prey to the worries and anxieties over which most people suffer as they live their lives. Having experienced this higher reality, a Sage has become liberated from all ignorance just as opening a door and looking into a room frees you from ignorance about the contents of the room.

True happiness comes when there is detachment from objects and worldly relationships, be they considered pleasurable or as sources of pain, and when there is "steadfastness" in the inner Self. When these qualities have been developed, peace and joy can be experienced at all times, such as in a Sage. True happiness and peace is experienced when the mind is not affected by the waves of desire, pleasure or pain. Therefore, a Sage is said to be *beyond the world, peaceful, independent and radiant.* Peaceful, abiding in the

Discovering
true
happiness.

Self always, independent, knowing him/herself to be an actor in the theater of creation and radiant, radiating the peace, love and joy that is experienced from being united (Yoga) with the source of all (God). Thus, a Sage is as *humble as a blade of grass* because he or she knows that human existence is fleeting and fragile. A Sage views the pride, arrogance and egoism of unenlightened personalities as manifestations of the state of ignorance of those persons, and thus is filled with boundless compassion and forgiveness for others, and a deep rooted desire to alleviate their pain and suffering, by showing them the way to self-discovery which is the supreme eradicator of all miseries. The Sage is not attached to anything in the world and does not need anything from the world to experience peace and happiness, therefore, a Sage is free from the world and any pain or sorrow which the world could inflict. Thus, a Sage is beyond all karmic entanglements, even while living in modern society. Many people consider themselves to be free individuals, yet they do not pursue their goals or act out of their true feelings because they are afraid of what others may say or feel about them. They are afraid of embarrassment, rejection or being otherwise hurt by others. This is because they have an egoistic need for acceptance and this need dominates their lives and determines their limitations, feelings, and thoughts. They live life in fear and do not realize their full potential or discover their deeper Self.

How a Sage views ignorance in others.

Also, the Sage is free from the desires which impel the soul to the varied experiences after death and lead to reincarnation, so the Sage is also free from the cycle of birth and death. A Sage can relieve misery because he or she is the embodiment of the experience which nullifies or neutralizes the pains and sorrows of human existence, enlightenment. The pains and sorrows of human existence exist only because you believe your self to be the ego-personality. You believe that the circumstances and situations of life are real and abiding due to your ignorance of your Higher Self. A Sage can show the way to discover the absolute reality which transcends ordinary human existence.

Being detached does not necessarily mean that there is spiritual enlightenment. Detachment without spiritual insight leads to greater ignorance and pain for the individual as well as society. Detachment is practiced as a discipline for retraining the mind to let go of its illusions and to attach to that which is real and abiding. Therefore, detachment does not mean to separate from loved ones or possessions. It does mean detaching from the desire to possess objects in a search for happiness and detaching from the illusion of loved ones as sources of happiness and as abiding realities.

There is no object which can bring you abiding peace just as there is no person or loved one who can bring you abiding peace and joy. In the end, all human personalities are just like yourself, souls wandering in ignorance who will someday leave the body (die) and move on in their spiritual journey. So why be attached to them? Why believe that they are sources of happiness? Why grieve when they die? Why act as if they existed but now will not exist any more? Why should you become elated when a person is born or depressed when they die? In the correct understanding of human relationships, there are no family members. In reality you are not the body, therefore you have no parents or siblings. In reality it is the body that has these relationships, and these occur as passing events of a dream-*Resu*. Why should you become elated when you acquire an object of desire and feel upset and angry when that object is out of your reach? Why should you struggle over material possessions when these are all manifestations of the Self which is also within you? These same material objects are perishable and cannot bring abiding peace and happiness anyway. The supreme, innermost reality of all living beings and of all objects in creation transcends the temporal physical manifestation. Therefore, when anything comes into manifestation and goes out of manifestation, the deeper reality is unaffected.

Dream- *Resu*
(see glossary)

With this wisdom, you should live in a detached manner, accepting all human beings as your kin since they are all manifestations of the Divine Self. You should strive to better your conditions and promote truth, justice and peace while keeping in mind that your innermost Self is not in any way affected by the outcome of your actions or the conditions you may find yourself in, be they adverse or prosperous. You should always strive to succeed in all of your endeavors while not depending on the outcome of your works as a source of happiness or satisfaction. If you depend on your activities as a source of happiness, you are bound to be disappointed because even the most monumental successes and riches do not guarantee happiness. In fact, if you are a person who has not learned to control the mind and senses, the wealth you gain will serve to allow you to get into more karmic entanglements, develop more attachments, and experience more disappointments and frustrations than a less well off personality. Further, whatever material wealth is gained can always be lost. However, the treasure of inner peace and contentment cannot be taken away if you learn the art of controlling your mind and directing it towards that which is true and real (Maat-God). Be happy in the present moment and give thanks for the opportunity to work for God and leave the outcome and results in the hands of God. In this manner, you will not be affected by the success or failure of the your efforts, but will always find fulfillment in the divine work-*Ari em hetep* itself, the service to humanity. Live your life with the feeling that you are one with the universe and that all living (people, animals, insects, etc.) and non-living (planets, galaxies, rocks, etc.) beings are your family. This wisdom is the basis by which you can develop universal love towards humanity and the entire universe. Anyone who acts with detachment born of self-knowledge will be dynamic, qualitative and inspiring. A Sage engenders these very qualities in others by their mere presence. Thus, the presence of a Sage is sought after by all who understand the teachings of mystical spirituality.

47. *Amen...Thou Being above who make the earth according to Thine own designs.*
48. *...at whose utterance the gods come into being, and food is created, ... and all things are come into being; the traverser of eternity, the old man who make himself young* (again) *through myriads of pairs of eyes and numberless pairs of ears...*

These verses are complementary to a different Egyptian hymn to God (in the form of Pa Neter) which states: *God's names are innumerable, manifold and no one knows their number.* It signifies that human beings, their names, bodies and their senses, are indeed expressions of the Divine. The eyes and ears of human beings are in reality the eyes and ears of the Divine. Further, this signifies that all of the innumerable personalities (people) that exist, existed and will exist are in reality different expressions of the Divine Self according to Divine Will. Though the Self is understood as ancient and primeval, this line shows that the Divine is ever-present and appearing before your eyes in ever more dazzling and imaginative forms. God, the Self, is not remote in antiquity, but is accessible in the eternal present moment.

At an elementary level when a person is first introduced to spirituality, especially religious spirituality, he or she is told to worship in a specific location, a church or temple. He or she is told to feel reverent when in the temple and to control the negative aspects of the personality because God is watching in that sacred place. With the deeper mystical understanding presented here it must be clear to you now that this entire universe is a temple and God is watching from every direction. The Ancient Egyptian temple was constructed in such a way that every aspect of it is a symbolic representation of Creation and as a reflection of Creation, it is a reflection of the Divine Trinity. Therefore, the Ancient Egyptian temple structure itself displays the wisdom of the Trinity for all who understand the mystic symbolism.

A Typical Complete Ancient Egyptian Temple Complex

Above: Temple at Luxor, Egypt-Africa, facade entrance showing two Pylons and the single opening. In an inscription at Edfu the pylons are referred to as Isis and Nephthys, the two goddesses of Osiris who raise him up to attain resurrection and immortality (picture below, left). The single opening symbolizes non-duality and singularity of consciousness. Thus, on entering into the Temple, there is a symbolic ritual-meditation leading toward a spiritual movement out of the world (duality - ISIS AND NEPHTHYS) and into the shrine wherein the underlying oneness of the universe is to be explored and is a place wherein the duality and multiplicity of human existence can be transcended. Therefore, the architecture of the temple, in and of itself, is a meditation on spiritual enlightenment and nonduality.

In the earliest Dynastic period, commonly known as the *Archaic Period,* the *House of God* or *ḥwt ntr* was composed of three parts. These were: the sanctuary (holy of holies), the Hypostyle hall (structure resting on pillars) and the courtyard. The sanctuary held the Divine image and was the scene of the innermost rituals for discovering the essence of the Divine. The sanctuary was not open to outside light. The further away from the sanctuary the other rooms were, the wider and taller they were. Also, they were more open to outside light. The pylons at the entrances were known as Aset and Nebthet, who **raise the Sun-God who shines on the horizon.**

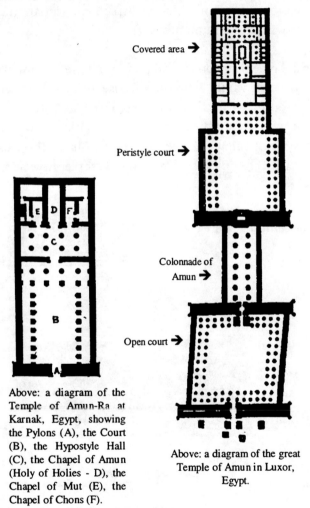

Above: a diagram of the Temple of Amun-Ra at Karnak, Egypt, showing the Pylons (A), the Court (B), the Hypostyle Hall (C), the Chapel of Amun (Holy of Holies - D), the Chapel of Mut (E), the Chapel of Chons (F).

Above: a diagram of the great Temple of Amun in Luxor, Egypt.

The Temple is a symbol of the universe. The bottom part represents the earth. From the earth sprout three plants: the papyrus, the lotus and the palm. These were depicted in the form of columns. The ceiling was vaulted (an arched structure, usually of masonry, forming a ceiling or roof) and painted or carved with forms of heaven, depicting stars and divine representations. Thus, the temple was a microcosm of the universe in the same way as the human being is a microcosm of the universe. In the temple, initiates and spiritual preceptors gathered for the purpose of intense initiatic studies and spiritual practice as well as to provide a focus for the education and management of society.

Thus, the construction of the ancient Egyptian Temple follows the format of creation, reflecting the Trinity and Triad aspect of the phenomenal universe, and the triune aspects of human consciousness through the three segments of the temple structure and the three sprouting columns. Out of the Duality (earth-heaven) come the three aspects of consciousness, subject-object-interaction. This same duality (Aset-Nebthet) acts as an enlightening factor which resurrects the initiate (i.e. the Sun, the Divine essence within the human being).

The typical Ancient Egyptian Temple was aligned on an east-west axis. In this manner the sun would symbolically rise and set between the pylon as they do the mountains in the horizon.. The two pylons at the entrance represent the two mountains in between which the sun travels (see hieroglyphic symbol below) in order to reach *Manu*, the west or abode of the blessed. Luxor Temple and Denderah Temple, however, have a north-south axis.

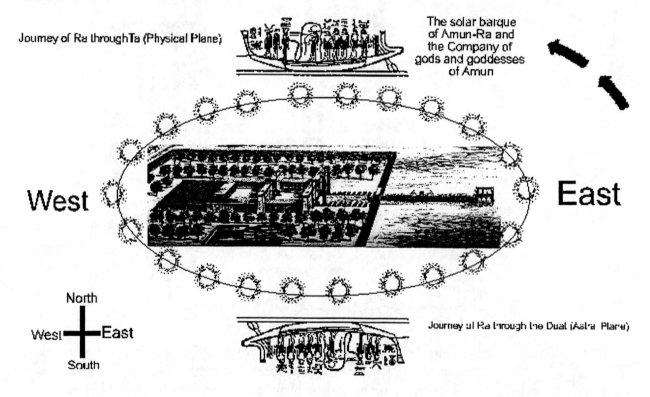

Journey of Ra through Ta (Physical Plane)

The solar barque of Amun-Ra and the Company of gods and goddesses of Amun

West

East

North
West — East
South

Journey of Ra through the Duat (Astral Plane)

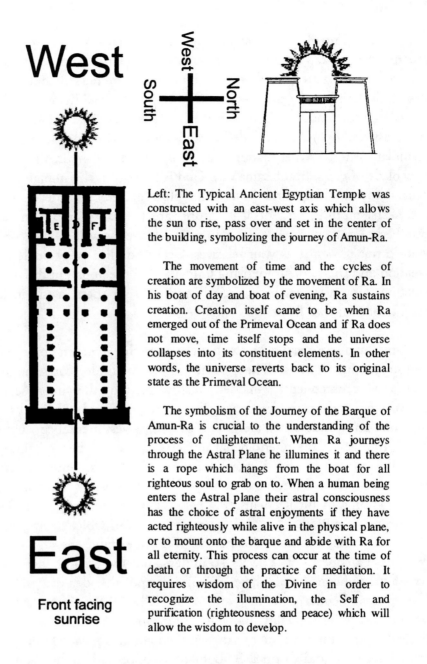

West

East

Front facing sunrise

Left: The Typical Ancient Egyptian Temple was constructed with an east-west axis which allows the sun to rise, pass over and set in the center of the building, symbolizing the journey of Amun-Ra.

The movement of time and the cycles of creation are symbolized by the movement of Ra. In his boat of day and boat of evening, Ra sustains creation. Creation itself came to be when Ra emerged out of the Primeval Ocean and if Ra does not move, time itself stops and the universe collapses into its constituent elements. In other words, the universe reverts back to its original state as the Primeval Ocean.

The symbolism of the Journey of the Barque of Amun-Ra is crucial to the understanding of the process of enlightenment. When Ra journeys through the Astral Plane he illumines it and there is a rope which hangs from the boat for all righteous soul to grab on to. When a human being enters the Astral plane their astral consciousness has the choice of astral enjoyments if they have acted righteously while alive in the physical plane, or to mount onto the barque and abide with Ra for all eternity. This process can occur at the time of death or through the practice of meditation. It requires wisdom of the Divine in order to recognize the illumination, the Self and purification (righteousness and peace) which will allow the wisdom to develop.

Allow yourself to be reflective, reverent, reserved, chaste, soft-spoken and cultivate the other virtues with the idea that you are always surrounded and permeated by Divinity, not just in the temple surroundings, but wherever you are. At first it may be difficult to keep this practice or even to believe that this is true. However, after a short time of living by the teachings, that is, listening to- *Meh mestchert*, reflecting upon-*Maui* meditating upon-*Uaa* and practicing them-*Maat* day to day and meditating daily, you will surely be convinced of this teaching by your own experience.

Another important element in this utterance refers to the relationship between the Self and Creation, but more specifically, between the Self and the individual human soul. It refers to God as: *the old man who makes himself young (again) through myriads of pairs of eyes and numberless pairs of ears.* This metaphorical hekau signifies that though existing since primeval times from a human perspective, God is ever renewing him/herself and becoming young, over and over again, because God is, in effect, all living beings which are born, grow and die. God is in the blade of grass that grows. God is in the grass when it dies and decays and God is also in the earth which assimilates the decaying matter, only to sprout up again in the form of a new blade of grass. In the same way, God is present in the human heart and causes growth, old age and death in the physical body and therefore, all the eyes, ears, mouths, etc., of all creatures are in reality God's, these being numberless and countless. God is in your relatives as well as in those whom you do not recognize as your relatives. God underlies every single atom in creation and this is the underlying unity behind the apparent differences in creation. However, nowhere is God more present than in the innermost reaches of your own heart.

God is present in the human heart.

Amun was represented first without form as the "Hidden Force" creating and supporting all things. The absence of a "form" underscores the teaching that the transcendental, hidden reality behind the universe, where everything is known to have a name and form, cannot be defined in terms of names and forms which are in and of themselves, mental concepts. That which transcends the phenomenal universe and exists beyond time, space and the range of the human senses and mental interpretations is transcendental of all mental concepts and modes of ordinary human understanding or intellectualism. Whenever the mind tries to understand something, it must have a point of reference from which to begin. These reference points are "mental concepts." To understand the idea of "up" it must have a concept of "down." To understand the idea of "here" it must have a mental concept of "there." To understand the idea of "you" it must have a mental concept of "me," and so on. All of these concepts are based on the idea of individuality. Individuality means that you see yourself as an individual in a universe full of other individuals and physical objects which are all separate and distinct. This mental concept of individuality arises when the soul forgets its connection to the universe, to the underlying unity in God, and sees itself as a separate entity with a unique personality, history, etc. However, all of the concepts of the human mind are illusory because they are based on limited information. The mind cannot comprehend the entire universe in a sweeping glance or enfold the universe with a single thought. Anything that is thought in the mind or perceived within the range of the senses is limited to the realm of time and space, and a small portion of it at best. The human mind and senses are like waves on the top of the ocean. They create an awareness of a wonder filled world of multiplicity, but they do not give insight into the depths which lie below.

Therefore, the human mind and senses cannot be relied upon to determine the truth about nature and human existence.

⎯𓏲𓏏𓅱𓀁
Dream -
vision- *Resut*
(see glossary)

The task of the spiritual aspirant is to grow out of the limitations of the mind and body and to discover the Cosmic Vision-*Resut,* which lies within. Therefore, an aspirant/initiate should seek to become a Sage by acting, feeling, speaking and thinking like a Sage. This does not mean copying a Sage's activities blindly, but seeking to develop those same qualities through true insight. When this is accomplished, there is a new perception of the universe and this represents the death of the human being and the birth of the Spirit, the Higher Self within. Until this most glorious and auspicious experience is achieved, you can only be said to have intellectual knowledge. Not until you actually experience that which transcends the mind and body can it be said that you have true knowledge about anything. All of the practices of mystical spirituality are leading to this most important experience of the transcendental, absolute reality (God). This is known as "communion" with the Divine. It is this experience that constitutes becoming truly "enlightened" and it is only through this experience that one can transcend the fear of death and the ignorance of human existence which leads to entanglements, pain, suffering and reincarnation. This is because, once the transcendental - absolute has actually been experienced, there is no more holding onto the relations or possessions of the mind and body, because you have discovered your true identity as transcending the mind and body. Until this experience is achieved, knowledge remains at the intellectual level and this level will not eradicate the mental complexes which cause egoism and bondage to the world of time and space.

You may travel to all of the holy sights, recite all of the prayers and perform all of the rituals and good deeds suggested in the scriptures, but not until you actually experience the transcendental and discover your true identity beyond your mind and body will you have a profound and permanent transformation in your life. This is why there are many people who profess to be "religious" or "spiritual" but when confronted with challenging situations or temptations in life, they are not able to cope or resist them. They cannot control their emotions and fall prey to the desires, fears and prejudices with which they have grown up. They have not discovered the kind of transcendental vision within themselves which allows a true Sage or Saint who has experienced the transcendental to have true peace in any situation or under any form of pressure or temptation. They have not experienced the form of vision which eradicates all illusions, ignorance and negativity which cause weakness and delusion. This is the kind of vision which allows a Sage or Saint to devote their lives to the upliftment of humanity and even sacrifice their lives in the cause of righteousness and love if necessary. They can do this because they "know" from experience, and not just from intellectual rationalization, that they are not just the body, but that they are part of a greater entity, and are one with the universe itself. In Egyptian Mythology, this experience is referred to as the "Opening of the Mouth" or "Becoming One with The God (Asar, Ra, Amun, or Aset, etc.)," "The resurrection" or becoming a living soul (Sahu). In mystical Christianity it is called the "Divine Marriage." In Indian philosophy it is called "Moksha" or "Liberation." In Buddhism it is known as "Nirvana" or the attainment of "Buddha Consciousness." It is a discovery of the eternal essence within you which transcends the temporal, mortal part of you. It can only be attained by profound meditation on the source of your being, through deep philosophical understanding and through control of the mind and senses which allows you to go beyond the awareness of your mind and body. This is the purpose of mystical philosophy and yoga meditation techniques. They allow you to first understand intellectually the mystical nature of your true being. This allows you to calm the mind and cleanse it from the complexes and erroneous notions which lead to negative experiences in life. Then the practice of meditation allows you to actually experience that transcendental nature within yourself until you become established in this nature. This attainment is called *Enlightenment.*

Glorious body which exists in heaven- *Sahu.* *(see glossary)*

When the various disciplines of yoga and mystical spirituality are practiced, the depths of the unconscious mind are discovered, and just as the water below the surface in the ocean is without any distinctive form, the deeper essence of the ocean of the mind is also without distinction. Here no forms exist. There are no large bodies of water or small bodies. There are no distinctive wave formations or shapes. There is only one essence, one mass, which underlies and supports the waves which are above and allows them to develop into various different forms, shapes and sizes. From the point of view of the ocean, the waves are not looked upon as separate individuals but as a wondrous display or expression of the infinite possibilities that exist. Likewise, the infinite possibilities that manifest in the form of human personalities and situations in life arise from within the depths of the human heart, the ocean of the Higher Self within. When the waves of multiplicity and the illusion of duality are cleansed from the mind, it is like a calm lake when there is no wind to stir up the waters and create waves. The mind can then accurately reflect that which is its underlying essence, the Higher Self, instead of being caught up in the external objects, desires and illusions. Though a seemingly impossible task, the human mind can be calmed by controlling the thoughts, feelings and desires through the disciplines of mystical spirituality.

A science of mental cleansing must be practiced which will clear the erroneous concepts of the mind and render it pure and subtle. As we have seen, through the various philosophical arguments, the principle, which underlies the universe, is singularity and not duality. Duality arises when the limited mind and sense are used and when there is ignorance of the deeper essence of existence, therefore, the process of spiritual evolution means developing the higher intellectual abilities of the mind and finally transcending the mind itself, thereby discovering the transcendental, formless and eternal essence of creation from which the forms arise.

The most important symbol of Amun is the ram. This symbol is so important because it communicates a direct relationship between the Self (God) and the human soul. This relationship goes beyond a family relationship or any other kind of relationship that can be conceived by the human mind. It is a most profound and sacred teaching in which all of the previous teachings culminate. The profound understanding of this teaching is the objective of all mystery philosophies and mystical practices.

Amun was depicted as a sacred ram (🐑), then in later times, as a ram-headed human, as shown above, and finally in a fully anthropomorphic form. In most forms, however, Amun wears the characteristic headpiece, the Sundisk, symbolizing Ra, and two tall plumes (symbolizing the dual goddesses who preside over the Life Force energy of creation: Aset and Nebthet (Aset and Nebthet), Uadjit and Nekhebet (serpent and vulture). Thus, Amun also encompasses the qualities of Ra, Horus and Ptah, hence the title "Amun-Ra-Ptah, Three in one."

The ram, (🐑), is also a symbol of the human soul (Ba), therefore, the true identity of every human soul is not the individual ego-personality, but Amun or the Universal Ba. In this manner, you are led to understand that the individual soul is in reality a manifestation of the Universal Soul, the High God Amun, who is the soul of everything and is symbolized as a ram-headed man. In its highest aspect, the individual soul cleanses itself from its association with the mortal body-consciousness and achieves identification with the Universal Ba - Amun.

THE TRINITY OF HINDUISM

As mentioned in the forward to this volume, in ancient times Northeast Africa was culturally and spiritually related to India thorough Egypt and Ethiopia (Nubia). This explains the large amount of mythological and linguistic correlations which we uncovered in the volume *Egyptian Yoga: The Philosophy of Enlightenment* and in the video presentation *Indus - Kamit - Kush: Yoga in Ancient Egypt and India*. Like Neberdjer: Amun-Ra-Ptah of Ancient Egypt, the Hindu tradition encompasses an understanding of a Trinity, which emanates from the absolute or Brahman. Hinduism also encompasses a teaching, which relates to the femaleness of the original essence from which the Trinity arose in order to form creation.

INUS
KAMIT
KUSH

(A): Parashakty - The Trimurti Mother.

In the early Hindu-Brahmanic period of Indian theology, Goddess Parashakty was revered as the original source from which the Trinity arises. In this aspect of Parashakty, she is equal to the Ancient Egyptian goddess Mehurt.

Figure B is an early depiction of *Brahma*, the first element of the Trinity. Brahma is the Creator of the universe.

Figure B-2 is a modern depiction of *Brahma*, sitting on the Lotus, which rises from the Primeval Ocean.

Figure C is a depiction of *Vishnu*, who represents the sustaining aspect of creation. Sustenance has two implications here. At every moment God sustains the existence of the physical universe just as waves are sustained by the ocean below. Also, when chaos in the form of evil and unrighteousness threatens to take over the world, God incarnates in order to combat the forces of darkness. For this reason Vishnu had ten important Avatars (Divine Incarnations), two of who were Rama and Krishna. In this respect, Asar, Aset, Horus and Djehuti of Ancient Egypt are also Avatars of the Divine Self.

Figure D is Shiva. Shiva represents the destructive aspect of creation, the time of dissolution which will give way to a new creation from Brahma. Also, Shiva represents the destruction of ignorance in a spiritual aspirant as represented by the opening of the Third Eye of Shiva, which is at the same time a symbolic reference to the opening of the spiritual eye of the aspirant or initiate of yoga. When the spiritual eye of an aspirant opens, the world as it was known before enlightenment is destroyed, giving way to Divine Consciousness.

The Indian Trimurti Mother and the Hindu Trinity

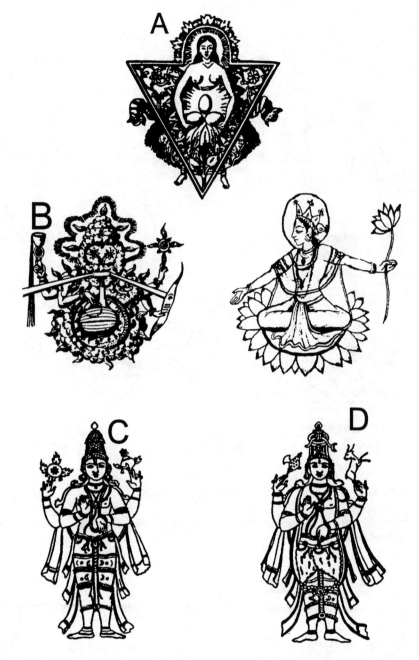

The remarkable correspondences between the Ancient Egyptian iconography related to the Trinity and the process of Creation will become evident when the Trinity symbols of India and Ancient Egypt are compared side by side.

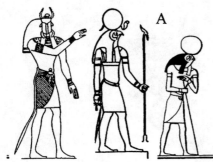

A- The three principal forms of Ra. From left to right: Khepri the Creator, Ra (Amun-Ra) the noon day sun (sustainer of Creation and Temu the setting sun, the cessation and consummation of a cycle of creation.

B- An Ancient Egyptian depiction of Horus-Nefertem God of Creation sitting on the primeval lotus which rises out of the primeval ocean. .

C- A modern rendition of the God Brahma sitting on the primeval lotus of Creation which arises out of the navel of Vishnu.

In mythological terms the Ancient Egyptian creator god Khepri-Nefertem corresponds to the Hindu Brahma. The Ancient Egyptian Temu corresponds to the Hindu Shiva.

D- Osiris is the essence of the primeval ocean and he rests on Sebek, who in this aspect represents the Life Force of the primeval ocean. From Osiris rises Horus, the new Sun (Creation). In this aspect Horus corresponds to the Hindu Brahma and Osiris Corresponds to the Hindu Vishnu. (B and D are Horus in the same aspect.)

Above: The Ancient Egyptian Supreme Being in the form of the evening sun (Tem), encircled by the serpent of "Many Faces" (infinity and multiplicity). The Serpent symbolizes the power or Life Force through which Creation is engendered. The Serpent, "Mehen" lives in the primeval ocean out of which Creation arises. Note the symbol, ꜈. It is an Ancient Egyptian determinative used to signify "limb," "flesh," "parts of the body." There are three symbols at the feet of Ra and next to these are the heads of the serpent. In mystical terms the meaning is that from the singular essence arise the three aspects, the Trinity, and from these arise the multiplicity of Creation. Thus, Creation is the very flesh or body of God. From his head is emerging Khepri, the Creator of the universe, who performs the actual act of creation. It is important to understand that the creation act is not something that happened once long ago. Khepri is said to create the new day every day. Thus, the implication is that creation is a continuous process, which sustains the universe at every moment just as you sustain your dream world at every moment during a dream..

Above: The Indian god Vishnu sleeps on the thousand-headed (infinity and multiplicity) serpent who lives in the milky primeval waters of Creation. From his navel arises Brahma, the Creator, in four-headed aspect, who causes the physical world to take

THE TRINITY OF CHRISTIANITY

Having fascinated scholars ever since their discovery in 1945, the 52 Gnostic texts found at Nag Hammadi, Egypt,[19] which date back to the time of the biblical Jesus have redefined the manner in which the social climate during the time of Jesus is being viewed. Up to the time of their discovery, it was known that many sects of Christian groups existed alongside each other until one of them (Roman Catholic) came to prominence and sought to establish itself as the only correct form of Christianity. These groups were considered to be outcasts and heretics by the Roman Catholic groups. It was also known that the early councils of the Roman Catholic Bishops had altered, edited and even omitted from the Bible, many existing scriptures of the time whose proponents had also claimed to be inspired directly by Jesus. By the time the Roman Catholic Church had compiled and canonized the scriptures, which would make up the present day Christian Bible, these works had undergone many revisions and changes. However, descendants of the Ancient Egyptians, known as the Copts, incorporated much of Ancient Egyptian Theology into the Coptic Christian Church. Likewise the religious system known as Gnosticism, which developed at around the same time, also incorporated many principles from Ancient Egyptian Religion. The decline of Ancient Egyptian society (1,000 B.C.E. to 300 A.C.E.) due to wars, internal corruption, and the normal cyclical decline of civilizations created a spiritual vacuum which elicited a reworking of the *Osirian* salvation story. This "reworking" emerged in the form of new religions of the Near East which included Christianity, the Eleusian Mysteries and others. The Eucharist ritual was a long-standing ceremony, which Christianity adopted from Egyptian religion. Prior to the dawn of Christianity the mystery of the Eucharist had transferred to all parts of the Roman empire (North Africa, the Near East, Greece and Rome) as it adopted the mysteries of Aset and Asar. The Eucharist ritual came to be practiced in the cults of Pythagoreans, Dionysus, Essenes, Mithras, and Attis prior to its adoption into the Christian Myth.

The Nag Hammadi scriptures of Ancient Egypt.

The Coptic Christians are the decedents of the Ancient Egyptian culture. The Coptic language and symbolism which was recorded during the early Christian era such as the painted coffins and winged pictures of the deceased as a free soul (called Ba in Ancient Egypt) along with the use of the Ancient Egyptian Ankh (☥) as a forerunner to the Christian crosses (☥☥) and certain modern traditions in the Coptic church clearly show the incorporation of the teachings from the Egyptian mysteries into Christian Theology. By the time when the Trinity teaching was formally incorporated

---

[19] For more on the Nag Hammadi scriptures and the practice of Christianity in Ancient Egypt see the book *Christian Yoga: The Mystical Journey from Jesus to Christ* and the video presentation *Introduction to Christian Yoga* by Dr. Muata Ashby

into Christian doctrine the church leaders were in Rome had developed a separate form of Christianity known as Catholicism and within this doctrine set out to eradicate not only other Christian sects but all other forms of religion or mystical spirituality. Thus, theological understanding was less important than the establishment of the Roman Catholic Church. So a dogmatic, patriarchal and segregative leadership emerged which sought to put aside older spiritual traditions in favor of the newer Christian doctrines. In this confusion, many teachings and rituals were assimilated from various religions. This was done in an effort to force other groups to acquiesce to the new religion. However, even though many of the teachings and rituals from other religions were assimilated, the leaders of the Catholic Church lost the mystical meaning behind them. This later became the source of much strife within the church as well as between European countries that followed different leaders within the church. The strife led to the separation of Christendom into three major divisions, the Western church in Rome, the Eastern church in Constantinople (Byzantine Empire) and the Coptic church in Egypt as well as the development of Protestantism and the creation of hundreds of Christian sects which opposed and broke away from Rome.

The doctrine of the Trinity in Christian mythology.

The doctrine of the Christian Trinity was stated in early Christian creeds to counter beliefs such as Gnosticism which followed the idea that each individual is a manifestation, and indeed one with God. The term *trinitas* first appears in the 2nd century A.C.E and was used by Tertulian, a Latin theologian. The concept was developed through the course of the debates, which sought to determine the nature of Christ (CHRISTOLOGY). it was not until the 4th century that the Orthodox Roman Christian Fathers finally formulated the doctrine. The doctrine taught that there was co-equally between the persons (God (Father)-Son-Holy Ghost) of the Godhead. St. Augustine's influential work in the 4th-century "De Trinitate" or On the Trinity, (400-16) compared the three-in-oneness concept of God with corresponding features in the human mind. He suggested that the Holy Spirit could be understood as a mutual love between Son and Father. Along with all this we must remember that the Egyptian Mysteries of Asar and Aset were popular throughout the Roman empire and it was not until the fifth century of the Christian era that their temples were closed by Christian zealots. Thus, in an effort to assimilate the followers of Shetaut Neter (Egyptian Mysteries) the Roman Catholic officials incorporated certain Ancient Egyptian religious traditions. The Eucharist, the resurrection, the cross and the Trinity were the most prominent of these.

Above: Three Christian symbols of the Trinity.

Below: Picture of the Christian Trinity containing The Holy Ghost (dove at top), God the Father (center) and Jesus the Son (foreground) by Albrecht Durer (1511).

Orthodox Christianity stated that God made man through the power of the Holy Spirit. In a sense this idea corresponds with ancient mystical philosophy because the Supreme Divinity did create the phenomenal world including human beings through a vehicle of three-fold nature. This is a teaching that was already expressed previously in the Ancient Egyptian Trinity. However, on a more subtle level, this is only the elementary understanding of the philosophy behind the Trinity. The church fathers could not explain the nature of this Trinity and their insistence on each character of the Trinity as being "equal". So they fell back on the notion of blind faith, saying that there is a mystery behind the Trinity and that believing in it was the duty of a true Christian. This seemingly complicated Triune notion of divinity along with church corruption and persecutions of other nations and religions opened the door to alternative religions such as Islam and the later Protestant movements.

The Christian Gnostics, and later the Sufis, on the other hand claimed that the phenomenal world is nothing but the Kingdom of Heaven itself and further, that the essence of every human being, the innermost self, is one with God. They emphatically stated that the individual must acquire the knowledge, which helps him or her to discover this essential truth which is masked by the ignorance of the mind. At the heart of this ignorance is the notion of the human ego. In order to discover one's innate oneness with the Supreme Being one must discard one's individuality and be absorbed (in consciousness) into the Divine in a mystical sense.

The church fathers staunchly opposed this view, stating that there would be a bodily resurrection and that each individual person (ego) would join God in heaven if they lived righteously. What is really meant here is that each individual would somehow come back to life (bodily) at the end of time and go to live in a spiritual world where they would be able to see Jesus and God on a throne and live happily ever after along side them. The mystical understanding of the Gnostics, Ancient Egyptians, Buddhists, Taoists and Vedantins was and is that the world and indeed the entire universe including human beings is one with that Supreme Being and that to truly come to know that Being is to become "like onto it." Traces of the mystical path may still be found in the present day orthodox Christian Bible. Three of the most important mystical passages come from the Gospels of John and Luke. They are rarely discussed in reference to their profound mystical meaning for each individual.

The popular understanding of the Christian Trinity.

Essentially, the Christian Trinity of The Father, Son and Holy Ghost are associated by most people with a mysterious and unseen God who sits in heaven on a throne from which he judges and punishes people. The second aspect of this Trinity is associated with Jesus, who is his son, who was born due to the mysterious impregnation of a mortal woman, Mary. The third aspect of the Trinity is a mysterious, unseen spirit force, which enlivens Creation. During the early years of the Christian church there was much debate and confusion over the idea of a Trinity. Some of the early sects of Christian followers held unto the notion of a Trinity because it had already been part of their tradition. However, the inner meaning was lost over time and due to the indoctrination of Roman Catholic dogmatic teachings without understanding the mystical implications of those teachings.

Prior to the advent of Christianity, Ancient Egyptian religion had given the Trinity teaching several thousands of years before through the various Ancient Egyptian Trinity systems presented in this volume. Christianity originated as a splinter sect, which broke away from Judaism. However, Judaism also developed previously as a splinter sect of Egyptians who began too reject Ancient Egyptian Religion in much the same way as the Hindu Trinity of Brahma-Vishnu-Shiva developed as a new movement away from an earlier system of Gods which included Indra as the Supreme Being. This is why the Hebrew and Christian Bibles state that Moses, the patriarch of early Judaism, was:

> *"learned in all of the wisdom of the Egyptians, and was mighty in words and in deeds."*
>
> The Bible Act. 7:22

Thus, Christianity is a combination of Jewish elements and Ancient Egyptian Religion which in the later period of the Ancient Egyptian dynastic times (400-0 B.C.E.) also gave birth to a new form of spirituality called Gnosticism and influenced many other religions in the Mediterranean as well as Asia Minor and the rest of Africa. However, as time passed and as the Sages of Ancient Egypt were shunned in favor of what at the time appeared as a fanatical cult (Christianity) which sought to eradicate all differing religions, the early Christian establishment systematically destroyed temples and silenced any priest or priestess from religions other than Christianity whom they could find. This over-zealousness and exclusivism led to the misunderstanding and forgetting of many mystical teachings related to much of the Christian doctrines, which had been assimilated from Ancient Egypt. The mystical wisdom of the Trinity was one of the greatest casualties to affect the church up to the present era. See the book *The Cycles of Time* by Dr. Muata Ashby.

Origins of Christianity.

CHAPTER IIII

PUTTING IT ALL TOGETHER

"I became from God one God(s) three"

The Mind
And
The Elements of
Human Consciousness

In Chapters 1 through 3 of this volume we have discussed at length the supreme wisdom related to the macrocosm. The mystical teachings related to the Trinity have been explored and we have seen how the Divine Self has come into existence as the universe as well as human consciousness. However, how does this consciousness operate from a practical point of view? How does the consciousness of the Divine Self, the Spirit, God, operate and manifest through the human personality? In this section we will begin to explore the mysticism of the human spiritual constitution in more detail.

The Mind and Its Origin

The questions of "Who is God?" and "Where do human beings come from?" were explored in a unique way in the book *Egyptian Yoga: The Philosophy of Enlightenment*. These ideas had been approached from a mystical view, reflecting the Ancient Egyptian teachings of mystical wisdom, for the first time. That book received such wide distribution and popularity that it spawned the creation of the present volume which delves even deeper into the heart of the mystical origins of life and how that wisdom may be used to discover and understand the mystery of life itself. What is the mind and what is its origin and purpose? This volume will present the Ancient Egyptian wisdom related to mystical psychology. It will show how the Sages of Ancient Egypt understood and recorded the highest knowledge of all, that which relates to the soul and the mind of a human being, and their relationship to the Higher Self.

In the books *Egyptian Yoga: The Philosophy of Enlightenment* and *The Hidden Properties of Matter* we explored the teachings related to the Primeval Ocean from which God emerged using a thought in his/her heart (mind). This thought and the subsequent ones that occurred caused everything to appear in Creation by the mere willing of the Supreme Being. This Primeval Ocean was and still is the undifferentiated mass of Pure Consciousness, devoid of thoughts or ideas. It just simply existed and therefore, had the potential to become anything. The original thought waves of the Supreme Being (the Cosmic Mind[20]) rippled through the Primeval Ocean, causing it to assume the appearance of the universe. Despite this appearance however, the essence of Creation remains the same as it was before the creation - Pure Consciousness or undifferentiated matter. The Supreme Being creates by reflecting his/her thought and willpower onto the Primeval Ocean of consciousness, thereby causing it to differentiate into different names and forms. The Cosmic Mind willed for life forms to exist and among these human beings came into existence. Human existence is special because

---

[20] The symbol of the Cosmic Mind is often given as *Maat* or *Djehuti*, transmitter of the will of God into words of Power or *Hekau*

human beings possess a nervous system, which can potentially reflect Cosmic Consciousness in its full state. However, the human mind is limited in its ability to process information gathered through the senses because of conditioning and the senses are also limited as we discussed previously. Therefore, the human being only reflects a small portion of the Cosmic Being, and unless enlightened, is not aware of the ocean of existence of which he or she is a part.

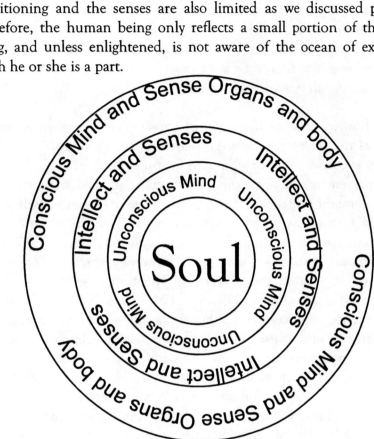

Above: A two dimensional schematic drawing of the mystical interpretation of the levels of human consciousness based on the Trinity system of Ancient Egypt.

The unconscious, intellect, mind, senses, sense organs and physical body constitute the ego-personality of a human being. The soul is eternal while the ego is transient and perishable. The ego is therefore a limited and temporary expression of the soul and not the absolute, abiding reality.

The problem lies with the conditioned human mind. Therefore, the solution lies with the same mind. For this reason, the teaching: *The mind is both the cause of bondage and source of release from the world of time and space* was developed. In a human being who is unaware of his/her divine nature, this state of mind is known as *ignorance*. This state of ignorance causes the individual to be bound to the sufferings of human existence even though in reality he or she is deep down connected to the Supreme, all-powerful

Ignorant-
Khemn

(see glossary)

Divine Self. Therefore, this state of being is also referred to as *bondage*. The soul, unaware of its divine nature, associates itself with the ideas of the mind and thereby believes itself to be a limited human being who originated at a particular point in history and who will cease to exist at some point in the future. The teachings and practices of yoga and mystical religion are designed to dispel the ignorance from which the soul suffers, thereby helping it to regain the knowledge and experience of its true nature which is immortal, eternal, and infinite.

Each human mind is like a ray of consciousness emanating from the Cosmic Mind. The mind may be understood as a bundle of thoughts. Thoughts are movements or vibrations in consciousness much like sound is a set of movements or vibrations. In the unenlightened state, the mind is beset by thought vibrations that prevent it from knowing itself as being connected to the vast ocean of consciousness. It is like a calm lake into which stones have been tossed. Just as stones cause agitation in the lake and stir up the sediments which in turn block the view from the surface to the bottom of the lake, these thought vibrations agitate the lake of consciousness of the mind and block its view of the Divine Self which is its deepest essence. They confuse the human mind and cause it to believe itself to be a separate and distinct individual. Due to the feeling of individuality, the mind experiences the plagues of egoism in the form of fear, anxiety, frustration, desire, sorrow, disappointment, etc. If it were possible to end the misunderstanding of the mind and calm the vibrations which result from its constant wants, needs and desires, people would discover themselves to be not only individual personalities, but also reflections of the Cosmic Self. This would end the sense of individuality and enable the expansion of that individual's consciousness, ultimately leading to the discovery of the Supreme Self. The individual would discover his/her identity not as a limited individual personality, but as an immortal, transcendental expression of the Divine. The individual would see the illusoriness of his/her individual human personality, and all that exists is a part of the Divine Self.

This theme of self-discovery is the underlying meaning of the Egyptian teaching wherein the initiate discovers his/her oneness with the universe in the **Book of Coming Forth By Day:**

> *"I am yesterday, today and tomorrow. I have the power to be born a second time. I am the source from which the gods arise."*

The Elements of Human Consciousness and The Personality

A human being is a complex of many elements, which together are referred to as the personality. The personality may also be referred to as the ego. All of the elements of the personality emanate or originate from the Universal Ocean of Consciousness (Divine Self). The ego is a unit of identity. It is the idea or self-concept of individuality (a wave) as opposed to the idea of universality (the ocean of consciousness). The *Triad* of mental experience is the basic factor of human existence. It is the factor that sustains the ego. However, the Triad is not the only factor operating in human consciousness. In order to have a more complete understanding as to the nature of human consciousness there needs to be a deeper study of the elements that compose the human personality. The following is a diagram to assist in understanding the relationship between the different levels of consciousness.

The Primeval Ocean
(Pure - undifferentiated consciousness)

The human ego is like a wave in the ocean. Both the ocean and the wave water are composed of the same constituents, but because they are being evaluated based on their gross forms and the names which they have been assigned (ocean vs. wave), they are viewed as being separate and distinct entities. Similarly, the human soul is a focus of Cosmic Consciousness, a wave of consciousness that arises from the ocean of consciousness. Just as the wave is essentially the ocean, so too the seemingly individual soul is in reality the same as the universal soul. Essentially they are one and the same.

Egoism -Duality
(Separation from the Self and attachment
to an illusory personality)

The human soul[21] the individual, being unaware of the Universal Self[22], sees itself as being separate, finite and limited. It is only in touch with its wavelike existence, and the existence of other waves around it. It is ignorant of its deeper essence and the deeper essence of all the other waves, the universal soul, the ocean. So it becomes attached to its ignorant understanding as well as its self-concept of being an individual in a world of individuals.

---

[21] Ancient Egyptian Term: Ba
[22] Ancient Egyptian Term: Universal Ba

Triad
(Seer, Seen and the instrument of sight and perception -
Also the realm of waking, dream and dreamless sleep
states of consciousness)

Ego-consciousness operates through the personality (mind, senses, feelings, desires, etc.). Since ego-consciousness is limited, the individual soul can never experience peace and happiness while identifying with its ego-consciousness. The individual soul, having experienced ocean-like, unlimited bliss, desires to rediscover that bliss. So it begins to search for ways to regain that experience, but having been tainted with the ignorance of egoism, does so not by discovering its true nature, but through the ego-personality. That ego-personality is held as the reality above all else. All thoughts and feelings are directed towards fulfilling the egoistic whims of the personality, thinking that these will lead to peace and happiness. The human personality is an effect of the **Error! Reference source not found.**[23] of mental experience based on subject, object, and the interaction between the two. However, since the personality is transitory, limited and weak, the search for true happiness and peace in human life becomes a frustrating and painful experience, intermixed with brief periods of relief and relaxation, but never true peace and happiness.

When the soul experiences bliss.

The Levels of Mind

All matter, be it sentient or inert, is sustained by Consciousness (God), however, a living[24] being reflects certain special qualities of Consciousness which give it varying degrees of intelligence according to the particular life form where the spirit energy is present. From plant life to animal life to human life, consciousness manifests in varying degrees of expansion according to the level of development of the nervous system of the particular life form. Human life reflects varying degrees of consciousness. This is why there are certain people who are more in touch with earthly values while others are more in touch with spiritual values. According to the level of purification, the subject may experience lesser levels of consciousness such as pain, misery, sorrow, loneliness, morbid thoughts, etc., or higher levels of consciousness such as harmony, peace, and happiness. Even while you are in a human body you can become one with The Divine in consciousness. This is the idea behind the teachings: *"Men are mortal gods, gods are immortal men"* (Egyptian proverb) and *"Know ye not that ye are gods"* (Jesus). The idea is that even though you are

---

[23] See Hymns of Amun Verse 13.
[24] human being, plants, animals, insects, etc.

associated with a lower vibratory state of matter (the physical body), you can raise your consciousness to the higher vibratory rate of the Supreme Self. The disciplines of yoga seek to transform the human body into a purified vessel wherein the subtle Spirit can fully manifest. Otherwise, the energy is distorted, and ignorance and other gross qualities of the lower self emerge. The human nervous system has the potential for reflecting the highest range of consciousness, Cosmic Consciousness or oneness with the mind of God.

Order of nervous system complexity:

Plant Life ➔➔ Animal Life ➔➔ Human Life ➔➔ Transcendental Experience

The mind is composed of three levels:

Unconscious ➔ Subconscious ➔ Conscious

The depth of the unconscious mind.

The unconscious level of mind is of unimaginable depth. It is the level in which the deepest impressions of the mind lie dormant. These impressions are gathered through life's experiences, not only in this lifetime, but in previous one's as well. It is this level of mind that determines your conscious thoughts, desires, beliefs and aspirations. These thoughts, desires, beliefs and aspirations only become evident when they appear in the conscious level of mind. If they are acted upon once they appear in the conscious mind, they translate into actions in daily life. Therefore, who you think you are is based on your impressions gathered in the unconscious an you are always acting out of these deepest beliefs about yourself. So if your beliefs are erroneous, your way of life will lead to frustration and sorrow. If your understanding is correct, your experiences will be positive and enlightening.

Unconscious impressions have been compared to seeds. When you had an experience in the past you had a certain feeling about it. This feeling was registered in the unconscious mind and remains dormant in the unconscious level of mind like a seed. At some point in the future that seed will sprout in the form of a subtle desire in the subconscious mind, the layer between the unconscious and the conscious level. It will then move into the conscious level where you become aware of it as a thought or desire. An example of an impression is as follows: In your previous lifetime you were a helpless, sickly child. You witnessed your family die from a plague. As a result, you gathered impressions of anger and fear toward disease, so in this lifetime you have an "unexplained" desire to become a doctor. The thoughts in your mind center around medical science and your aspirations draw you toward this field. You may not remember the actual experiences, which propel you to act in a certain manner, but the feelings that have registered deeply in your unconscious mind.

Thoughts, desires, beliefs and aspirations are what lead people to the varied positive and negative situations in which they find themselves throughout life. Impressions lead to desires, desires lead to thoughts and thoughts lead to performing activities in an effort to gain what is desired. These activities may be successful or unsuccessful. If you gain what is desired you feel elated and become greedy, craving for more and desiring more. If the actions were unsuccessful they create feelings of disappointment, anger and frustration. Elation, greed, craving, frustration and anger create more impressions that will compel the mind to more actions. These lead to more entanglements in the world, which is in reality is as illusory as a dream. Thus people become entangled in the web of human existence, while alive, and are led, compelled by their unconscious impressions, even after death, to continue seeking to satisfy their ego based thoughts, desires, beliefs and aspirations. These eventually lead to repeated reincarnations for that soul.

The externalized movements and desires of the mind keep the conscious self distracted with worldly pursuits and therefore, there is no time for introspection or inward reflection. Thus, there is no awareness of the inner self. The ego with all of its desires and fancies leads the intellect into interaction with the world. The intellect leads the soul on a misguided quest for the fulfillment of egoistic desires. The soul remains as a quiet observer, forced to follow along with the whims of the ego and weak intellect. The soul *identifies* itself with the intellect and ego and believes: *These are my thoughts and my desires, so I must go along and pursue them.* This is the situation that occurs when the mind is beset by ignorance. In a healthy human being, the soul should be the ruler of the intellect and the intellect should be the director of the ego. In this way, the intellect and ego would become instruments of the soul and not the other way around. This is the correct order of mastership in the human psyche. In addition, on the spiritual path, as you access your greater self who is the Cosmic Soul, then that Self becomes the true master of your intellect and physical body.

The externalized movements and desires of the mind.

Therefore, in order to engender a real transformation in the conscious level of the mind, the unconscious level of mind must be transformed. The conscious level of mind is where the thought vibrations in your mind become fully realized. This is the level of mind in which you can exert control over your mental thoughts. In this system of Integral Yoga, practicing the Yoga of Wisdom facilitates this process.

In order for this profound transformation of the mind to occur, you must first have a firm grasp of what you should accept as truth. Most people accept the information given to them by their senses, but upon closer inspection, this information is found to be faulty and illusory. The Ancient Egyptian philosophy of Maat provides a guideline to understand what is real: *That which is unchanging.* If you reflect upon this idea you will realize that what is constantly changing cannot be real. Only that which is abiding is real. Upon closer inspection of your sensory organs, you will discover that they are constantly changing and your perceptions are never exactly the same. We already noted that the human senses are limited in their information gathering ability. Also, if you have a cold or if you become injured, your perceptions are different. Therefore, the conditioned mind, senses, human life and egoistic feelings cannot be trusted as means for discovering what reality is. The mind has the potential to discover reality, but only when it is pure, devoid of the taints produced by egoism and ignorance. Rather, you need to discover the deeper aspect of your mind so that you may discover the illusoriness of thoughts, desires, beliefs and aspirations.

Most people live life according to their thoughts, desires, beliefs and aspirations, believing them to be real. However, as we have seen, the entire universe is a dream-like expression of the Divine, so therefore, what is there to think about, desire, or aspire from this world? Your attempts to gain anything from the world are like gaining something in a dream. What use is it to find a treasure in the dream world? When you wake up it is of no use to you.

Yogic dispassion.

By developing deep yogic dispassion towards the world, the unconscious impressions of thoughts, desires, beliefs and aspirations become nullified. When this occurs the unconscious mind becomes purified, leaving the conscious mind free of distracting thoughts, desires, beliefs and aspirations, be they of a positive or negative nature. This state will allow you to have clear insight into the transcendental level of mind that goes beyond the conscious, subconscious and unconscious.

The most important point to understand from this teaching is that all of your ego-based desires are like desires in a dream, and therefore, they should be abandoned. Rather, you should desire only to know the Self, even as you carry out the normal duties of life which sustain your practical realities. You may continue to go to work and have material wealth as needed for your sustenance. However, deep down you should remain aware of the illusoriness of desires, the true nature of physical matter and you should develop increasing aspiration for discovering the Self rather than for gaining worldly things. Whatever you need for your spiritual evolution will come to you in a spontaneous manner if you put forth self-effort towards your spiritual practices. Therefore, never hold ideas of fear or worry over how you will be provided for, or how you will survive and so on. Rather, concentrate on doing your daily work and spiritual practice and the Divine grace will shine upon you.

Thoughts, desires, beliefs and aspirations have the ability to lead people to experiences of pain and sorrow in life because they are deluded into believing in these as real. From one thought to the next, people are caught in a cage as it were, created by their own experiences based on forgetfulness of their deeper Self. Thus, ignorance is the true cause of delusion in the mind. So ignorance in the mind is the element which must be eradicated. Developing a deep insight into the nature of the mind by experiencing its transcendental levels through the practice of meditation and self-control does this. Therefore, you should strive to become sensitive to the thoughts that enter the mind and reflective as to their worth. Thoughts and desires should be subjected to the scrutiny of your higher intellect, *Saa*, and then dealt with accordingly though wisdom and understanding. You will not successfully transcend your desire if you simply brush off a desire and say: "This is wrong for me because Muata[25] said so." You must develop an insight into it and discover its illusoriness for yourself, thereby becoming free of it. Eventually, having become free from all desires, your consciousness will expand beyond the confines of the mind. This is because it is only due to the illusion of fulfillment in the illusory world of time and space that you have you become entangled with the mind and its thoughts, desires, beliefs and aspirations. In reality you are infinite, eternal and devoid of desires. What does the ocean need to desire from the waves? As the Self you are all encompassing and vast. You are that mystical primordial ocean, encompassing all the wave-like objects of Creation. Your association with the mind (unconscious-subconscious-conscious) has caused you to believe that you are limited to a human personality and bound by its circumstances. Thus you must purify the mind and then transcend it. You must leave the ignorance of the mind behind and discover the Self within. A Sage who has purified the mind is said to have "no mind." The term "no mind" does not mean that there is no mental activity in a Sage, otherwise how could a Sage think in order to interact with the world? It means that the mind is translucent, devoid of illusions, ignorance and egoistic desires that lead to pain, sorrow, error and delusion. The purification of the mind means an absence of egoism in the mind.

The practice of yoga wisdom involves reflecting on your thoughts, feelings and desires even as you are performing actions. With practice you can come to a state of mind wherein you are aware of your thoughts as they come into the mind. From this position you can then "observe" them in a

is wisdom deified- *Sa*
or *Såa*

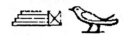

To Know- *Såa*.

To not Know, weakness, evil- *Såaa*

(see glossary)

---

[25] The author of this volume.

detached manner and maintain a neutral state of mind that will not be affected by the pressure of egoistic desires. Latent desires are elicited when you come into contact with objects that you have developed a longing for deep within. The contact with the objects sets into motion a process where you are led to attempt to possess those objects. This impulse causes unrest in the mind. This unrest is sometimes referred to as unhappiness or dissatisfaction. Of course this entire process exists in the mind due to ignorance of the fact that there is no object or person that can be possessed which will bring abiding happiness and satisfaction. There is always something missing. The object of desire is never enough even when you are able to acquire it. In a short time there is complacency and boredom in the mind. Therefore, by understanding the content of desires and their illusoriness, it is possible to turn away from these and discover the true object of desire, the Self. Desires waste much of the mental energy. The distraction and agitation prevent you from discovering the Self within because the attention is drawn from one thought to the next in the Waking State, and from one illusory world to another when you enter into the Dream State.

Madness, folly, insanity, delusion- *Riba*

(see glossary)

So it is ignorance of the Self within that leads to desire. Desire leads to actions that will move one towards the fulfillment of desire. When desires are not fulfilled there is either suppression or longing. Suppression is when you can't get what you want and you say, "Oh well, I don't really need that any way." In reality you have not dealt with your desire and it will remain latent until another provocative event occurs. For instance, you may see the object you desire often because a friend possesses it. This could be a car, an article of clothing, etc. The more you see it the more pressure your desire places on you. Then the suppressed desire leads to anger over the inability to acquire the object. If you do not suppress the desire then there develops longing and fancies about the object: "How happy would I be if I could only get it," and so on. The constant pressure in the mind from longing, anger, desire, etc. renders the mind dull and gross. It is difficult to see the error because the mind is beset with ignorance about the objects of desire. Also, such a mind is incapable of exercising reason because the intellect is clouded with the delusions or erroneous beliefs in the mind. The object cannot permit happiness to be experienced, except for a short time. Since this happiness is only serving to engender new impressions to sprout into more egoistic desires and longings which will keep the mind in a constant state of vibration, unable to discover true peace and contentment, it is not seen as true happiness, but pain in disguise. This type of happiness that occurs as a result of some occurrence in the world is termed as elation. Both elation (excitement) and depression (sadness) are seen as pain because they lead the mind to a distracted, agitated state which distorts the mind's understanding of the world and of its own identity. Thus, both elation and depression prevent the mind from perceiving the Divine Self as the innermost essence of the mind as well as the essence of Creation. This is the state known or referred to as "spiritual ignorance."

When there is a longing to have worldly experiences there can be little spiritual discovery, because this requires focusing (concentrating) one's attention on the Divine within as well as outside of yourself. Therefore, you must understand that the witnessing consciousness within you which is aware of the thoughts, feelings, desires, etc., is at the same time separate from them. When you completely realize your separation from the contents of the mind, the varied states of consciousness and the physical body, you will gain an awareness of who you really are. This is the true goal of life, to discover your true identity and the fullness of life.

Fullness here implies that you will have a deeper, richer experience of happiness and bliss which cannot be experienced through the mind and senses. The paradox here is that in the state of enlightenment you experience more peace and happiness than you could ever hope for in ordinary life. This is what everyone is really looking for and hoping to find. It is greater than any positive worldly situation, such as coming into material riches or traveling to the most beautiful spot on earth and being treated as a king or queen.

Fullness of happiness.

There is no peace and happiness like the peace and happiness that comes from absolute desirelessness. Spiritual peace and happiness are related to an expansion in consciousness while the peace and happiness of human existence are based on experiences of the senses and body which are fleeting. Thus, most people, as they get older and the body and senses do not function as they did before, experience more and more instances of sadness and depression. When your consciousness associates with the mind and body it must constrict itself to a single personality, a single body and the possibilities of one lifetime of experiences. However, the expanding consciousness of a spiritual aspirant transcends the individual personality to encompass the entire universe. Then what is there to desire? What is there to long for in the world of human experience? What is there to possess?

The mind is like a lake. When the mind is calm there is no agitation, no movement. It is like a lake that can reflect an image clearly. However, when the mind is agitated, the mental substance is put into vibration and these vibrations are what constitute thoughts and perceptions of the senses. Thus, consciousness in the state of rest reveals one image, one essence, one being. When the mind moves, seeking to fulfill desire after desire, it is like a lake into which a rock has been thrown. Many waves ripple through the surface, breaking up the image and creating the illusion that there are many pieces instead of the one. These ripples are the thoughts of the mind. When there is constant agitation and vibration in the mind it is not possible to perceive the Self clearly. So there is only a limited experience of peace and joy. However, when the mind is calmed by practicing the wisdom teachings,[26] detachment, humility, dispassion and meditation, in everyday life, the true identity within becomes revealed.

Mind of an Enlightened Person

When a human being becomes an enlightened Sage, there is awareness of infinite expansion and oneness with all things. This feeling transcends the awareness of the body and mind even though these continue to exist even as a waking (lucid) dream continues after one has woken up mentally within the dream. An enlightened person sees all things as part of himself or herself and therefore, feels no need to desire an object or the company of any person in particular to be happy. On the other hand, an enlightened person also does not feel a need to keep objects or persons away from themselves to be happy. There is indifference, detachment and dispassion due to inner contentment. This is true freedom from the world as well as from the cycle of birth and death. This is because there are no unconscious desires or illusions which will impel the mind to continue seeking happiness and satisfaction from the realms of relative existence (Astral or Physical planes) which are governed by the triad of consciousness. There is no ignorance in the mind about their true identity, therefore there is no desire to be an individual, seeking to fulfill egoistic needs or experiencing the disappointments and sorrows of that individual existence. An enlightened Sage lives in constant awareness that all levels of mental experience, waking, dream, dreamless sleep, conscious, subconscious and the unconscious, are nothing but ripples or vibrations in the ocean of pure Consciousness. They are a wonderful display of multiplicity and the myriad permutations of infinite possibilities. However, a Sage realizes that they are fleeting and illusory like a dream, so a Sage does not allow attachment to grow in the mind nor harbor illusions about objects or people. A Sage is the supreme witness of the spectacle of the world, having discovered the reality that transcends it. Being anchored to that reality, nothing in the world can hurt them or add anything to their feeling of contentment.

The absence of ignorance in the mind of a Sage.

As an aspirant, your task is to control your mind by engaging in the various practices outlined here. With patience and perseverance you must move forward on your quest for self-discovery through studying the teachings, reflecting upon them constantly and meditating on them as often as possible. If these practices are undertaken as outlined here, you will eventually be able to control your mind and discover the hidden inner

---

[26] Integral Yoga.

realms within it, leading to discovery of the Supreme Self, your true identity.

Consciousness and the Three States

"The Mind, being builder, does use the fire as tool for the construction of all things, but that of man only for things on earth. Stripped of its fire (awareness of the innermost Self) the mind on earth cannot make things divine, for it is human in its dispensation. And such a soul, when from the body freed, if it has fought the fight of piety—to Know God and to do wrong to no one—such soul becomes entirely mind (pure Consciousness). Whereas the impious soul remains in its own essence (conditioned), chastised by its own self (leading itself to suffering by its own will)."

Ancient Egyptian Proverb

As introduced earlier, consciousness expresses in three states, waking, dream and dreamless-sleep. The study of these states will provide deep mystical insight into the nature of human existence, the nature of God and the nature of creation. Throughout the following study we will follow the plan laid out in the Hymns of Amun based on the Trinity symbolism of Amun-Ra-Ptah.

When you normally think of yourself you point to your body and say, "this is me." This is called body consciousness. However, how can you say this is me when your body is inseparable related to the elements of the earth and these are related to the elements of the entire universe?

Every human being is composed of three personalities and not just the body and ego-self of which most people are aware. How is this possible? The wisdom of yoga philosophy shows the way to reason this out. The understanding of this most important teaching will lead to spiritual enlightenment.

When you are awake you refer to your physical body and say that this physical body is *"me"* and this is *"my"* life, and so on. However, when you are asleep the waking life is tossed aside in favor of a new personality with new problems, a new body and an entirely new world. Further, when one is experiencing deep sleep, in other words, when one is neither awake nor dreaming, there is another personality that manifests. It is oblivious to any forms of experience. This is the deep unconscious personality. Therefore there are three distinct personalities which every human being experiences on a daily basis. These are the waking personality, the dream or astral personality and the unconscious personality. So which one of these are you? When you wake up in the morning after sleeping you say that the dream was not real, but when you go to sleep at night and the dream personality arises, aren't you saying the same thing about the waking personality? When you are dreaming you believe the dream personality to be the real you. So which is real and which is unreal?

The Waking Personality - *Ptah*

The waking personality is aware of the physical reality. It is the state in which Consciousness uses the gross senses in order to experience gross physical objects. However, as we discussed in the *Egyptian Yoga: The Philosophy of Enlightenment* (Volume I) and in Part I of this volume, gross physical objects are in reality not physical at all. This finding which mystics have hailed for thousands of years has been confirmed by modern physics. In reality, physical objects which are experienced in the Waking State of consciousness are no more real than the objects experienced in a dream. The factor which makes them appear real is Consciousness. In association with the senses, Consciousness lends reality to the world depending on the state (lucid, agitated, or dull) in which it is. This is why you believe that the waking world is real and while in your dream you believe the dream world to be real. However, neither is real from an absolute point of view. They are relative realities that have expressed or emanated out of the mind, as a thought, imagination, or daydream arises.

The waking personality wants physical objects for its experience. It desires worldly objects and worldly experiences for its enjoyment and to interact with through the senses.

The Dream Personality - *Ra*

The dream personality is characterized by an astral existence. This means that the experiences here are subtler than in the Waking State. However, they are no less real or intense while they are occurring. In this astral plane, events do not occur with the same causal law as the waking. Events don't occur as a result of other events in a progressive manner as in the waking. In the Waking State if you want to do something like go across town, you have to walk or get in a car, turn it on, drive, etc. In the astral plane you can just think it and you are there.

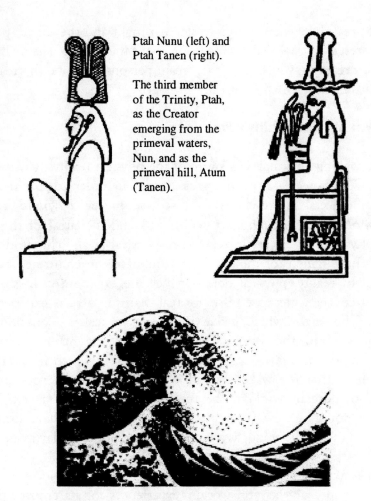

Ptah Nunu (left) and
Ptah Tanen (right).

The third member
of the Trinity, Ptah,
as the Creator
emerging from the
primeval waters,
Nun, and as the
primeval hill, Atum
(Tanen).

"Ptah conceived in His heart (reasoning consciousness)
all that would exist and at His utterance (the word - will,
power to make manifest), created Nun, the primeval
waters (unformed matter-energy).

Then, not having a place to sit Ptah causes Nun to emerge from the
primeval waters as the Primeval Hill so that he may have a place to
sit. Atom (Atum) then emerges and sits upon Ptah. Then came out of
the waters four pairs of gods, the Ogdoad

The astral personality experiences with the subtle senses while the
waking personality experiences with the gross physical senses. This is why
there is experience in the dream even though your body may be sound
asleep and oblivious to noises or sensory stimulation in the waking world.

The astral plane is the plane in which the mind and intellect function. It
is the plane where your personality feels fulfilled by good thoughts or where
anguish, worry or sorrow burden it. It is the plane of words, ideas and
thoughts. The substance of which the mind is composed is subtle forms of

undifferentiated matter[27]. Thoughts arise in the form of differentiated clumps of subtle matter, which the mind has learned to recognize as particular thoughts and ideas based on the concept of assigning and then recognizing names and forms in nature.[28] Also, it is the plane in which the personality holds onto its self-concept (egoism) instead of recognizing its transcendental underlying essence. This holding on reflects in a gross manner through the physical body and senses that hold onto physical possessions and the idea of body consciousness.

Since all matter is in reality the same subtle substance in different states of coagulation from subtle to gross, in reality there is no differentiation in matter except through the power of the mind. So it is the mind which lends reality to duality in the world through the power to recognize differences in the appearance of material objects in the waking world as well as in the astral world of dreams and ideas.

The astral personality is the level in which desires and longings are harbored and manifest in the forms of thoughts and feelings. These in turn lead the person to certain actions that the person believes will allow them to discover the object of their desire and achieve satisfaction. However, since the desires of the mind are endless and can never be satisfied, the person is led on a seemingly endless and futile journey through life in search for happiness and satisfaction. When the object that provides true satisfaction cannot be discovered in a lifetime, the astral personality survives even though the waking aspect of personality dies. It then seeks for fulfillment in the astral plane through astral experiences. Then, after some time, it becomes associated with another body and becomes born into the Waking State again. This process is called reincarnation or the cycle of birth and death.

The astral plane and the Dream State.

As stated earlier, the astral plane is also experienced in the Dream State. However, this is a negative experience because you are just as much caught here as you are in the Waking State. In meditation, the astral plane can be experienced consciously. Have you ever had a waking (lucid) dream or a situation in which you were between waking and sleep and suddenly your body is paralyzed even though you are aware? Rarely, people sometimes experience a dream and are aware that they are having a dream. They are "conscious" of the astral plane and not of the waking body or waking personality. The objective of meditation is to discover the astral plane in a

---

[27] Matter refers to gross physical matter: the elements, water, air, fire, earth as well as their chemical components, i.e. the periodic table of elements. The periodic table is a tabular arrangement of the elements according to their atomic numbers.

[28] It is important to understand that nature does not assign or recognize anything. Only the human mind, when beset with ego consciousness, assigns names an ascribes value to objects.

positive, conscious way and to thereby allow the mind to expand and understand that the waking and astral planes are merely reflections of your consciousness. In reality, just as you experience a dream universe and when you wake up from the dream you realize that that entire existence was within your mind, in the same way, when you wake up from the dream of the world of time and space by attaining enlightenment, you discover that the existence of the world of time and space also occurs within your consciousness. In reality you are not an individual, finite and minuscule speck in the vast ocean of the universe. In truth, the universe is within you. It is an emanation of your consciousness. You are the source and sustenance of the entire universe.

The Deep Unconscious - *Amun*

When you are asleep and the dream-state of consciousness ceases, where are you? This is the deep unconscious state. It is characterized by a deep experience of peace and transcendentalness. This is why, upon waking up, you might say that you experienced a profound rest. You cannot say where you were, or what happened, but you know that it was total peace and rest. This is because you were temporarily in a state of transcendence beyond any form of dualistic consciousness that is experienced in the dream-astral and waking-physical states of consciousness. In the deep dreamless Sleep State there are no sense experiences. Thus consciousness experiences undifferentiated existence, that is, existence when there is no duality (you-me, up-down, here-there, male-female, yes-no, etc.). This is the true state of consciousness and it is the true state of all existence. In other words, consciousness is in reality undifferentiated and free from all associations with duality, bodies, senses, problems, family, etc. However, this state, when experienced in the dreamless sleep, is only a dull memory upon waking up. This is why people do not become spiritually enlightened by the experience. What is necessary is to explore this area of consciousness in a positive way through understanding, brought about by study and reflection upon the mystical teachings, and then by actual experience through the practice of meditation.

Transcending the experience of duality.

On an ordinary level, this state of consciousness is experienced by people in the form of peace and bliss. Have you ever experienced a deep peace, contentment or satisfaction which you cannot explain intellectually? This is the deeper feeling at the deep unconscious level. It is beyond the mind, intellect or the level of awareness wherein there is reasoning, memory, thoughts, etc.

The Transcendental Personality - *Neberdjer*

> "The sleep of the body is the sober watchfulness of the mind and
> the shutting of my eyes reveals the true Light."
>
> Ancient Egyptian Proverb

All of the states of consciousness described above are relative. They are all relative because they are not abiding. They are in the realm of duality, multiplicity and segmentation of consciousness. They depend on and are sustained by an underlying essence which is the only reality. The underlying essence is absolute, immutable and real. Beyond the waking, dream and unconscious personalities lies the transcendental state. Attaining this state is the objective of all spiritual disciplines. It is the highest achievement of all Sages and Saints. This is the underlying essence of all the states of consciousness discussed above. This is the level of awareness wherein there is a discovery that all of the states of consciousness, waking, dream and dreamless sleep, are in reality emanations or aberrations of the transcendental state which is without distinctions or differentiations of any kind. Therefore, from un-differentiation comes differentiation, from non-duality comes duality. However, as we have seen, the underlying essence of duality is non-duality, therefore, the supreme reality, the transcendental Self, is present in all states. In reality duality is merely an illusion sustained by the unenlightened mind which is caught in constant movement from state to state. When there is a discovery of the transcendental state, the human being is no longer caught in any of the states of relativity. This means that it is not possible for him or her to be caught up in the experiences of the waking, dream or deep Sleep States. Therefore, they will not experience the pains and sorrows or the elations of ordinary human existence. Instead, they will experience pure, unobstructed peace and bliss (Hetep). Also, they will not be subject to becoming caught in the cycle of birth and death, reincarnation, because there will be no more desire in the mind to impel it to seek for either astral, waking or unconscious experiences.

In the transcendental state there is no segmentation, no time and no space, no differentiation and no duality. There is only one unitary consciousness, which encompasses all existence. This is why in the state of deep dreamless sleep as well as in the state of deep meditation there is no awareness of the passage of time or of events in space. In other words, you are not a subject relating to objects through a mind, senses or a personality. This is why the dreamless Sleep State is so restful; duality draws mental energy while non-duality is restful, peaceful and invigorating. Therefore, the rest experienced at the astral (Ra) and physical (Ptah) planes cannot be compared with that experienced in the deep unconscious plane (Amun).

Going beyond the conditioning of the mind.

195

The big difference between the experience of the deep Sleep State (Amun) and that of the deep meditative state is that the meditative state (Neberdjer) is a state of heightened awareness while the Deep Sleep State is a state which is blanketed by a veil of ignorance (ego-individuality). The meditative state is not passive like the Sleep State. In reality it is a state of positive awareness which allows the mind to be cleared of the thoughts that cloud the reflection of the truth. Using the metaphor of the lake, the mind is like the water. If it is beset with thoughts, desires and ignorance, it is murky and muddy like a lake in the midst of a raging storm. If it is purified with understanding and calmed through the practices of Maat[29] (balance, equanimity, meditation in action), then it clearly reflects the light of the Self which pervades every corner of the universe, just as when the lake is calm and the mud settles, one can see the bottom clearly.

Through the practice of yoga, that is, by listening to the teachings, reflecting upon the teachings and meditating upon the teachings, it is possible to consciously discover this transcendental state that is beyond the waking, dream and dreamless Sleep States and the physical, astral and deep unconscious planes of existence. When this accomplished, the darkness that was enveloping the mind is lifted and the ignorance which once held you in the degraded state of the three personalities becomes like a soft mist which can be dispersed by a mere thought. This purified mind can reveal the glory of the Supreme Self that shines throughout every plane of existence as the non-dual, transcendental reality. This is the power of the mind which is trained in the disciplines of yoga. When the enlightenment of the mind is perfected, the transcendental state (undifferentiated universal awareness) overpowers all of the relative states (waking, dream, and dreamless sleep) and there is a continuous experience of peace and bliss at all times. This is the resurrection of the soul which occurs in the Ausarian Mysteries, the Unveiling of Aset (Isis) in the Asetian Mysteries of Ancient Egypt, the Enlightenment of the Buddhists, The Moksha or Kayvalya (liberation) of the Vedantins, the Christhood (divine marriage or discovery of the Kingdom of Heaven) of the Christians, etc.

The power of a mind that is trained by the disciplines of Yoga.

There is a picture, related to the Ancient Egyptian epic story of *The Ausarian Resurrection*,[30] which shows the character Heru (Horus- the higher Self) and Set (lower self) as sharing one body with two heads, that of Heru and that of Set. The Heru-Set figure leads us to understand that Heru and Set are not two separate individuals, but two aspects of the same character. The entire story of the Ausarian Resurrection hinges on this very point. It mystically symbolizes the plight of every human being that is struggling to

---

[29] See the book *The Wisdom of Maati* by Muata Ashby

[30] For the complete rendition of the epic see the book *The Ausarian Resurrection* by Dr. Muata Ashby.

conquer his or her lower nature and to become the master of his/her own life.

"Body's sleep becomes the soul's awakening, and closing of the eyes - true vision; pregnant with good my silence, and the utterance of my word begetting good things."
Ancient Egyptian Proverb

Another picture depicting the union of Heru and Set is most important. It symbolizes the union of Heru and Set which is a mystical code for the uniting or harmonizing the lower and Higher Self in the individual human being. It means achieving inner harmony and peace with the universe, the culmination of the Ancient Egyptian injunction: *Know Thyself.* Set is not a devil or an evil force to be destroyed. He is the principle of the uncontrolled, untrained ego with its rampant desires and selfish thoughts. Thus, in order to conquer Set, it is necessary to control the impulses of the lower self. This is accomplished by allowing oneself to be nurtured and protected by Aset, which means listening to the mystical stories and myths, studying the wisdom teachings through the initiation process and practicing Maat by leading a life based on virtue, order, correctness, justice, balance and peace.

From the previous study, the following schematic diagram may further assist the mind in understanding the nature of existence, the mind and consciousness.

Waking
↑
Dream
↑
Dreamless sleep
↑
Differentiated consciousness - Duality -
Ignorance of the transcendental -
Subject to time and space

_____

↑
Undifferentiated consciousness -
The underlying essence
(Transcendental Supreme Peace, Universal, Eternal, Infinite and Bliss)

Spiritual enlightenment consists of discovering that the waking, dream and dreamless Sleep States of consciousness are only relative realities. In fact, all of them constitute the ego personality of a human being in various states of expression. When there is knowledge of the absolute, transcendental reality, the relative states are discovered to be only passing expressions of consciousness as a dream or as a thought. The Absolute is discovered to be the true identity and body consciousness is dissolved in the ocean of the Cosmic Self.

The Voyage of Ra and The Journey of the Soul

The Ancient Egyptian Creation Myth tells of the emergence of Ra out of the Primeval Ocean. The ocean was unformed, undifferentiated matter. The emergence of Ra was synonymous with the coagulation of matter into various forms. In so doing, Ra established Maat (order) in the place of chaos. This statement may be understood as the establishment of form out of that which is unformed. This idea may be better understood by using an example water and ice. In the liquid state, water is unformed, undifferentiated. When it is cold enough, it turns into ice and thereby takes on a particular "form" or "differentiation" which sets it apart from the rest of the water. However, the water is not really transformed into the ice. That is, water has not been permanently changed into another substance altogether. The change is merely a temporary appearance. In the same way Creation was explained by the Ancient Egyptian Sages as an ocean. This ocean is a metaphor which refers to the ocean of consciousness. All matter is in reality neither liquid, gaseous, solid nor abiding. The underlying essence of matter is in reality "non-existence," as modern physicists would call it. Modern physics experiments have concluded that matter, when broken down to the most elemental levels, is in reality energy. This idea may be understood through the diagram below.

"And now that thou hast learnt these lessons, make promise to keep silence on thy virtue, and to no soul, make known the handling on to you the manner of rebirth, that we may not be thought to be calumniators."

Ancient Egyptian Proverb

(A)

(B)

(C)

Matter and Anti-matter collide in a modern physics particle accelerator.

When positively charged protons (matter) and negatively charged protons (anti-matter) are crashed into each other (A), the two cancel each other out and the particles of matter temporarily go out of existence. Modern physicists believe that it transforms into energy (B). It then transforms back into matter again (C).

The mystical explanation, based on the teachings of Yoga and Mystical spirituality, is that the matter reverted back to its true, undifferentiated, form as subtle matter. It did so in much the same way as human consciousness takes on various forms while in the Dream State and then reverts back to the unformed state when there is deep dreamless sleep.

The voyage of Ra symbolizes the differentiation of matter or consciousness into the various forms which human beings have come to know as Creation. However, since matter is not "real" as we have seen and it is nothing more than the manifestation of Divine consciousness, Creation must be understood as the essence of the Divine. In other words, Creation is an expression of the mind of God, the Supreme Being. The following diagram outlines the differentiation of matter according to the Ancient Egyptian Creation myth.

Shetai - Neter Neteru - Neberdjer
(Unseen, hidden, omnipresent, Supreme Being,
beyond duality and description)

Ra-Tem
⇩
Hathor
Djehuti
Maat
⇩
Shu ⇔ Tefnut
⇩
Geb ⇔ Nut
⇧   ⇩   ⇘
Set — Nebthet   Asar ⇔ Aset   Asar ⇔ Nebthet
⇩   ⇩
Horus   Anubis

The process of Creation is explained in the form of a cosmological system for better understanding. Cosmology is a branch of philosophy dealing with the origin, processes and structure of the universe. Cosmogony is the astrophysical study of the creation and evolution of the universe. Both of these disciplines are inherent facets of Ancient Egyptian philosophy through the main religious systems or Companies of the Gods and Goddesses. A company of gods and goddesses is a group of deities, which symbolize a particular manifestation of the cosmic forces or principles which emanate from the all-encompassing Supreme Being, from which they have emerged. The Self or Supreme Being manifests creation through the properties and principles represented by the *Pautti* company of gods and goddesses–cosmic laws of nature. The Company of Gods and Goddesses of Anu is regarded as the oldest, and forms the basis of the Osirian Trinity.

The diagram above shows that the *Psedjet* (Ennead), the creative principles which are embodied in the primordial gods and goddesses of creation, emanated from the Supreme Being. Ra or Ra-Tem arose out of "*Nu,*" the Primeval Waters, the hidden essence, and began sailing the "*Boat of Millions of Years*" which included the company of gods and goddesses. On his boat emerged the "Neteru" or cosmic principles of creation. The Neters of the Ennead are Ra-Atum, Shu, Tefnut, Geb, Nut, Asar, Aset, Set, and Nebthet. Hathor, Djehuti and Maat represent attributes of the Supreme Being as the very *stuff* or *substratum* that makes up Creation. Shu, Tefnut, Geb, Nut, Asar, Aset, Set, and Nebthet represent the principles upon which creation manifests. Anubis is not part of the Ennead. He represents the feature of intellectual discrimination in the Osirian myth. "Sailing" signifies the beginning of motion in creation. Motion implies that events occur in the realm of time and space, thus, the phenomenal universe comes into existence as a mass of moving essence we call the elements. Prior to this motion, there was the primeval state of being without any form and without existence in time or space.

The voyage of Ra is depicted as two boats. One travels through Nut (the heavens) during the day, shining upon the physical world as symbolized by the morning and noon-day sun. The other travels through the Duat (Astral Plane-Netherworld) at night, as symbolized by the setting sun, providing the light of consciousness which shines in the astral world. This light of the astral consciousness (Dream State) which illumines the thoughts of the mind is an effulgent subtle light, not to be confused with physical forms of light such as that which is given off by a light bulb. So Ra illumines the physical world as well as the astral world.

The voyage through the heavens corresponds to the Waking State of human consciousness. The Duat represents the cosmic astral plane that corresponds to the Dream State of human consciousness. Thus we are led to understand that Ra, the Self, traverses through the different states of consciousness and encompasses all of them. In Chapter 17 of the *Ancient Egyptian Book of Coming Forth By Day*, it is stated that the Divinity within the "Common Folk," that is to say, ordinary human beings, is none other than

Ra, the Supreme Self. Therefore, it is in reality Ra who is moving from plane to plane and it is Ra, the light of consciousness, who is the ultimate reality in every human being. Thus the ego in a human being is an illusory development based on ignorance of the higher underlying reality. The soul of every human being is Ra, the Supreme Being.

The Barque of Ra-Tem, *Mandjet* 🛶 (the movement of the Self), courses through all regions of existence including the earth (physical plane or realm) and the *Sekhet-hetepet* or *Duat* (astral plane or realm). Ra possesses another barque known as the *Mesektet*, the boat that travels in the nighttime through the Duat or Amentet of disembodied souls and the transcendental world that is the peaceful abode of those who join with Ra (God). Those who achieve entry into the intermediate world must be equipped with the proper qualities because they must be ready to recognize and welcome the Divine. In line 19 of the *Hymn to Ra-Tem* from the *Papyrus of Mut-hetep*, mystical insights into the Duat, the voyage of Ra and its significance to every soul are given.

19- The gods of the land of Amentet rejoice and lay hold upon the cords of the *Sekhtet* boat, and they come in peace; the gods of the hidden place who dwell in Amentet triumph.

When souls leave the physical realm or when, through spiritual practice and having attained purity of heart, they are able to achieve psychic contact with the intermediate world (Daut, or Netherworld), they can go close to the region of Amentet and wait for the time when the barque will pass. This waiting period is beset with dangers from demons that would like to not only stop the voyage of Ra, but stop the spiritual movement of souls. These demons are a figurative way to describe the unconscious failings and demoniac tendencies in the human psyche such as anger, fear, desire, greed, depression, gloom, and desires of all kinds for earthly pleasure and experiences of the senses. Through the purifying process of the spiritual disciplines, the mind (heart) can be purified, and thus prepare the soul to grasp the *cords of the Sekhtet boat* when the time comes. This taking hold of the cords symbolizes the will of the initiate to direct his/her mind toward the Divine through recitation of hymns, oblations, offerings, loving devotion, study, reflection and meditation on the teachings which lead to a direct experience of recognition and identification with the Divine. The act of joining Ra in his barque is a metaphor of the human being who has transcended all levels of creation (differentiated matter in the Physical-Waking, Astral-Dream and Causal-Unconscious). Going onto the barque is a symbol of dissolving the consciousness of duality and the Trinity in order to become one with Ra.

"Indeed they who are yonder (those who live righteously will join GOD after death), will be living Gods, punishing anyone who commits a sin. Indeed they who are yonder will stand in the boat (barke of RA) causing the choicest offerings in it to be given to the temples. Indeed he who is yonder will become a sage who will not be hindered from appealing to GOD whenever they speak."

Ancient Egyptian Proverb

Reincarnation and Enlightenment

In Ancient Egyptian Mystical Symbolism the Journey of Ra is symbolic of the journey of the soul. Just as the sun is born in the east, traverses the sky and then dies in the west, a human being is said to come into existence (birth), live life and then die as well. Thus, it is beneficial to go to the west and stay there because this is the abode of the blessed. This is the abiding place of light, peace, joy and Divinity itself. However, those who are not ready to remain in the west due to their previous actions (karmic entanglements) and spiritual ignorance will be reborn again. Therefore the aspiration or desire is not to go to the east because the east symbolizes the land of reincarnation. It is the portal to a renewed human existence with its incessant struggles and futile search for desire and fulfillment. Thus, going to the west after death is a metaphor meaning that a person has become spiritually enlightened and will not be reborn again. This is the ultimate goal of life.

"The Race is never taught, but when God willeth it, its memory is restored by the Creator. You will see within yourself the Simple Vision brought to Birth by the compassion of God; no one can be saved before Rebirth."

Ancient Egyptian Proverb

The Elements of the Human Personality

This section will concentrate on the subtle human anatomy and the anatomy of all existence. It will discuss the Physical, Astral and Causal planes of existence and their inner workings as they relate to the elements that compose the human personality. First we will review the themes and essential wisdom developed in the book *Egyptian Yoga: The Philosophy of Enlightenment*. Then we will proceed to look into the nature of the subtle spiritual Self with more detail and depth. The Ancient Egyptian concept of the spiritual constitution recognized nine separate but interrelated parts that constitute the personality of every human being.

(1) THE SAHU:

Figure 10: The Sahu

The hieroglyphs of the word Sahu are the door bolt, meaning consonant "s" or "z," the arm, meaning the guttural sound "ain," the intertwined flax, consonant "h," the chick is the vowel "u," the determinative cylinder seal, meaning "treasure" or "precious," the "t" and the determinative of the "corpse" or "body." The Sahu is the "glorious" spiritual body in which the Khu and Ba dwells. When the elements are integrated (person reaches enlightenment), the spiritual and mental attributes of the natural body are united and deified. The Sahu is the goal of all aspiration. It is the reason for human existence – to become Godlike while still alive.

(2) THE BA:

Figure 11: The Ba

The hieroglyphic symbol of the Ba is the Jabiru bird. The Jabiru is a stork. It symbolizes the nature of the soul to spread its wings and take flight, and exist apart from the body. The Ba is the heart or soul which dwells in the Ka with the power of metamorphosis. Sometimes described as the "Soul" and "Higher Self," it is seen as a spark from the Universal Ba (God). The Ba may be dialogued with and can be a spiritual guide to the developing individual. It is the equivalent of the Hindu "Atman." It is the indestructible, eternal and immortal spark of life. It is not affected by anything that may happen to the senses, body, mind or intellect (higher mind).

Through the mind, the Ba (soul-consciousness) "projects" and keeps together an aggregate of physical elements (earth, air, water, fire) in a conglomerate that is called the psycho-physical personality. When the soul has no more use for the physical body, it discards it and returns to the Universal Ba if it is enlightened. If it is not enlightened, it will tune into another aggregate of elements to make another body (reincarnation).

(3) THE KHU or AKHU:

Figure 12: The Khu or Akhu

The hieroglyph of the word Khu is the "crested ibis." The ibis is representative symbol of Djehuti, the god of reason and knowledge. As such it relates to the pure spiritual essence of a human being that is purified by lucidity of mind. The Khu or Akhu is the spirit, which is immortal; it is associated with the Ba and is an Ethereal Being. The Khu is also referred to as the "being of light" or "luminous being." The Khu illumines the personality and without this light the personality and the mind cannot function. It is the light of consciousness itself.

(4) THE KHAIBIT:

Figure 13: The Khaibit

The hieroglyphs of the word Khaibit are the "sunshade" and the consonant "t." The sunshade produces a shadow when the light is reflecting on it. Similarly, the shadow of a person is produced when the light of their true essence (Akhu) is shining forth through their personality. The Khaibit is a subtle manifestation of the elements of the personality that acts somewhat as the resistor in an electronic component. A resistor causes a shadow in a manner of speaking, when it is placed in an electric circuit. In the same manner, the Khaibit and the other elements of the personality consume spiritual energy from the spirit and produce a particular image thereafter referred to as the individual personality of a human being. The Khaibit or Shadow is associated with the Ba from which it receives nourishment. It has the power of locomotion and omnipresence.

(5) THE KA:

Figure 14: The Ka

The hieroglyph of two upraised arms that are joined is the Ka. It is the abstract personality or ego-self. It is the source from which subconscious desires emerge. It is also considered to be the ethereal body possessing the power of locomotion. It survives the death of the physical body. It is the ethereal double containing the other parts of the personality. The concept of the Ka was known in India and the word was also known. The Indian God Brahma had a Ka (soul-twin). This teaching of the Ka in Ancient Egypt and in India shows that there is a keen understanding of the reflective quality of the personality. In reality the physical personality is a reflection or more accurately, a projection of the astral body. The Ka is associated with the Sekhem in that it is the dynamic aspect of a person's personality in the Astral Plane. It is the dynamic aspect of the vital force in the body of a human being.

(6) THE SEKHEM:

Figure 15: Sekhem

Sekhem is the Life Force or Power that exists in the universe. The symbol of sekhem is the hand held staff pictured above. When used in worldly terms it refers to a scepter that means physical power, authority and strength. In spiritual terms the Sekhem is the power or spiritual personification of the vital Life Force in humans. Its dwelling place is in the heavens with the Khus, but all life draws upon this force in order to exist. Sekhem also denotes the potency, the erectile power or force used in fashioning one's own glorious new body for resurrection.

(7) THE AB:

Figure 16: The Ab

"The conscience (Ab) of a man is his own God."

The Ab or conscience is the source of Meskhenet (Karma) and the mother of reincarnation. The Ab represents the heart. It is the symbol of the deep unconscious mind, the conscience and also the repository of unconscious impressions gathered in past experiences from the present life and previous lives. As desires can never be fulfilled by experiences or from objects in the world of time and space, at death, the ignorant soul will harbor impressions of unfulfilled desires which will lead to further incarnations in search of fulfillment. This point is described in Chapter 30, line 3, from the *Egyptian Book of Coming Forth by Day: "My heart, the mother of my coming into being."* The mind is seen as the source of incarnation (coming into being) because it contains the desires and illusions which compel a human being to be born to pursue the fulfillment of those desires. In the judgement scene from the *Book of Coming Forth By Day*, the Ab undergoes examination by Djehuti, the god of reason. In other words, one's own reasoning faculty will be the judge and judged. The heart (mind) itself metes out its own judgement based on its own contents. It is one's own heart which will fashion (*mother*) one's own fate (*come into being*) according to one's will and desires, which are based on one's understanding (wisdom) about one's true Self. Thus, the new embodiment is fashioned in accordance with what a person has done during previous lives and what they desire for the future. A desire for worldly experience will cause embodiment. A desire to go to the west and join with God will bring spiritual enlightenment.

(8) THE KHAT:

Figure 18: The Khat

The hieroglyphs of the word Khat are the fish meaning "dead body" and the consonant "k," the vulture meaning the vowel "a," the symbol of "bread" and the consonant "t," the egg-like determinative symbol of "embalming" and the determinative symbol of the "mummy," "corpse" or "body." The Khat is the concrete personality, the physical body. It refers to the solid aspect of a human being (bones, skin, blood, sense organs, etc.) which is transient and mortal.

(9) THE REN:

Figure 19: Ren

The Ancient Egyptian word Ren means "name." The name is an essential attribute to the personification of a being. You cannot exist without a name. Everything that comes into existence receives a name. This is an essential quality of that which comes into the realm of time and space. The Ancient Egyptian symbols that signify name are the "mouth" and "water." The name is sometimes found encircled by a rope of light called a cartouche, which is associated with the Shen (a symbol of eternity), the top part of the Ankh Symbol. The cartouche represents a rope of sunlight or Life Force harnessed into the form of a circle. It is the most impregnable structure to protect one's name against attack. The ⬭, means mouth.

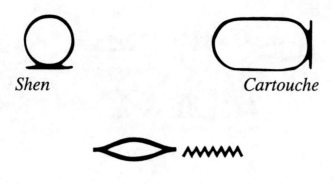

Shen *Cartouche*

"R" and "N"

or "REN"

The symbol of the mouth is of paramount importance in Ancient Egyptian Mystical wisdom. The symbol of the mouth refers to the consonant sound "r," and it is a symbol of consciousness. It is the mouth which is used in two of the most important mystical teachings of Ancient Egyptian Yoga, *The Creation* and the *Opening of the Mouth Ceremony* of the *Book of Coming Forth By Day*. God created the universe by means of the utterance of his own name. In the *Book of Coming Forth By Day*, the mouth is manipulated so as to promote enlightenment. Why is the mouth so important to this mystical symbolism?

Consider the following. When you think of anything you attach words to your thoughts. In fact, it is difficult to think without words. Therefore, words are the symbols that the human mind uses to group thoughts and which constitute intellectual forms of understanding. However, thoughts are conditioning instruments. This means that when you think, you are actually differentiating. The differentiation process allows the mind to be conscious or aware of differences in matter. It labels these differences with different names based on the form or function of the object or the relationship it has to it.

Thought as a differentiating act of the mind.

The mind learns to call objects by names. For example, a chair is an aggregate of matter just like a rock. However, the mind has learned to call it a particular name and associate the name "chair" with a particular kind of object which looks in a particular way and serves a particular function that is different from the rock.

When the mind goes beyond words, it goes beyond thoughts and thereby experiences undifferentiated consciousness. This is the deeper implication of the opening of the mouth ceremony. It signifies opening the consciousness and memory of the undifferentiated state of existence. At a lower state of spiritual evolution, consciousness appears to be differentiated, even though the underlying essence is undifferentiated. However, when intuitional realization or spiritual enlightenment dawns in the human mind, words are no longer viewed as differentiating instruments, but merely as practical instruments for the spirit to operate and interact with the world through a human personality. This is the difference between a human being who is spiritually enlightened and one who is caught in the state of ignorance and egoism.

The vocal capacity in a human being is intimately related to the unconscious level of the mind. This is why those who do not practice introspection and self-control often blurt out things they do not wish to say, and later regret. For this reason, the teachings enjoin that a spiritual aspirant should practice the disciplines of virtue which lead to self-control through right action and righteous living. In this manner, one's speech becomes *maakheru*, the highest truth. When one's speech becomes truth, one's consciousness is truth. When one's consciousness is truth, it is in harmony with the transcendental truth of the universe which is symbolized by the Ancient Egyptian goddess Maat. Thus, becoming true of speech is a primary goal for every spiritual aspirant. It is synonymous with coming into harmony with the universe and thus, refers to spiritual enlightenment itself.[31]

The symbol of the water recalls the image of the Primordial Ocean of Consciousness. Thus, Ren relates to consciousness manifesting through names, words and sound itself.

---

[31] For a detailed examination of the principles embodied in the neteru or cosmic forces of the company of gods and goddesses, the reader is referred to the books *The Hidden Properties of Matter, The Ausarian Resurrection* and *The Mystical Teachings of The Ausarian Resurrection* by Dr. Muata Ashby.

The Mystical Implications of the Elements of the Personality

This section will provide a more detailed classification of the human being in an attempt to understand the underlying origin and cause of human existence. Also, it will seek to bring forth a deeper understanding of how the Cosmic Forces operate through the human constitution at gross and subtle levels.

As discussed earlier, the Universal Soul, God, Pure Consciousness, emanates Creation and all that is within it, all that is. The human being is like a ray of that emanation which refracts into several parts composing all of the levels of existence. Human consciousness may be compared to a reflection of the sun in a pool of water. Human consciousness is a reflection of divine consciousness in the pool of the mind which operates through the brain and nervous system. This idea is also reflected in the relationship between the parts of the spirit called BA and AB.

$$BA \Leftrightarrow AB$$

The Ab is the heart or seat of the mind, and it is in the mind where the soul, Ba, reflects. So the mind has no independent existence without the soul's sustaining life force and consciousness, and the individual human soul has no independent existence without the Universal Soul.

$$\text{Universal Ba} \Rightarrow \text{Individual Ba} \Rightarrow \text{Individual Ab}^{32}$$

These levels of existence transfer into the four states of consciousness and various levels of psycho-spiritual psychology related to the Uraeus-Serpent Power system (see the book *The Serpent Power* by Dr. Muata Ashby).

The Universal Ba or Soul, or in other words, the consciousness of the Supreme Being, emanates and sustains each individual human being through the various parts of the human spirit. There are three basic parts to the human being. These are further broken down into more specific parts.

The three basic parts of the human being are:

Universal Self
↓
Causal Body
↓
Astral Body

---

[32] (**Human heart and mind**)

↓
Physical Body

These bodies also relate to the bodies of the universe:

Neberdjer (Universal Self)
↓
Heaven
↓
Duat
↓
Earth

Sages of ancient times who were able to discern, through their spiritual eye, the different levels of vibration and psychology within all human beings, have set forth this teaching about the constitution of the human being.

Duality and the three states of mind.

An important point to note is that each of the lower three states involves duality while the highest state involves non-duality. The human soul is a projection of the divine into the realm of duality (physical-astral-causal planes). The human soul forgets its divine origin and believes itself to be a creature among other creatures; hence, the idea of duality arises. The ignorant human being is not aware that he/she is at all times most intimately connected to the Universal Self, as are all objects and all other human beings. Just as each wave in the ocean is essentially the same as the ocean, each wave-like human personality and all the objects in Creation are essentially the Primeval Ocean, the Self. Ignorance of this then gives rise to the various egoistic feelings. The ignorant human being, not aware of his/her storehouse of innate potential to experience fullness and peace within, goes on seeking for fulfillment in the worlds of duality instead of seeking to know and experience the only source of true fulfillment, the Universal Self, which encompasses all other realms. Non-duality is experienced as absolute oneness and interconnectedness to all that exists. There is no feeling of you and me, here and there, male or female; there is no desire for objects because all objects are one with the Self. There is only the experience of awareness of the Self. Human words and concepts are not capable of describing the actual experience of oneness with the Self, therefore, all mystical descriptions are transcended in the actual experience. They are like a map, but you must take the journey and arrive at the destination by your own will and self-effort. Thus, they serve as guides to lead the mind toward, the understanding of yogic philosophy.

The nine major elements or parts of the human personality espoused by the Ancient Egyptian Sages may be classified as follows within the three basic bodies for the purpose of study and understanding: The Causal Body, the Astral Body and the Physical Body. God is also understood to have three bodies: Universal Causal Body, Universal Astral Body, Universal Physical Body, the three aspects of universe or planes of existence. Within these bodies are the constituent elements, totaling nine in number. God also has nine elements. However, unlike those of the human being which are limited and characterized by their individuality, the divine elements are universal and all pervading in their respective level of existence. Thus we are told in the Ancient Egyptian scriptures that God has a Universal Individual – Ba, a Universal Sahu, a Universal Khu (Akhu), a Universal Khaibit, a Universal Ka, a Universal Sekhem, a Universal Ab, a Universal Khat, and a Universal Ren. Thus, the individual elements that compose the personality of each individual human being emanate from the same Supreme Being.

Classifying the elements of the personality.

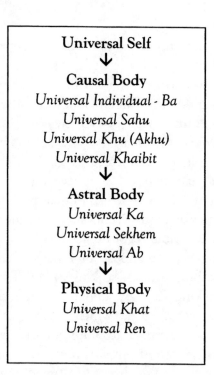

Human Constitution ↓	Universal Self ↓
Causal Body	**Causal Body**
Individual - Ba	*Universal Individual - Ba*
Sahu	*Universal Sahu*
Khu (Akhu)	*Universal Khu (Akhu)*
Khaibit ↓	*Universal Khaibit* ↓
Astral Body	**Astral Body**
Ka	*Universal Ka*
Sekhem	*Universal Sekhem*
Ab ↓	*Universal Ab* ↓
Physical Body	**Physical Body**
Khat	*Universal Khat*
Ren	*Universal Ren*

It should be noted that while the gross elements of the ego-personality are evident at the level of the physical body, the original cause of the existence of the individual and his/her separation from the Divine occurs at the level of the Causal Body. Many people erroneously think of their soul as existing within their physical body. However, the opposite is true. The soul emanates from the Self. It in turn creates the other parts of the personality. All of this creation occurs within the Divine Self and not the body. The Causal Body is where the slightest tendency towards thought and desire

The physical body exists within the soul.

occurs. It is here where the deep unconscious impressions cause the other parts of the body to emerge. When the physical body of an un-enlightened person dies, the gross elements of the ego (name and personality used in a particular lifetime) also die. The Astral and Causal bodies survive with the unconscious impressions collected from that lifetime. Through these bodies the soul continues the pursuit of fulfillment of desire (unconscious impressions lodged in the Astral-Causal mental subtle matter). The pursuit to fulfill the desires may continue in the Astral plane (Duat-Underworld) for a time, where the individual experiences pain or pleasure (heaven or hell) according to his/her Meskhenet (karmic basis composed of impressions gathered from feelings, actions and desires of many lifetimes).

The task of an aspirant is to cleanse the Physical, Astral and Causal planes of the mind so as to regain conscious perception of the Universal Self. Since the Universal Self is non-dual, immortal, eternal and the source of all planes and all objects within those planes, the union with the Universal Self bestows omniscience and boundless vision of infinity, immortality and a feeling of non-duality and connectedness to all things great and small. The correct practice of the various yogic disciplines are designed to accomplish this cleansing process. If successful, the soul comes into communion with the Self (Universal Ba, Asar, Ra, Aset, etc.) while still alive, and after death the soul of the enlightened person dissolves in the ocean of pure consciousness from whence it came originally. This is the meaning behind the teaching of *merging with the maker* presented in the Ancient Egyptian story known as *The Story of Sinuhe*.[33]

Earlier we discussed the fact that in the process of embodiment, the Universal Ba* itself becomes the individual Ba of every human being due to its association and identification with the feelings of the emotional body *Ka* and the cravings of the physical body, *Khat*. If this is true, then how is it possible that the Universal Self (*Ba*) is also non-dual, meaning without a second, one and alone, all-encompassing as well as transcendental? At this more advanced level you must understand that all of the parts of the body are merely emanations from that same divine Self, just as you emanate a dream in your sleep or an idea in your Waking State, out of the depths of your consciousness.

---

[33] See Egyptian Yoga: The Philosophy of Enlightenment (Egyptian Yoga Volume I)

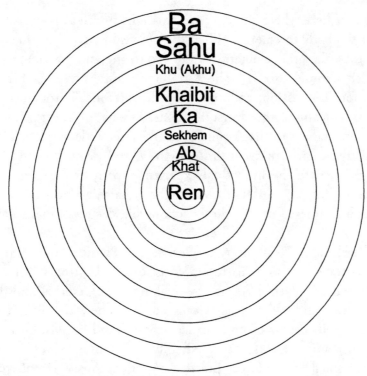

Above: A two dimensional depiction of the elements of the personality.

In the same way this entire universe and everything in it is nothing but the emanation of God's consciousness. All that exists is ethereal, subtle matter, the Self. The process of thought has the effect of coagulating matter in a form as directed by the thought. In this way you have created your body and mind along with all of the other parts of your individual existence. In reality these parts are nothing more than subtle energy held together by your thoughts and ultimately, every one of those parts are not yours, but are parts of the Self. Thus, nothing exists outside of the Self, God. Therefore, even though there appears to be many objects, colors and differences in creation, the underlying essence of it all is the Self. Think about it, if there was something other than the Self, then the Self could not be all-pervasive, all-encompassing and all-powerful. Its movements, would be restricted. The idea that there is a devil or some evil being who is the nemesis of God is erroneous because there can be no other being outside of the Self. The Self is the soul or substratum of all that is.

Ren=Name
Khat=Form

Name and form are the basis of physical existence.

The idea of a "devil" who is a counterpart or nemesis of God who is "all good" was a development out a dualistic way of understanding life and mythology. This dualistic view is contrary to the teachings of mystical spirituality. It is the basis for egoism and misunderstanding in the practice of true religion. True religion means that you look for a connection, a oneness between yourself and God. For this to be possible you need to discover that your ego-personality is only a superficial expression of the deeper reality which is God. When you discover the depths of your own being you realize that you are not an individual, separate from the universe and God. You discover that underneath the apparent separation there is oneness. A dualistic view looks for differences and affirms that there is a separation between God, creation and humankind. Thus, a practitioner of dualism prays to God, looks to God for salvation and believes he exists as an individual while the non-dualist practices the teachings that lead to the understanding that the innermost reality in the heart is God. God is in all things everywhere, and nothing exists besides God.

If you were to let go of your thoughts related to your body consciousness, you would discover that you are separate from your body. In the advanced stages, you could dematerialize and materialize it at will as well as perform other feats that are considered as miracles or psychic powers. The parts of the spiritual body are in reality like layers of clothing on your true Self. Therefore, in the *Gospel of Thomas*, Jesus exhorts us to strip without being ashamed and on that day we will see him (our own Christhood, Enlightenment).

42. His disciples say to him: "On what day wilt thou appear to us, and what day shall we see thee?" Jesus says: "When you strip yourselves without being ashamed, when you take off your clothes and lay them at your feet like little children and trample them! Then {you will become} children of Him who is living, and you will have no more fear."

All of the elements of the personality come together and create a conglomerate which collectively makes up likes and dislikes, opinions, feelings, thoughts, and desires of an individual. All of them constitute a conditioning[34] of the individual consciousness. This conditioning is referred to as egoism. The ego must be dismantled and stripped from the mind. When this occurs you will discover that what seemed so real and concrete (Astral Body, Physical Body) is nothing more than condensed thoughts. This discovery will free you from them as a bird is freed from a cage. When you take them off, what is left is the true Absolute you. All Creation has that same Absolute Self at its core. Therefore, you must seek to transcend all of the layers of ethereal matter so as to discover your true Self. This is accomplished by the practice of all of the disciplines of yoga presented here.

When we speak of "conditioning" here, we are referring to the conditioning of consciousness into the forms of the parts of the spirit in the same way as consciousness becomes conditioned into the forms (subjects, objects and interactions) a dream. What is holding it all together? The

---

[34] See also Egyptian Yoga: The Philosophy of Enlightenment (Egyptian Yoga Volume I)

subtlest parts of the body: *Khaibit, Individual - Ba, Sahu,* and *Khu or Akhu* are the deepest level of the unconscious mind. Contained in them is the cause of separation between the individual soul and God. This individuation principle is called *ignorance.* Therefore, ignorance, based in the causal body, is the primary "cause" of the astral and physical bodies (ego) coming into being. This is why it is called the causal body. It causes the other bodies to come into existence. When this ignorance is removed, all of the bodies become as if transparent, as when you wake up in a dream even when you are still asleep. The dream continues, but you "know" it is a dream, so you witness it as a dream and not as reality. This is the reason why the Sages consider the body and the phenomenal world as an "illusion." Upon waking from a dream you discover that even while things seemed to be so real, they were not. You were not even moving; you were placidly lying on the bed. In the same way, a Sage discovers that the Self is not moving; only the thoughts, senses and body controlled by those thoughts can be said to be moving. Does a dream move? No. In the same way the real you is not located in the body and is not moving. Therefore, you are the "Unmoved Mover." You are Atum, the creator who causes movement but itself does not move. Plato and Aristotle elaborated on this idea in later years but it originated in Memphite Theology, which they studied as initiates of the Ancient Egyptian mystical teachings. Essentially, the teaching explains that while the world exists and is characterized by movement and change, it has a deeper basis that is unchanging and undisturbed. This is the support or unmoving cause that supports the existence of Creation. This teaching can also be found in the great Indian Yoga text known as the Bhagavad Gita. It states that a Yogi who has become established in the awareness of the Self becomes indifferent, unmoved by the changes that seem to appear in matter, the senses no longer interested in the illusion created by ignorance.

Gita 14

23. Seated like one indifferent, he is not disturbed by the gunas; he knows that the gunas[35] alone operate and not the Self, and thus, being established in the Self, he moves not.

Thus, the Sage looks on the body as a marionette, created with thoughts by the Self, or as a projection as in a dream. Having awoken from the dream, when the physical body dies, the Sage who has discovered his/her oneness with the Self remains as the Self and does not create any more bodies to further incarnate. This is because he/she has discovered their essential nature and there are no more desires for experience as a human being. Thus, there is no cause for the creation of a new ego-personality. This

---

[35] Note- Gunas are the three qualities of matter: Rajas-active, Tamas-passive, and Sattwa-harmony.)

is the state that Sages experience with respect to the waking world of ordinary human beings. They are no longer caught up in the illusion of the world. This is called Liberation, Salvation, Horushood, Waking up, Meeting Asar, Resurrection, Nirvana, etc. This is the loftiest goal of human life.

> *"Knowledge derived from the senses is illusory, true knowledge can only come from the understanding of the union of opposites."*
>
> Ancient Egyptian Proverb

If you look at yourself objectively, you will realize that every cell in your body is changing from moment to moment and that you are never the same as you were a moment ago. Even solid objects are changing and decaying, albeit at a slower rate, but eventually they will decompose into their constituent elements. In much the same way, the human body is changing and constantly moving towards extinction. But is this real? Is this change a quality of your inner Self? Upon closer examination, the real you is not changeable; the real you is Pure Consciousness and one with the Supreme Being who is eternal. Remember the teaching: *"The Great God inside the common folk"* from Chapter 17 of the *"Book of Coming Forth By Day."* This is what it means. Your inner Self is one with the Divine Self. Initiatic science shows that the real you, the innermost Self, is unchanging.

What is it that is constantly moving, constantly restless from the time you wake up until the time you go to bed again? This is the thinking mind with all of the worries, all of the desires, all the beliefs, all of the ambitions and all of the regrets. These thoughts, worries, desires, beliefs, ambitions and regrets constitute your mental conditioning, your personality, and your ego-self concept. Through the process of your human experience in the world, your mind has become conditioned to expect to see reality in a certain way and therefore, it perceives life according to its conditioning. This conditioning, your ego, is what is holding you back from being able to realize your innermost Self, which is all encompassing, all-knowing, and all-blissful contentment and peace.

Your ego-personality is like a movie character that emerges at the beginning of a movie and fades away at the end. The movie screen remains in order to receive images from other movies. In the same way your personality emerged out of your mental conditioning at the time of your birth and since then it has never stopped changing, moving, craving and searching for fulfillment. Egoism is the feeling of separation from the Self and attachment to an illusory personality that arises out of the dream quality of consciousness. It is intensified by to the distraction of the mind due to the pursuit of fulfillment of sensual desires. At the time of your death it will cease to exist but the impressions it created in the unconscious will leave you still craving for the unfulfilled desires. This is because the deep unconscious mind with its conditioned impressions of desire, survives death and follows you into the Netherworld (astral plane) until you finally are born again in the earth plane to once again continue seeking fulfillment.

> *"Get thyself ready and make the thought in you*
> *a stranger to the world-illusion"*
>
> Ancient Egyptian Proverb

The concept of relativity of time is expressed in the hieroglyphic text entitled, *The Songs of The Harper*. In one verse the relativity of the passage of time is explained as follows:

> "The whole period of things done on the earth is but a period of a dream."

Consider your dreams. They may seem to occur over a period of hours. You may even experience the passage of years within your dream, and yet upon waking up you realize that the entire time you were in bed asleep for a few hours. In the same way, the entire period of the existence of the universe is nothing but the span of a short dream in the mind of God.

From an advanced perspective, neither time nor space can be said to exist as something that is real, just as time, matter or physical objects within a dream cannot be called "real." The entire dream world exists in the mind and does not require real time or space. The phenomenal world, which is experienced in the Waking State of consciousness, is also not real and does not exist except in the mind of God. This teaching is not only confirmed by the *Hymns of Amun* but it is also a primary teaching of Memphite Theology that is presented in the *Shabaka Inscription*.[36] In reality only eternity is real and God is eternity. Since all matter is in reality constituted of the thought energy of God, and the changes in matter are called time, it must be clearly understood that God is the only reality that exists.

God is eternity itself. The limited perceptions of the unenlightened human mind and senses are what human beings refer to as "time" and "space" awareness. However, the perception of time and space is due to the limitations and conditioning of the human mind and body. If it were possible to perceive the entire universe then you would discover that there is only oneness, an eternal view that is not restricted to time and space. This is the view that God has towards Creation. The task of the spiritual aspirant

---

[36] See also Egyptian Yoga: The Philosophy of Enlightenment (Egyptian Yoga Volume I)

is to grow out of the limitations of the mind and body and discover the Cosmic Vision that lies within. When this is accomplished there is a new perception of the universe. This represents the death of the human being and the birth of the spiritual life in the human being.

God has assumed the form of the Neteru or Pautti. These "neteru" are cosmic forces, energies that sustain the universe and which constitute "physical matter." Therefore, this "physical" universe is in reality the body of God and everything in it is Divine, from the smallest atom to the largest celestial bodies in the heavens.

In this process, *The Universal Ba*[37] itself becomes the individual Ba of every human being due to its association and identification with the feelings of the emotional body *Ka* and the cravings of the Physical body *Khat*.

By practicing the disciplines of Maat, the initiate is able to curb the wanton desires of the ego and thereby strengthen the will of the intellect. The science of practicing virtue in life will serve to assist the aspirant to purify the heart (mind), to cultivate peace of mind, and thereby to develop insight into the innermost Self. At this stage, the movement or vibration in the Primeval Waters which caused the world to be, would subside. Just as a calm lake reflects a pure image, the mind will reflect the clarity of the Cosmic Soul. The waves, caused by movements of the mind, would once again become just as the waves in the Primeval Ocean before creation: silent, at rest, at peace.

Your inner Self, the Cosmic Soul, is constantly interacting with the world through the mind. If you had yellow sunglasses on, when you look at anything you would see a yellow tinge. In the same way, when you look at the world through your conditioned mind and senses, your vision reflects the tinge of egoism and divergent thoughts, but most of all, ignorance of your true Self which causes body identification. If you were to eradicate your mental conditioning, you would see a different reality. This is the goal of the various disciplines of yoga, to purify the intellect, *Saa*. By developing your higher intellectual ability to cut through the illusions of life with the ax of wisdom, you purify your subconscious mind from all of the conditioning. It is this purification of Saa, which can lead you to awareness of the Higher Self.

The philosophy of the four states of consciousness is of paramount importance for the spiritual aspirant. A profound understanding of this teaching will lead you to develop subtlety of intellect in discerning the

---

[37] The terms: The Universal, World Ba, Pa Neter, Amun, Nebertcher are to be understood as being synonymous.

reality of the thoughts in your own mind as well as that which is real around you. In the book *The Cycles of Time*, we explored in depth, the practices of how this teaching is applied in everyday life in order to realize its significance at the deepest levels of the mind through virtuous living, the practice of Maat.

Maat philosophy provides us with a guideline for determining what is real and what is not. This is crucial to the correct operation of the mind because the mind supports whatever reality it believes to be true. You experience the world through your mind and senses. You have learned that these are valid criteria to determine the validity of the world and of your inner experience. Everything must be known through your rationalizing mind once it has been perceived by your senses. However, as we showed in the books *Egyptian Yoga: The Philosophy of Enlightenment* and *The Hidden properties of Matter*, what is normally considered to be real and abiding, solid matter is nothing more than energy in its grosser states of being. It must be clearly understood that mental perceptions are not direct perceptions of matter. Your hand which you use to hold an object is itself a swirling mass of energy which is connected to other masses of energy conduits that lead to the brain. Sensual stimulus is an interaction between different forms of energy that registers in the brain centers in a specific manner. The mind perceives these stimuli by reacting to the centers and then acknowledges a perception. Therefore, perception occurs in the brain itself and not in the hand. Consider for a moment the situation of a paralyzed person or your own experience if a limb has fallen "asleep." In these eventualities, there is still a limb, but there is no perception. Why? because the perception media, the senses, are incapacitated. Consider the possibility of the disabled limb coming into contact with an object. Did any interaction occur? From the standpoint of the observation yes there was some sort of interaction between two objects, but not from the standpoint of the person with the disability.

Now consider the Dream State of consciousness. When you have dreams you perceive various objects, you touch them and you may even feel you own them. They appear to be real and "feel" very solid and true. However, upon waking you realize that they did not exist and never did. They were simply energy forms, which you created out of the subtle astral matter and perceived through the deluded mind. They were fleeting masses of subtle energy that arose out of your own mind and perceived by your own mind. You developed an illusory triad of consciousness during your Dream State and from this arose an entire world. Your waking ego self-concept dissolved and you became a new subject. This "new" you used the subtle senses to perceive objects which you yourself imagined to exist. This is the triad of *seer, seen and sight.* When you woke up, this triad dissolved into your waking consciousness as if it never existed.

The *triad* of human consciousness arises out of your inability to perceive reality without the mind and senses. The mind and senses along with your soul form the three elements of the triad. If you were to transcend the mind and senses you would perceive reality directly through your soul. Only through direct perception is it possible to know the truth or reality. The teaching of the triad is expressed in the symbolism of the Divine Trinity, which arises out of the Primeval Ocean.

The whole idea here is that the world you perceive as real is illusory. The senses, which you use to perceive the world are illusory, and the mind, which you use to perceive the world is also illusory. Therefore, there is only one factor left which qualifies as real. That factor is the *witnessing consciousness* that perceives all of the different states. Through spiritual practices (yoga of wisdom, yoga of action, yoga of devotion and yoga of meditation) you can gradually lead your mind to deeper and deeper levels of perception of the truth until you discover the Absolute Truth beyond all of the illusory layers of the mind.

May you discover the glory of the Mystical Hymns of Amun and the Trinity of consciousness within yourself.

INDEX

GLOSSARY OF ANCIENT EGYPTIAN
MYSTICAL PSYCHOLOGY
Selected Ancient Egyptian Mystical
Psychology Terms and their definitions

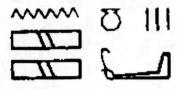

Agitated, disturbed- *Neshsh*

Agitation, trembling- *Tchefi*

Anger- *Ken*

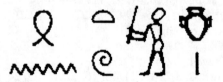

Angry, to be wroth, to quarrel- *Sheni ab*

Assembly, reunion, gathering- *Smait*

Beings of light- *Akhu*

Beloved one or love itself God- *Merr*

Dense Dull of heart- *Wmet htp ab*

Dream - vision- *Resut*

Dream- *Resu*

Egyptian Yoga- *Smai Taui*

Evil person- *Tuta*

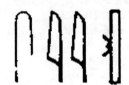

Fullness, satiety- *Si*

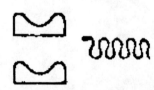

God of evil- *Apep or Set*

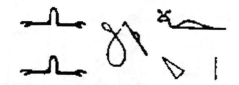

Growthless, barren- *Nrutef*

Hatred, cursing- *Kenau*

Ignorance, simple, stupid- *Ukha*

Ignorant- *Khemn*

Ignorant- Khemm

Innermost Heart Horus- *Abtelab Heru*

Joy Expansion of heart three (manifold)-fold- *Aut ab htp*

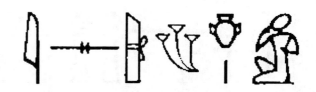

Light-minded man, unstable- *Ass ab*

Lucid, to be bright to see- *Beq*

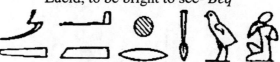

True of thought, word and deed- *Maak-heru*

Madness, folly, insanity, delusion- *Riba*

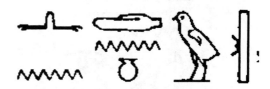

Non-duality- *Nntenu*

Object of love longed for wished for desire- *Ab*

Object of love longed for wished for desire – *Mer*

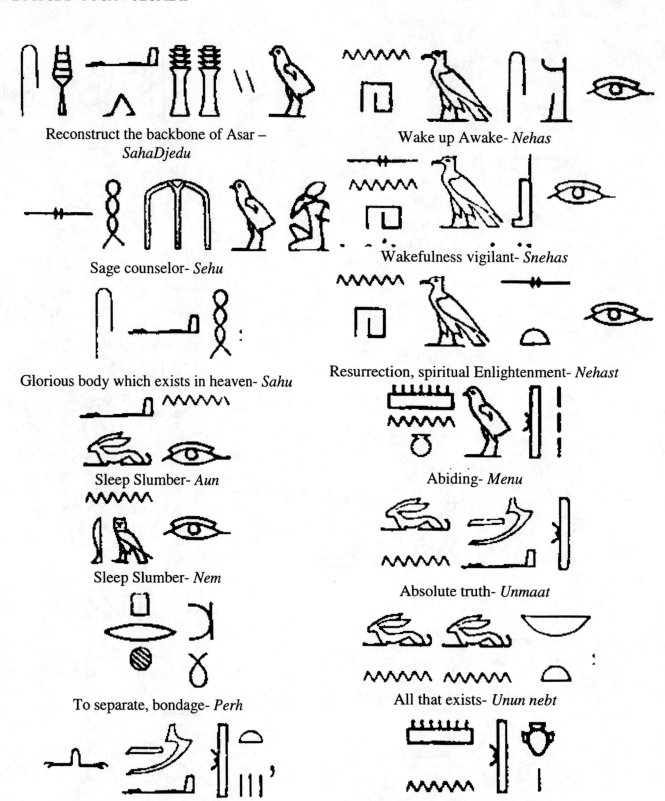

Reconstruct the backbone of Asar – *SahaDjedu*

Wake up Awake- *Nehas*

Sage counselor- *Sehu*

Wakefulness vigilant- *Snehas*

Glorious body which exists in heaven- *Sahu*

Resurrection, spiritual Enlightenment- *Nehast*

Sleep Slumber- *Aun*

Abiding- *Menu*

Sleep Slumber- *Nem*

Absolute truth- *Unmaat*

To separate, bondage- *Perh*

All that exists- *Unun nebt*

Unrighteousness- *N maat*

Firm of heart, resolute- *Men ab.*

Sluggard, lazy, innert, dull man- *Neni.*

Sluggishness, sedentary- *Nen.*

Evil hearted man- *Un ab.*

Devoted to God- Uah abr Neter.

Devotion, Set the heart on something -Uah ab.

Fill the ears, listen attentively- Meh mestchert.

Forget, to make to forget- Smeht.

Forgetfulness- *Smekh.*

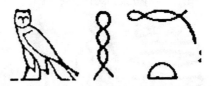

Fullness- *Meht.*

Fullness of heart, contentment, satiety- *Meht ab.*

Health, vigor- *Senbi.*

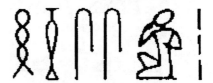

Hymns, praises, songs- *Hessu.*

Chant, sing repeatedly praises- *Hesi.*

Imagination, let fancy run free in mind- *Ab.*

Mental anguish, sorrow, pain- *Mesqeh.*

Still of heart (title of mummy or initiate) - *Urti-hat.*

Still of heart (title of Asar)- *Urti-hat.*

is wisdom deified- *Sa or Såa*

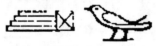

To Know- *Såa.*

To not Know, weakness, evil- *Såaa.*

Work contentedly- *Ari em hetep.*

Work rightly, lead life of integrity- *Arit maat.*

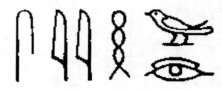

Ecstacy, religious - *Seh.*

Swoon or subsiding during religious ecstacy - *Heft.*

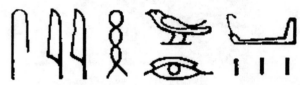

Hipnotized - *Sihu.*

Visible image of god – *bes neter*

Innermost Heart, Horus - *Abtelab Heru*

Live again-Reincarnation – *Uhem ankh*

Other Books From C. M. Books
P.O.Box 570459
Miami, Florida, 33257
(305) 378-6253 Fax: (305) 378-6253

THE YOGA AND MYSTICAL SPIRITUALITY BOOK SERIES

This book is part of a series on the study and practice of Ancient Egyptian Yoga and Mystical Spirituality based on the writings of Dr. Muata Abhaya Ashby. They are also part of the Egyptian Yoga Course provided by the Sema Institute of Yoga. Below you will find a listing of the other books in this series. For more information send for the Egyptian Yoga Book-Audio-Video Catalog or the Egyptian Yoga Course Catalog.

Now you can study the teachings of Egyptian and Indian Yoga wisdom and Spirituality with the Egyptian Yoga Mystical Spirituality Series. The Egyptian Yoga Series takes you through the Initiation process and lead you to understand the mysteries of the soul and the Divine and to attain the highest goal of life: ENLIGHTENMENT. The *Egyptian Yoga Series*, takes you on an in depth study of Ancient Egyptian mythology and their inner mystical meaning. Each Book is prepared for the serious student of the mystical sciences and provides a study of the teachings along with exercises, assignments and projects to make the teachings understood and effective in real life. The Series is part of the Egyptian Yoga course but may be purchased even if you are not taking the course. The series is ideal for study groups.

Prices subject to change.

EGYPTIAN YOGA:
THE PHILOSOPHY OF ENLIGHTENMENT

An original, fully illustrated work, including hieroglyphs, detailing the meaning of the Egyptian mysteries, tantric yoga, psycho-spiritual and physical exercises. Egyptian Yoga is a guide to the practice of the highest spiritual philosophy which leads to absolute freedom from human misery and to immortality. It is well known by scholars that Egyptian philosophy is the basis of Western and Middle Eastern religious philosophies such as *Christianity, Islam, Judaism,* the *Kabbalah,* and Greek philosophy, but what about Indian philosophy, Yoga and Taoism? What were the original teachings? How can they be practiced today? What is the source of pain and suffering in the world and what is the solution? Discover the deepest mysteries of the mind and universe within and outside of your self.
216 Pages 8.5" X 11" ISBN: 1-884564-01-1 Soft $18.95 U.S.

THE AUSARIAN RESURRECTION:
The Ancient Egyptian Bible
The Ancient Sages created stories based on human and superhuman beings whose struggles, aspirations, needs and desires ultimately lead them to discover their true Self. The myth of Aset, Asar and Horus is no exception in this area. While there is no one source where the entire story may be found, pieces of it are inscribed in various ancient temples walls, tombs, steles and papyri. For the first time available, the complete myth of Asar, Aset and Horus has been compiled from original Ancient Egyptian, Greek and Coptic Texts. This epic myth has been richly illustrated with reliefs from the temple of Horus at Edfu, the temple of Aset at Philae, the temple of Asar at Abydos, the temple of Hathor at Denderah and various papyri, inscriptions and reliefs.

Discover the myth which inspired the teachings of the *Shetaut Neter* (Egyptian Mystery System - Egyptian Yoga) and the Egyptian Book of Coming Forth By Day. Also, discover the three levels of Ancient Egyptian Religion, how to understand the mysteries of the duat or Astral World and how to discover the abode of the Supreme in the Amenta, *The Other World.*

The ancient religion of Asar, Aset and Horus, if properly understood, contains all of the elements necessary to lead the sincere aspirant to attain immortality through inner self-discovery. This volume presents the entire myth and explores the main mystical themes and rituals associated with the myth for understating human existence, creation and the way to achieve spiritual emancipation - *Resurrection.* The Osirian myth is so powerful that it influenced and is still having an effect on the major world religions. Discover the origins and mystical meaning of the Christian Trinity, the Eucharist ritual and the ancient origin of the birthday of Jesus Christ.
200 Pages 8.5" X 11" Hard Cover ISBN: 1-884564-12-7 $29.99 U.S. Soft Cover ISBN: 1-884564-27-5 $18.95

THE MYSTICAL TEACHINGS
OF
THE AUSARIAN RESURRECTION

This Volume will detail the myth of the Osirian Resurrection and The Story of Horus and Set and their mystical implications in the life of the aspirant/initiate. Then this volume will turn to a line by line mystical reading of the myth in order to uncover the mystical implications of the epic story. Mythology will come alive as a message from the Sages of ancient times to the initiates and not just as stories for entertainment. This Volume is special because it links the individual student to the myth and thereby gives her/him deep insight into his/her own true nature and how to practice the religion of Asar, Aset and Horus. This volume may be used as a companion to the book *The Ausarian Resurrection: The Ancient Egyptian Bible* by Muata Ashby (see the description above). **232 pages 5.5"x 8.5" ISBN: 1-884564-22-4 $15.99**

THE PROPERTIES OF MATTER:
Egyptian Physics and Yoga Metaphysics.

This Volume will go deeper into the philosophy of God as creation and will explore the concepts of modern science and how they correlate with ancient teachings. This Volume will lay the ground work for the understanding of the philosophy of universal consciousness and the initiatic/yogic insight into who or what is God? **200 pages. 5.5"x 8.5"   ISBN 1-884564-07-0 $14.99**

INITIATION INTO EGYPTIAN YOGA:
The Secrets of Sheti

Sheti: Spiritual discipline or program, to go deeply into the mysteries, to study the mystery teachings and literature profoundly, to penetrate the mysteries.

☥ You will learn about the mysteries of initiation into the teachings and practice of Yoga and how to become an Initiate of the mystical sciences.

This insightful manual is the first in a series which introduces you to the goals of daily spiritual and yoga practices: Meditation, Diet, Words of Power and the ancient wisdom teachings.
150 pages 8.5" X 11" ISBN 1-884564-02-X   Soft Cover $16.99 U.S.

THE GLORY OF INITIATION

A brief discussion of the theme of Initiation which was introduced in the book *Initiation Into Egyptian Yoga*. This volume explores the need for initiation and how a person is initiated into the teachings of mystical spirituality. Many new important topics are introduced such as: The Ancient Egyptian "Guru," The Mystical Sphinx, The Life of an Initiate of Yoga, The Importance of the Spiritual Name, Initiation With a Spiritual Preceptor and The Initiation Ritual. 40 pages $3.99 ISBN: 1-884564-37- 2

THE WISDOM OF ISIS
GOD IN THE UNIVERSE, GOD IN THE HEART
Who is God in the light of
Yoga Philosophy?

Through the study of ancient myth and the illumination of initiatic understanding the idea of God is expanded from the mythological comprehension to the metaphysical. Then this metaphysical understanding is related to you, the student, so as to begin understanding your true divine nature. **243 pages 5.5"x 8.5" ISBN 1-884564-24-0 $15.99**

THE BLOOMING LOTUS OF DIVINE LOVE
The Process of
Mystical Transformation and
The Path of Divine Love

This Volume will focus on the ancient wisdom teachings and how to use them in a scientific process for self-transformation. Also, this volume will detail the process of transformation from ordinary consciousness to cosmic consciousness through the integrated practice of the teachings and the path of Devotional Love toward the Divine. **225 pages 5.5"x 8.5" ISBN 1-884564-11-9 $14.99**

MEDITATION
The Ancient Egyptian Path to Enlightenment

Many people do not know about the rich history of meditation practice in Ancient Egypt. This volume outlines the theory of meditation and presents the Ancient Egyptian Hieroglyphic text which give instruction as to the nature of the mind and its three modes of expression. It also presents the texts which give instruction on the practice of meditation for spiritual enlightenment and unity with the Divine. This volume allows the reader to begin practicing meditation by explaining, in easy to understand terms, the simplest form of meditation and working up to the most advanced form which was practiced in ancient times and which is still practiced by yogis around the world in modern times. **268 pages 5.5"x 8.5" ISBN 1-884564-27-7 $16.99**

THE WISDOM OF MAATI:
Spiritual Enlightenment Through the Path of Virtue

Known as Karma Yoga in India, the teachings of MAAT for living virtuously and with orderly wisdom are explained and the student is to begin practicing the precepts of Maat in daily life so as to promote the process of purification of the heart in preparation for the judgment of the soul. This judgment will be understood not as an event that will occur at the time of death but as an event that occurs continuously, at every moment in the life of the individual. The student will learn how to become allied with the forces of the Higher Self and to thereby begin cleansing the mind (heart) of impurities so as to attain a higher vision of reality. 210 **pages 5.5"x 8.5" ISBN 1-884564-20-8 $15.99**

EGYPTIAN TANTRA YOGA:
The Art of Sex Sublimation and Universal Consciousness

This Volume will expand on the male and female principles within the human body and in the universe and further detail the sublimation of sexual energy into spiritual energy. The student will study the deities Min and Hathor, Asar and Aset, Geb and Nut and discover the mystical implications for a practical spiritual discipline. This Volume will also focus on the Tantric aspects of Ancient Egyptian and Indian mysticism, the purpose of sex and the mystical teachings of sexual sublimation which lead to self-knowledge and enlightenment. **203 pages 5.5"x 8.5" ISBN 1-884564-03-8 $15.99**

EGYPTIAN PROVERBS: TEMT TCHAAS

Temt Tchaas means: collection of Ancient Egyptian Proverbs

> ♀ How to live according to MAAT Philosophy.
>
> ♀ Beginning Meditation.
>
> ♀ All proverbs are indexed for easy searches.

For the first time in one volume, Ancient Egyptian proverbs, wisdom teachings and meditations, fully illustrated with hieroglyphic text and symbols. EGYPTIAN PROVERBS is a unique collection of knowledge and wisdom which you can put into practice today and transform your life. **160 pages. 5.5"x 8.5"** **$9.95 U.S   ISBN: 1-884564-00-3**

MYSTICISM OF USHET REKHAT:
Worship of the Divine Mother

The Supreme Being may be worshipped as father or as mother. *Ushet Rekhat* or *Mother Worship*, is the spiritual process of worshipping the Divine in the form of the Divine Goddess. It celebrates the most important forms of the Goddess including *Nathor, Maat, Aset, Arat, Amentet and Hathor* and explores their mystical meaning as well as the rising of *Sirius,* the star of Aset (Aset) and the new birth of Hor (Horus). The end of the year is a time of reckoning, reflection and engendering a new or renewed positive movement toward attaining spiritual enlightenment. The Mother Worship devotional meditation ritual, performed on five days during the month of December and on New Year's Eve, is based on the Ushet Rekhit. During the ceremony, the cosmic forces, symbolized by Sirius ✶ and the constellation of Orion ✶✶✶, are harnessed through the understanding and devotional attitude of the participant. This propitiation draws the light of wisdom and health to all those who share in the ritual, leading to prosperity and wisdom.

$9.99 - 146 pages. 5.5"x 8.5"   ISBN 1-884564-18-6

HEALING THE CRIMINAL HEART
Introduction to Maat Philosophy, Yoga and Spiritual Redemption Through the Path of Virtue

Who is a criminal? Is there such a thing as a criminal heart? What is the source of evil and sinfulness and is there any way to rise above it? Is there redemption for those who have committed sins, even the worst crimes?

Ancient Egyptian mystical psychology holds important answers to these questions. Over ten thousand years ago mystical psychologists, the Sages of Ancient Egypt, studied and charted the human mind and spirit and laid out a path which will lead to spiritual redemption, prosperity and enlightenment.

This introductory volume brings forth the teachings of the Ausarian Resurrection, the most important myth of Ancient Egypt, with relation to the faults of human existence: anger, hatred, greed, lust, animosity, discontent, ignorance, egoism jealousy, bitterness, and a myriad of psycho-spiritual ailments which keep a human being in a state of negativity and adversity.

40 pages   5.5"x 8.5"   ISBN: 1-884564-17-8 $3.99

EGYPTIAN YOGA EXERCISE WORKOUT BOOK
Thef Neteru:
The Movement of The Gods and Goddesses

Discover the physical postures and exercises practiced thousands of years ago in Ancient Egypt which are today known as Yoga exercises. This work is based on the pictures and teachings from the Creation story of Ra, The Osirian Resurrection Myth and the carvings and reliefs from various Temples in Ancient Egypt. **130 Pages 8.5" X 11" ISBN 1-884564-10-0 Soft Cover $16.99 Exercise video $19.99**

Figure 20

THE SERPENT POWER:
The Ancient Egyptian Mystical Wisdom of the Inner Life Force.

This Volume specifically deals with the latent life Force energy of the universe and in the human body, its control and sublimation. How to develop the Life Force energy of the subtle body. This Volume will introduce the esoteric wisdom of the science of how virtuous living acts in a subtle and mysterious way to cleanse the latent psychic energy conduits and vortices of the spiritual body. **204 pages 5.5"x 8.5" ISBN 1-884564-19-4 $15.99**

THE CYCLES OF TIME:
The Ancient Origins of Yoga in Egypt and India

This Volume will cover the ancient origins of Yoga and establish a link between the cultures of Ancient Egypt and ancient and modern India. This Volume is of paramount importance because it shows that Egyptian Philosophy began over 30,000 years ago and did not die out along with Egyptian society but that it was carried on by the Sages and Saints who left Egypt at the time of its social collapse. **200 pages. 5.5"x 8.5" ISBN 1-884564-13-5 $14.99**

THE MYSTERIES OF SHETAUT PAUTI
The Mystical Teachings of The Ancient Egyptian Creation Myth

Discover the mystical teachings contained in the Creation Myth and the gods and goddesses who brought creation and human beings into existence. The Creation Myth holds the key to understanding the universe and for attaining spiritual enlightenment.
ISBN: 1-884564-38-0 40 pages $5.99

GROWING BEYOND HATE
The Mystic Art
of Transcending Hate and Discovering
Spiritual Enlightenment Through Yoga

What is the source of animosity between human beings? What is the basis for negativity in the human heart and is there a way to deal with it? How can the teachings of Yoga Philosophy be used to resolve animosity and to transcend hatred in order to attain spiritual enlightenment and promote harmony in society.

Human Relations is an important issue in modern times. This volume is an introductory guide to understanding why people engage in various forms of animosity including hatred, hostility, racism, sexism, etc. towards others. It provides insights into the nature of the mind and the process of spiritual development which leads to purity of heart and spiritual emancipation. 64 Pages ISBN: 1-884564-34-8 $5.99

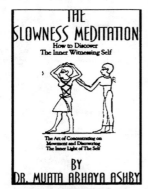

THE SLOWNESS MEDITATION
How to Discover
The Inner Witnessing Self

The Slowness meditation is the art of concentrating
on
movement and discovering the inner light of the Self

What is the *Inner Witnessing Self* and how can slowness lead a person to discover it? What is *automatic consciousness* and what does it operate in the mind of most human beings?

Discover the discipline of meditation which will allow you to go beyond the mundane realities of life so that you may discover inner peace, expansion of consciousness, inner fulfillment and contentment.

This is the Slowness Meditation Program 40 Pages
ISBN: 1-884564-36-4 $4.99

THE STORY OF ASAR, ASET AND HERU:
An Ancient Egyptian Legend

Now for the first time, the most ancient myth of Ancient Egypt comes alive for children. Inspired by the books *The Ausarian Resurrection: The Ancient Egyptian Bible* and *The Mystical Teachings of The Ausarian Resurrection*, **The Story of Asar, Aset and Heru** is an easy to understand and thrilling tale which inspired the children of Ancient Egypt to aspire to greatness and righteousness.

If you and your child have enjoyed stories like *The Lion King* and *Star Wars you will love* **The Story of Asar, Aset and Heru.** Also, if you know the story of Jesus and Krishna you will discover than Ancient Egypt had a similar myth and that this myth carries important spiritual teachings for living a fruitful and fulfilling life.

This book may be used along with *The Parents Guide To The Ausarian Resurrection Myth: How to Teach Yourself and Your Child the Principles of Universal Mystical Religion.* The guide provides some background to the Ausarian Resurrection myth and it also gives insight into the mystical teachings contained in it which you may introduce to your child. It is designed for parents who wish to grow spiritually with their children and it serves as an introduction for those who would like to study the Ausarian Resurrection Myth in depth and to practice its teachings. **41 pages 8.5" X 11" ISBN: 1-884564-31-3 $8.99**

THE PARENTS GUIDE TO THE AUSARIAN RESURRECTION MYTH:
How to Teach Yourself and Your Child
the Principles of Universal Mystical Religion.

This insightful manual brings for the timeless wisdom of the ancient through the Ancient Egyptian myth of Asar, Aset and Heru and the mystical teachings contained in it for parents who want to guide their children to understand and practice the teachings of mystical spirituality. This manual may be used with the children's storybook *The Story of Asar, Aset and Heru* by Dr. Muata Abhaya Ashby. **64 pages   5.5"x 8.5"   ISBN: 1-884564-30-5 $5.99**

The Egyptian Yoga Guide is a comprehensive pamphlet which helps you to navigate through the Egyptian Yoga Book Series as well as the program of yoga and or religious studies based on the book series. The Egyptian Yoga Guide assists you in understanding the meaning and purpose of Egyptian Yoga by introducing the main concepts and goals. Then the guide helps you to determining what kind of personality you have and what form of spiritual study and practice is best suited for you. Then the guide helps you to understand the process of spiritual evolution and the way to promote spiritual knowledge through the integral Egyptian Yoga Studies program. $2.95   ISBN 1-884564-29-1

Ushet I: The Daily Woship and Meditation Audio Cassette

Featuring The Hymns of Amun

THE EGYPTIAN YOGA GUIDE
Introduction to Egyptian Yoga and the Egyptian Yoga Book Series

What is Religion? What is Yoga? What is Spirituality?
How can I end pain and sorrow in my life?
What is my purpose in life?
Is it really possible to discover peace and immortality?
How can I discover my Higher Self and benefit humanity?
How do I become a practitioner of Yoga?
and
How can the Egyptian Yoga Book Series help me to discover my spiritual path?

Many people have written and called us asking these questions. In response we have created a small and easy to read volume called the *Egyptian Yoga Guide*.

Begin each day by centering yourself to the wisdom of the Hymns of Amun. The tape contains related Words of Power for Aset, Hathor and Maat for strength and positive vibrations during your day. The tape also contains short silent meditation segments which will allow you to go within yourself as you are guided through the Ushet (worship) of the Divine.

ABOUT DR. ASHBY

Sehu Maa (Reginald Muata Ashby) was born in New York City but grew up in the Caribbean. Displaying an early interest in ancient civilizations and the Humanities, he began to study these subjects while in college but put these aside to work in the business world. After successfully running a business with his wife for several years they decided to pursue a deeper movement in life. Mr. Ashby began studies in the area of religion and philosophy and achieved doctorates in these areas while at the same time he began to collect his research into what would later become several books on the subject of the origins of Yoga Philosophy and practice in ancient Africa (Ancient Egypt) and also the origins of Christian Mysticism in Ancient Egypt.

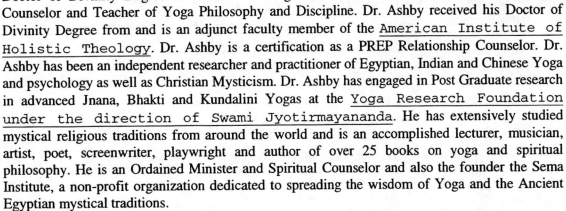

Muata Ashby holds a Doctor of Philosophy Degree in Religion, and a Doctor of Divinity Degree in Holistic Healing. He is also a Pastoral Counselor and Teacher of Yoga Philosophy and Discipline. Dr. Ashby received his Doctor of Divinity Degree from and is an adjunct faculty member of the American Institute of Holistic Theology. Dr. Ashby is a certification as a PREP Relationship Counselor. Dr. Ashby has been an independent researcher and practitioner of Egyptian, Indian and Chinese Yoga and psychology as well as Christian Mysticism. Dr. Ashby has engaged in Post Graduate research in advanced Jnana, Bhakti and Kundalini Yogas at the Yoga Research Foundation under the direction of Swami Jyotirmayananda. He has extensively studied mystical religious traditions from around the world and is an accomplished lecturer, musician, artist, poet, screenwriter, playwright and author of over 25 books on yoga and spiritual philosophy. He is an Ordained Minister and Spiritual Counselor and also the founder the Sema Institute, a non-profit organization dedicated to spreading the wisdom of Yoga and the Ancient Egyptian mystical traditions.

Sehu Maa began his research into the spiritual philosophy of ancient Egypt and India and noticed correlations in the culture and arts of the two countries. This was the catalyst for a successful book series on the subject called "Egyptian Yoga". Now he has created a series of musical compositions which explore this unique area of music from ancient Egypt and its connection to world music.

ABOUT THE EDITOR

Karen Clarke-Ashby "Vijaya-Asha" is the wife and spiritual partner of Muata. She is an independent researcher, practitioner and teacher of Yoga, a Doctor in the Sciences and a Pastoral Counselor, the editor of the Egyptian book series. Dr. Ashby has engaged in Post Graduate research in advanced Jnana, Bhakti and Kundalini Yogas at the Yoga Research Foundation. She is a certified Yoga Exercise instructor and teacher of health and stress management uses of Yoga for modern society. Also, she is the author of *Yoga Metaphors* and co-author of *The Egyptian Yoga Exercise Workout Book.*

Sema Institute
P.O. Box 570459, Miami, Fla. 33257
(305) 378-6253, Fax (305) 378-6253 ©1997

Order Form

Telephone orders: Call 1(305) 378-6253. Have your AMEX, Optima, Visa or MasterCard ready.

Fax orders: 1-(305) 378-6253

Postal Orders: Sema Institute of Yoga, P.O. Box 570459, Miami, Fl. 33257. USA.

Please send the following books and / or tapes.

ITEM

_____Cost $_____
_____Cost $_____
_____Cost $_____
_____Cost $_____
_____Cost $_____
_____Cost $_____
_____Cost $_____
_____Total $_____

_____Please send the latest *Egyptian Yoga Catalog* to me FREE.
_____Please add my name to the *Sheti Association* so that I may receive more
information on upcoming Yoga Seminars and other events.

Name:_____

Address:_____

City:_____ State:_____ Zip:_____

Sales tax: Please add 6.5% for books shipped to Florida addresses

Shipping-.

_____Book Rate: $2.00 for the first book and 75 cents for each additional book
(Surface shipping may take three to four weeks)
_____Air Mail or UPS: $3.50 for first book and 1$ for each additional

Total of the order: $_____

_____Payment:_____
_____Check_____
If Paying by check include your drivers license
number_____

_____Credit card: _____ Visa, _____ MasterCard, _____ Optima,
_____ AMEX.

Card number:_____

Name on card:_____ Exp. date:_____/_____

*Donations: I would like to Donate $_____ to the Inmate Education Program.
*Donations: I would like to Donate $_____ to the Yoga Center Book program.
Tax Deductible.